THE RACING PORSCHES

A TECHNICAL TRIUMPH

THE RACING PORSCHES

A TECHNICAL TRIUMPH

Paul Frère

ARCO PUBLISHING COMPANY, INC.
New York

Published by Arco Publishing Company, Inc.
219 Park Avenue South, New York, N.Y. 10003

© 1971 Motorbuch Verlag, Stuttgart
© 1973 Patrick Stephens Limited, Cambridge

First edition May 1973
Reprinted January 1974

Library of Congress Catalog Card Number 73-76831

ISBN 0-668-02972-2

Printed in Great Britain

First published in Germany
under the title
'Das Rennen vor dem Rennen'

Contents

Foreword

IN HIS BOOK Paul Frère gives a very unbiased account of the racing car development by our company in the last eight years. Though the author views the problems almost exclusively from the racing point of view, there is no doubt that his book will be of interest to others besides motor racing enthusiasts, as it also reflects the dynamic progress of automobile engineering in the light of the recent past of our company in which racing and production car development go hand in hand.

Thanks to this almost unique policy, our experience gained in racing is quickly applied to production cars and benefits the private owner.

I extend my warmest thanks to Paul Frère for his clear and frank report which is of a high technical standing.

Dr F. Porsche

Photographs and illustrations: Frère (7), Porsche (128), Weitmann (2), Van Bever (1)

Front jacket photograph: General Racing Inc; back jacket: Geoffrey Goddard

Jacket design by Martin Treadway

Introduction

IN THE PORSCHE FAMILY the motor sport tradition is nearly as old as this century and nearly 50 years older than the Porsche company itself. Ferdinand Porsche senior was a very young man when long before the First World War he drove competition cars of his own design, long before the little Sascha he had created for the Austro-Daimler company won its class in the 1922 Targa Florio, long before Hans Stuck became the European Mountain Champion in the Porsche-designed Austro-Daimler, long before Rudolf Caracciola won numerous races on the supercharged SSK designed by Porsche when he was with Mercedes. To the man in the street, however, the name Porsche remained unknown until the then quite revolutionary P-Wagen hit the headlines. This was the first design of the newly-founded Porsche Technical office. The design was bought by the German Auto-Union concern and, together with the contemporary Daimler-Benz racing cars, lifted Germany to an unassailable position in international motor racing. The P-Wagen was the first successful racing car with the engine amidships and it was soon followed by another equally successful car: the Volkswagen Beetle, which introduced basically quite similar design principles into a completely different class of vehicle. There were two important differences, however; one was that the whole engine-gearbox unit had been turned round to make more room for the occupants of the car and the other was that for the first time air cooling was successfully used in a mass-produced car.

After the Second World War the Porsche Technical Office was extended to incorporate a small factory. The first model to be produced there, the famous Type 356, was designed by Professor Porsche's son, known today as Dr Ferdinand Porsche or more popularly as Ferry Porsche, and was based on the Beetle. Professor Porsche made the name of Porsche famous; his son Ferry created a world-famous factory. This is now run by Professor Porsche's descendants and has been developed into one of the industry's most technically advanced manufacturing companies, especially starting with the years in which the technical leadership was held by Professor Porsche's grandson Dipl-Ing Ferry Piëch.

Porsche's position in the motor industry is a very special one, for the company is owned entirely by the founder's family and is ruled mainly by engineers. This is borne out not only by the technical perfection of the production cars but also by the methods used for developing racing cars. All too often racing car designers seem to forget that the performance of a competition car does not only depend on the power of the engine, but also to a quite considerable extent on how efficiently the available power is used. Many years ago the cars from Zuffenhausen showed that the combination of a good chassis, light weight, good adhesion of the driving wheels and a well-shaped aerodynamic body can go a long way towards compensating for the lesser power of a smaller engine. The policy of putting the available power to the best possible use is being continued even today when the racing cars produced by Porsche are as powerful as any. The main reason for this is that better results can be expected today from putting the available power to good use, than from a further increase in the specific power output of an engine. Extremely high specific outputs can be achieved reliably only by very complicated engines which cannot serve as a basis for future production units. This is contrary to Porsche's racing policy which aims at gaining as much experience as possible, later to be incorporated into production models. This is the main reason why the racing department and the experimental department of the company are a single unit. The principle that racing should be of as much practical value as possible to the production cars also explains why Porsche have shown comparatively little interest in Formula 1 racing. The races are too short, the aerodynamics of single-seaters have nothing to do with those of road-going cars and the minimum weight required for today's Formula 1 racing cars is much higher than Porsche would like to aim at. The recent introduction of a minimum weight for racing sports cars was one of the important reasons why the Porsche company decided to retire from sports car racing and to build a Group 7 racing car to Can-Am specification.

The wide variety of approaches by the Porsche racing and experimental department to building successful racing cars, makes an insight into the development story of the competition models built in Zuffenhausen particularly interesting. It is difficult, in a book covering nearly ten years of development, to give a true idea of the enormous amount of work that went into the development of the cars over that period, but I hope to convey to the reader at least a part of the fascination of the constant search for progress which is required to achieve success in racing over a period of years.

I am very indebted to Dr Porsche who permitted me to compile this book and would particularly like to thank Dipl-Ing Ferdinand Piëch, and his successor Dr Ernst Fuhrmann, for giving me access to a great number of documents and experimental data which usually remain hidden behind the doors of a jealously-guarded experimental department. I am equally indebted to the current Development Chief H. Bott and to the experimental engineers Mezger, Flegl, Singer, Hänsle and Falk and to their colleagues, who went to great pains to answer the many questions that cropped up as this book was written and thus allowed me to report on the various developments as truthfully as possible. Neither should the Porsche photographic department remain unmentioned for it supplied most of the photographs reproduced in this book.

Paul Frère

1

904: the first of the 'moderns'

IN THE HISTORY of Porsche racing cars the Type 904, also known as the Carrera GTS, marks a turning point. The first racing cars built by Porsche which were not developments of the series production Type 356 were the two mid-engined coupés which ran at Le Mans in 1953, one of which was driven by Richard von Frankenberg and myself. These cars, which finished equal first in the 1,500 cc class (the second car being driven by Hans Herrmann and Helm Glöckler), made history not only by being the first real racing cars built by Porsche, but also because they were the first mid-engined cars ever to run at Le Mans. For Porsche, however, they were only transition models as at that time the development of the four-camshaft engine, later to be known as the Carrera had progressed so much that it was soon ready to replace the pushrod engine, still used at Le Mans, which was a direct development of the current Volkswagen power unit. The combination of this new engine, designed by Porsche's current Technical and Managing Director, Dr Fuhrmann, and an improved version of the tubular chassis of the Le Mans cars became famous as the RS Spyder from which, for the next ten years, all two-seater Porsche racing cars and even the single-seater Formula 2 cars were developed.

In contrast, the 904, evolved under the leadership of Dr Tomala, was a completely new design except for its engine. Originally even this was to have been new: it was intended to be a development of the six-cylinder engine of the then brand-new Type 911 production car. This explains why the engine bay of the 904 was actually too big for its four-cylinder engine; but in the meantime the Carrera engine had been developed to produce 180 hp, so the old engine was finally preferred to the not yet fully developed racing version of the 911 engine. The gearbox, however, was taken from the Type 911, except for the gear sets which were tailored to suit racing conditions. In order to meet the homologation requirements of the CSI, which stipulated that 100 units of a given type had to be produced for the model to be accepted as a Gran Turismo car, it was decided to produce a first series of the required number. The very low price of 29,700 DM asked for this very promising competition car finally attracted far more than 100 customers and another 20 cars some of which were kept by the factory for development purposes, had to be produced to meet the demand. Ten cars of the 904 series were actually fitted with the six-cylinder engine, which they were originally intended to take, and an eight-cylinder engine was dropped into another six cars of that type. This eight-cylinder unit was a development of that used in the 1962 Formula 1 car. Even before the 1964 racing season began, the entire production of the 904 model had been sold and no Porsche racing car could be bought, except secondhand, before the Carrera 6 (officially known as the 906) came on the scene in 1966.

It was not only the low price which was responsible for the success of the Porsche 904. It was also the fact that in 1964 it was still possible to build a successful sports racing car that was not strictly confined to the race tracks. The 904 was successfully used in international rallies and also the factory insisted that the 904 could be driven on the road to and from the circuits, saving its owner the expense of a trailer or a transporter. Some customers were even expected to use the 904 as a normal road car. This is indicated by the fact that a Webasto petrol heating system was standard equipment (it was certainly necessary for winter rallies), while the instruction manual recommends that 'in the winter period', cars used mainly for city driving or short distance driving should have the engine oil replaced every 2,500 km !'

It is also of interest to note that the 904 was normally delivered with 165HR-15 Dunlop SP radial-ply tyres. Racing tyres were only supplied on request and had to be purchased by the customer direct from the manufacturers. In this case the use of rear wheels having 6-in wide rims was recommended. It is typical of the extremely quick development of tyre design during the last few years, that the standard 904 used the same size of wheels front and rear having a rim width of only 5 in. This is only half as much as the rear rims of the Type 907 raced by the factory only three years later in the same class, and is also narrower than the wheels which became standard equipment on 911 models from 1969.

Beginning in 1953, when the first competition car not developed from the Type 356 was produced by the factory, all Porsche competition cars, not directly based on the 356 or 911 models, have had a frame made of welded tubes. The only exception was the 904. In view of the relatively large number of units to be made, production considerations dictated the use of a pressed steel frame. Another deviation from previous Porsche practice was the use of a glass fibre body bonded to the frame. The body thus became a structural part of the car which improved the rigidity of the chassis. This proved to be a doubtful asset, however, as the torsional stiffness varied quite considerably from one car to another, due to variations in the body panel thickness, while rigidity tended to decrease with time, due to the progressive deterioration of the bonding between the chassis and the body.

The pressed steel chassis and the glass fibre body of the 904 were thus still relatively unknown quantities, and very thorough tests were made even before the first prototype was constructed. In its original form, the pressed steel frame was considerably more flexible than the tubular space frame of the then newest Porsche Spyder. Even after it had been reinforced, the pressed steel frame was still about twice as flexible as the older tubular steel space frame but it was expected that the body would raise the stiffness to about the same figure as for the older space frame. These expectations were confirmed by the finished product, which means that the rigidity of the pressed steel frame was about doubled by the plastic body bonded to it.

It might seem surprising that a very light plastic body could contribute to such an extent to the rigidity of the complete vehicle. It must be remembered, however, that the central part of the 904 body was particularly stiff, thanks to the construction of the seats which were part of the body structure. In conjunction with the rear bulk-head, the side walls and the floor, they formed an extremely stiff central section· As a result of this form of construction the seats could not be moved, so that the pedals had to be made adjustable and a telescopic steering column had to be used.

Before the car was put into production, three prototypes were made. All were fitted with the 160 hp version of the Carrera engine, internally known as the 718/2, as used in the Carrera-Abarth car, since the more powerful 718/3 engine was still under development. One of these prototypes was first tried on August 29 and 30 1963 on the Porsche steering pad in Weissach. It was then taken to the Nürburgring and to the Hockenheim track where it was submitted to development tests for the next three months. The main aim of the two-day trials in Weissach was to set up the car and rectify any serious fault which might be discovered before the three prototypes were taken to the two race tracks.

The first trials at Weissach showed that the movable pedal carrier did not function properly and that the gear change was sticky. The driving position was criticised and the racing tyres were rubbing on the front wings when the car cornered hard. With 5.50-15 Dunlop racing tyres, the time on the 190-metre diameter circular pad was 19.8 s, equivalent to a lateral acceleration of 0.99 g.

The first trials on the Nürburgring took place on September 10/12, during which time about 640 km (equivalent to 400 miles) were covered. The faults which showed up are typical for the first trial runs of a competition car. They show that even a car designed by a company with such a brilliant racing background as Porsche does not always initially generate boundless enthusiasm from the test crew. Even though the 904 was later to become extremely successful, no fewer than 27 faults were re-corded, some of which were very important. Here are a few examples of them:

the body became detached from the chassis in several places due to insufficiently strong bonding;
body cracked at door opening;
front wheels touched wings before suspension stops were reached;
brake cooling insufficient on all wheels;
chassis box section cracked at the attachment point of one of the rear upper wish-bones;
chassis transverse member around gearbox cracked;
chassis cracked at engine support;
steering gear bracket cracked;
changes of gear ratios impossible without removing the gearbox from the car;
gear change sticky;
gearbox support broken;
final drive pinion shims destroyed;
gearbox oil temperature too high;
great quantities of oil lost through gearbox vent;
chassis transverse member carrying the engine broke several times;
steering kicked and was too high-geared;
brakes grabbed;
brakes faded; and so on . . .

On the occasion of these trial runs, the car was run both on Dunlop 165-15 radial-ply tyres and on Dunlop R6 D12 5.50-15 front and 6.00-15 rear. With the latter combination, a time of 2 m 36.2 s was obtained on the southern loop of the Nürburgring, while the northern loop was covered in 9 m 55.3 s, both on a dry track.

The car was then rectified in the light of the findings and went back to the Nürburgring from October 2/5 1963. After 580 km (about 360 miles) had been covered, the clutch disc (which had already had a hard life on the test bed) was destroyed. Otherwise the car proved very much more reliable than during the first test runs. Except for the clutch disc and a cracked steering gear holding bracket, no important part broke, either in the course of this second test run, or during the third test run which took place from October 7/11 on the 'Ring and during which 1,080 km were covered. Strong criticism was still expressed on several points: for instance the too-quick steering, the bad gear change and the fact that the gearbox occasion-ally jumped out of gear due to over-soft engine mountings. The brakes still tended to grab (the remedy suggested by the test team was to use light alloy brake calipers and wheels) and they faded badly. The tyres still rubbed on the front wings too.

Modifications were also suggested to enable the engine and the gearbox to be removed separately from the vehicle.

Front brake seals failed because of too high temperatures and these also caused the Ferodo DS 11 racing brake pads to wear very rapidly. They were worn down almost completely after only 840 km had been covered on the Nürburgring. Considerable aerodynamic lift was also noted which reduced front wheel adhesion at speed, resulting in bad straight line stability. The lift on the front axle was 20 mm at 180 kph and as much as 45 mm at 220 kph. In this connection, however, it should be mentioned that the front suspension had been raised compared with its design height in order to prevent the front tyres from rubbing on the wings too often. Reducing the static height of the front suspension by 20 mm brought about a considerable reduction of the aerodynamic lift, but the straight line stability remained poor. A considerable aerodynamic lift was also suspected to exist over the rear axle but no check was made. The amount of lift at the front was measured by attaching a rod to the front suspension and leading it through a hole in one of the front wings so that the driver could see it. The rod was marked in different colours along its height and the driver was asked to observe which colour showed above the level of the wing at a given speed.

Though the car was still far from perfect, a lap of the southern loop of the Nürburgring was covered on a 50 per cent wet surface in practically the same time (2 m 36.5 s) as had been achieved on a dry track during the first trials. On the northern loop which was dry, the previous time was bettered by 10 s despite road works which in one place forced the drivers to slow down. Here are extracts from the observations and suggestions made on this occasion by the development engineers:

Front axle: the reaction to road irregularities is poor. The fluidblock wishbone pivots, consisting of two rubber spheres, should be replaced by Silentbloc bushes (concentric steel bushes with a rubber interlayer, working in torsion but allowing practically no radial movement) in conjunction with a softer spring. A more precise geometry could be expected from the Silentblocs while the softer springs would compensate for the torsional stiffness of the Silentblocs themselves.

Rear suspension: the anchorage of the radius arms in rubber blocks is unsatisfactory because the deformations of the rubber blocks produce toe-in variations. Static tests showed that these can reach as much as half a degree either way. The rubber joints should be replaced by metallic Unibal joints. These are spherical joints with a hard plastic bearing surface needing no servicing.

To avoid excessive shocks being fed back from the wheels into the transmission, the Nadella halfshafts (halfshafts with needle bearing universals) should be made solid instead of tubular and of smaller diameter in order to act as a shock-absorbing torsion bar. Other suggestions were to use Giubo rubber universals (the so-called doughnuts) or even the special Nadella universals as used on the Type 911, which allow some axial movement.

Steering: the steering was described as too quick, and very severe reactions were transmitted to the steering wheel. The drivers also said it was too heavy, especially around the central position. Lower gearing was suggested, along with more elasticity. The test team also recommended reducing the one degree negative camber of the front wheels.

Brakes: the rate of wear of the brake pads was so high that, although the car could have gone through a 1,000 km race at the Nürburgring or through the whole Le Mans race without changing tyres, a change of pads would have been necessary. The brakes were also described as excessively heavy. The test team suggested reducing brake disc temperatures with various sorts of air scoops, using a main brake cylinder of smaller diameter for lighter operation and trying thicker brake discs. **Gearbox:** the new vent on the differential housing allowed even more oil to escape than the original one. Additionally, various improvements were suggested for the gear change linkage.

On the occasion of these test runs the front and rear suspensions were adjusted to get the best possible results, but the data obtained were changed again later as a result of other modifications. It should be mentioned, however, that the data were obtained on front wheels of only $4\frac{1}{2}$ in width, because the intended 5-in rims fouled the lower wishbone.

These tests were made in mid-October and the first production cars were to be delivered not later than the end of the coming February in view of the forthcoming Sebring 12-Hour race. Consequently things were getting very urgent and only two weeks later more tests were done with a partially improved car. These, however, had to be interrupted because a connecting rod broke, although they were soon resumed on the Nürburgring.

The main object was to develop the braking system which had shown itself so unsatisfactory. To make operation lighter, the original twin circuit master-cylinder of $\frac{7}{8}$ in diameter was replaced by one of $\frac{3}{4}$ in. As the drivers had also complained of premature locking of the rear wheels, larger front wheel cylinders were used, the rear ones remaining unchanged at 35 mm diameter. The correct distribution of the front and rear braking forces was arrived at by weighing the car in order to locate its exact centre of gravity, after which the exact weight transfer for the retardation obtainable on a dry road was calculated. This led to the replacement of the 45 mm front cylinders by 48-mm diameter cylinders. With these, however, the fluid capacity of the system proved to be too large for the smaller twin master-cylinder now used, and, as a makeshift measure, this was replaced with a single master-cylinder of equal diameter, taken from a Type 356C production car. Simultaneous locking of the front and rear wheels could then be obtained with the fuel tank, located over the front axle, approximately 80 per cent full.

It is symptomatic of the fact that the Type 904 was also to be used on the road, that all the tests were carried out on radial-ply tyres on which the mean maximum braking retardation obtained was 0.83 g. Other combinations of front and rear brake cylinders were tried and even better results were obtained by using rear wheel cylinders of 33 instead of 35 mm diameter which, unfortunately, produced dangerous premature front wheel locking with a nearly empty fuel tank. These findings led to the plea for the use of a pressure limiting valve which, however, never went into the car.

Following the earlier Nürburgring tests, a new experimental car (904 002) was fitted with thicker $\frac{1}{2}$-in (12.7 mm) instead of the previous 10.5 mm discs which brought the temperature down by about 70° C. In spite of these, front disc temperatures still reached between 550 and 650° C on the southern loop of the Nürburgring, exceeding the temperature of the 10.5 mm rear discs by some 150-180° C. This resulted in a wear rate of the Ferodo DS 11 brake pads which was about four times greater at the front than at the rear. Just how much the temperature accounts for pad wear can be judged by the fact that on the northern loop, where the front disc temperature doesn't usually exceed 450° C, (peaks of about 600° C being only reached down the road to Wehrseifen) the front to rear wear rate was only about two to one. Blanking off the air scoops caused the temperature to rise by approximately 60° C front and rear, but direct ventilation by ducts from the outside of the body did not make any measurable difference. An improved system worked satisfactorily but the pressure which had to be applied to the pedal was still considered to be too high, while test driver Herbert Linge said that at high speed it was impossible to lock the brakes due to high speed fade. Pressure of time, however, led to the decision to produce the car with the existing braking system except that discs of 10.5 mm thickness were used on all wheels, special precautions being taken to provide the brakes with adequate ventilation, especially the front ones. Thanks to the better cooling, it later proved possible to go back to the larger brake master cylinder for the works cars, while the production cars were delivered with the $\frac{3}{4}$ in cylinder, in the interests of lighter brake operation. The brake calipers were cast iron, except on the works cars when they were entered in the prototype class.

Other problems proved equally difficult to solve. In the course of 400 km of testing on the Hockenheimring, one litre of oil again leaked from the transmission and a newly developed ball valve venting system caused such a pressure build-up that the oil escaped through all the joints and packings of the transmission. The gear change again came in for unfavourable comment and the frame once more cracked at the engine mountings.

As a result of previous experience, the second car 904 002, which was tested over 1,340 km on the Nürburgring at the end of October 1963, was fitted with hollow rubber bump stops acting as auxiliary springs front and rear. At the front, these shortened the suspension travel too much, however, and the car proved to be quite undrivable. When they were removed the underside of the car scraped the road in various places, even when fitted with racing tyres which were slightly larger in diameter than the radial-ply tyres. This led to a modification of the rear suspension of which the attachment points on the chassis were lowered 13 mm (about $\frac{1}{2}$ in).

Increased front wheel castor noticeably improved the straight line stability of the car under heavy braking, but in spite of lower gearing obtained by lengthening the steering arms, the steering was still being criticised for its severe kick-back and excessively quick response. More rigid anti-roll bar attachments were required by the test team, in the interests of quicker response and cleaner dynamic behaviour, when the car was driven into a corner. Despite these faults, the southern loop of the 'Ring was lapped in 2 m 31.5 s, about 5 s faster than on the occasion of the first test runs six weeks earlier.

A modified car was taken to the Nürburgring in mid-November for the last time before the model was put into production. The rear radius arms were now pivoted on metallic Unibal joints and the Fluidblock joints of the front suspension had been replaced by radially stiffer Silentblocs. This resulted in much improved handling. The entry into corners was now more progressive and braking no longer called for steering corrections. Straight line stability was also notably improved and such corrections as were called for could be performed with more smoothness and precision.

After jumping diagonally over a hump the car now landed all square with no noticeable roll around the longitudinal axis. A rubber doughnut joint in the steering column did the trick of both reducing kick-back and making the response less excessively quick.

The final data for setting up the running gear were only obtained after the first production cars had been built. Five-inch wide rims were used all round to take the 165HR-15 radial-ply tyres although for racing tyres 6-in wide rear rims were recommended. Negative camber was used all round, 50' at the front and 2° 10' at the rear, while damping was approximately equal on rebound and compression at the front but rebound was considerably more damped than compression at the rear. In starting grid trim, with the driver on board, the front wheels had 25' toe-in. This

Left: There is a lot of unused space under the 904's bonnet which had been originally designed to take a six-cylinder engine.

Centre: Nurburgring 1963. An old-style eight-cylinder Spyder with aluminium body, drum brakes and steel girder frame. Behind the car are Porsche team manager H. von Hanstein, works drivers Linge and Abate and the (spectating) British driver Dickie Stoop.

Bottom: A standard Carrera GTS, Type 904, of which 120 were built.

The 904 proved its all-round roadworthiness by finishing second overall in the 1965 Monte-Carlo Rally, driven by Bohringer and Wutherich.

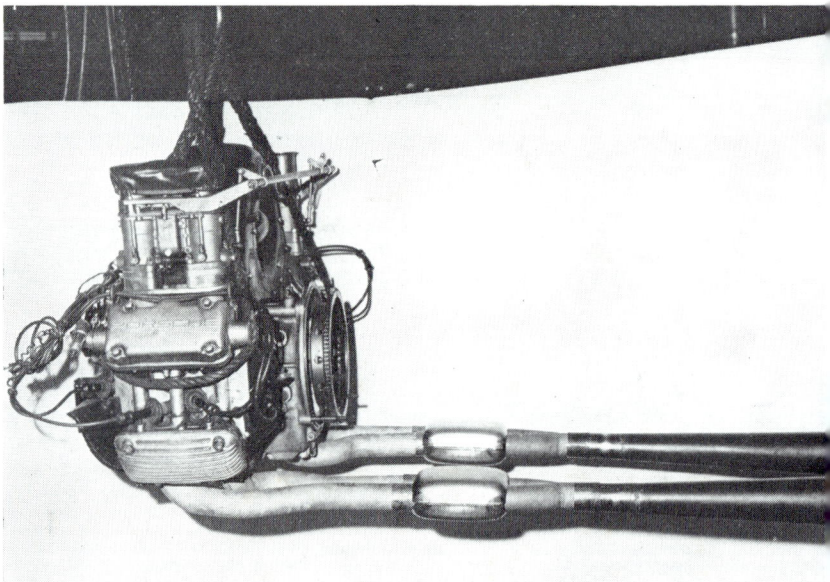

The Type 587/3 engine of the 904 in its 1965 version with twin exhausts.

Box section pressed steel frame of the 904 in prototype form. In production examples, the rear radius arms were pivoted on spherical Unibal joints rather than rubber.

became nil at full bump and was increased to 1° at full rebound. The rear wheels had 20' toe-in and the recommended tyre pressures were 31.5 psi front and 34 psi rear for both road and racing tyres.

As already mentioned briefly, the aircooled flat four engine of the 904, as it was homologated in the GT group, was taken from the special lightweight Abarth-bodied version of the Carrera 2. In contrast to the first Carrera engines of 1,500 and 1,600 cc and the corresponding racing versions used in various forms, the 904 engine (known internally as 587/3) had plain main and big end bearings. The entire engine structure was made of light alloy. The aluminium alloy cylinders had an iron working surface and were known as ferral cylinders. There were four camshafts driven by transverse shafts and bevel gears and rockers were interposed between the camshafts and the valves (two per cylinder) which had an included angle of 78°. Two entirely independent ignition systems fired two plugs per cylinder and carburation was by two twin-choke downdraught type 46 IDM 2 Weber carburettors. The engine torque was transmitted by a Fichtel & Sachs 200 mm single dry plate clutch to the five-speed gearbox which had separate gear sets. These could be chosen individually to alter any gear ratio without changing the final drive bevel gears giving a 7:31 ratio. The car could be delivered with an exhaust system for road use or with the so-called Sebring racing exhaust system which improved the engine performance considerably: with the latter 180 hp was obtained at 7,200 rpm with a maximum torque of 20 mkg (146 lb/ft) at 5,000 rpm but these figures were reduced to 155 hp at 6,900 rpm and 17.2 mkg (125 lb/ft) at 5,000 rpm by the road going exhaust system. The claimed maximum speed was 164 mph with the racing exhaust and 155 mph with the silencer. In Spring 1964 a car was put at our

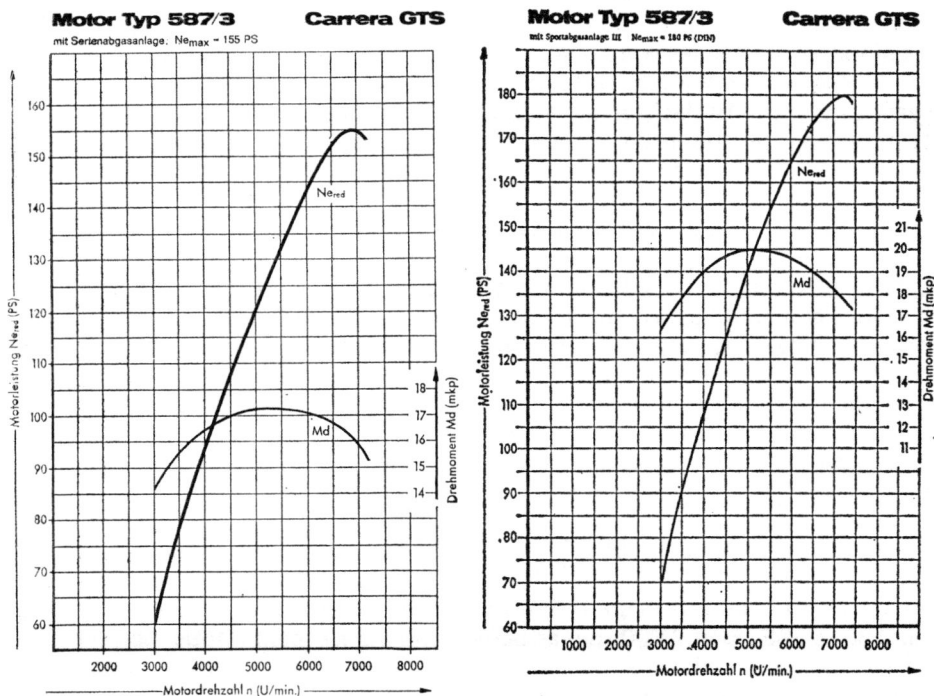

Power and torque curves of the 587/3 engine, 1964 version. Left with street exhaust, right with racing 'Sebring' exhaust system.

B

disposal for a road test. It reached a mean maximum speed of 157.5 mph and did a kilometre from a standing start in 24.6 s, with two up, racing exhaust and racing tyres. The gearing was the standard set, suitable for the Nürburgring.

For the sake of accuracy, it should be added that at the end of the 100-car production run, some examples were fitted with the newer 46 IDA 2/3 Weber carburettors (identical to the 46 IDM 2 except that they were pressure moulded rather than sand cast) and due to a shortage of Webers some cars were also delivered with Solex type 44 P11-4 carburettors.

Racing and developing the Type 904 GTS

In spite of its hurried development and its well-known weaknesses, the 904 production model became an extremely successful car. Especially for Abarth, who shortly before the 904 was announced had produced a series of 100 2-litre sports cars, the latest from Zuffenhausen was a hard nut to crack. The Abarth had a very good twin overhead camshaft four-cylinder engine of Abarth's own design and according to our own findings, its performance matched that of the Porsche: it did a kilometre from a standing start in 24.9 s and had a maximum speed of 163 mph. In contrast to the Porsche, its engine was overhung at the back and the car was based on a chassis suitably developed from the Simca 1000. Its handling was hopelessly inferior to the Porsche's and in racing it just couldn't hold a candle to it. However, in the Mont Ventoux hill-climb Hans Herrmann once succeeded in heading Mitter's six-cylinder Porsche to win the event, driving an Abarth.

So many orders came in for the 904 that a second production run of 100 units was seriously contemplated, many parts being actually purchased for their manufacture, among them 100 complete sets of suspension parts. In the end, however, only 20 cars of this second series were built, some of which were fitted with six- and eight-cylinder engines for development purposes and entered by the factory as prototypes in various events. The decision not to build another series of 100 cars coincided with the take-over of the experimental department by Dipl-Ing Ferdinand Piëch, Dr Ferdinand Porsche's nephew. He did not see much future in this model, a compromise between a road-going and a racing car. Also, for reasons which will be explained later, he wanted to go back to the tubular space frame type of chassis.

As the works felt that it would have been rather hard on customers who had bought a 904 to produce better and faster cars only a year later, and as the 904 had no serious competitors anyway, it was decided not to produce a new car for 1965. Some modifications, however, were developed and they could be incorporated in existing cars at a reasonable cost. The chassis remained basically unchanged, but in the course of time some cracks and breakages were detected on several cars, mainly around the wishbone attachments, the spring abutments and the steering gear supports. On all cars which went back to the factory for servicing, these were attended to and suitably reinforced.

While the factory devoted its attention mainly to the six- and eight-cylinder engines, the four-cylinder was being further developed in order to keep the existing cars competitive for 1965. The modifications, which were incorporated in the works cars and also, on request, in privately-owned cars, increased the power by 3 per cent from 180 to 185 hp at 7,000 rpm as before, and a 5 per cent torque increase, from 146 to 153 lb/ft still at 5,000 rpm, was obtained. The improved performance resulted from the following modifications:

A new twin exhaust system, entirely separate for the right- and left-hand banks of cylinders. The megaphones contained new radial reinforcement baffles used up to the last version of the unsupercharged 917.

The diameter of the intake valves was increased from 49 to 50 mm.

New camshafts were used: the inlet camshafts were entirely new while the previous year's inlet camshafts were now used on the exhaust side. The timing was changed as follows:

	1964	1965
Intake valve opens/closes	79° btdc/93° abdc	90° btdc/94° abdc
Exhaust valve opens/closes	88° bbdc/60° atdc	100° bbdc/72° atdc

Disregarding the valve clearance of 0.15 mm, the valve lift was in both cases 12.25 mm on the exhaust side and 12.26 mm on the inlet side.

Right from its first race, the sporting career of the 904 was a success story. Even before it could be homologated as a GT car, Briggs Cunningham and Lake Underwood won the 2-litre class in the Sebring 12-Hour race, the car still running as a prototype. A month later, now running as a GT car, it won the Targa Florio driven by Colin Davis and Antonio Pucci, a gentleman-driver from Sicily, while Herbert Linge and Gianni Balzarini drove a similar car into second place. This rather unexpected victory was a tribute to the reliability of the 904 which outlasted the eight-cylinder 2-litre Porsche Spyders and most of the much more powerful Ford 4.7-litre-engined Cobras which were severely handicapped by their much inferior handling.

The remarkable reliability of the 904 was confirmed in many other important international championship races: in the Spa 500 km event eight started, seven finished without any unforeseen pit stops, the eighth car being black flagged as a result of the insufficient ability of its driver! In the Le Mans 24-Hour race all five, and in the Reims 12-Hour race all eight, 904s which started finished the race. In all those cases they were also the first 2-litre cars home, heading the corresponding prototypes. In the ADAC 1,000 km race on the Nürburgring, a 904 won the 2-litre GT class and was third overall.

The reliability of the 904 did not show up only on the race tracks, however; in the Tour de France four cars took third to sixth place overall behind two 3-litre Ferrari GTOs, after covering more than 6,000 km on French main and secondary roads and over 1,500 km racing on tracks and hill-climbs. A few months later Böhringer and Wütherich took an astonishing second place in the Monte Carlo Rally. At the end of 1964 the 904 also first appeared as an eight-cylinder using the well-proven 2-litre Type 771 engine which will be described later. This was in the Paris 1,000 km race in which Edgar Barth and Colin Davis came home third overall behind two 3.3-litre Ferraris, while once more a series production 904 won the 2-litre GT class. For the third year running Porsche took the World Championship in the 2-litre class which in those days was attributed on the basis of GT results.

Thanks to the improved engine, the 904 remained supreme in the 2-litre GT class in 1965. In view of future developments, however, the main interest lies with the cars which were entered as prototypes by the factory in various races and which all took part in the 1965 Targa Florio where four 2-litre Porsches followed behind the victorious 3.3-litre Ferrari driven by Vaccarella and Bandini:

Second place was taken by Colin Davis and Gerhard Mitter driving an open model using the 904 frame and a Type 771 eight-cylinder engine, a 2-litre version of the 1962 Formula 1 engine. An interesting experiment in this car was the use of needle roller bearings for the pivots of the suspension wishbones.

Third were Umberto Maglioli and Herbert Linge in a 904 coupé fitted with a six-cylinder engine developed from the Type 911 production unit.

Fourth were Jo Bonnier and Graham Hill in a similar 904 but using an eight-cylinder Type 771 engine.

Fifth overall and winner of the GT general classification were Günther Klass and Antonio Pucci in a series production 904.

Of these prototypes the six-cylinder proved to be particularly successful in long-distance racing; in addition to taking third place in the Targa Florio, it finished fourth overall in the Le Mans 24-Hour race and additionally won on Index. The reason for running this car was mainly to develop the Type 911 engine for racing. The racing version produced about 210 hp and, except for the camshaft boxes, all its structural cast parts were magnesium alloy instead of aluminium with the object of saving weight. The experience gained with the racing engine was later transferred to the production unit; since 1969, these engines have used a crankcase pressure-cast in magnesium alloy (AZ 91) which, thanks to its lighter weight, has considerably improved the handling of the 911 with its overhung rear engine.

In contrast the eight-cylinder unit lacked the reliability required for long-distance racing. Having originally been conceived as a pure racing unit, it produced some 30 hp more from the same capacity as the racing 911 and this made it ideal for hill-climbs where durability is not essential. On one such occasion, the Ollon-Villars Hill-Climb of 1965, it was dropped into a completely new tubular space frame built in record time but, in this case, the object of the exercise was mainly the chassis which was to be the basis for the future 906 (also called the Carerra 6), rather than the engine, to which the factory only turned its attention later when the six-cylinder reached the end of its development possibilities. A later chapter deals with this interesting eight-cylinder engine in more detail.

2

The development of the Type 906

THE 906 OR CARRERA 6 is the first competition series production car that was designed and developed by the team responsible for all the racing models produced by Porsche up to and including the 917. Originally the 904 had been designed to take a six-cylinder engine developed from the Type 911 production unit and ten such cars were actually built and successfully run in 1965. Internally these six-cylinder engined 904s were already known as 906, this number being actually used as a prefix to their chassis number. Consequently, to avoid confusion we shall call the production 906 model the Carrera 6 as it was to be catalogued.

It would have been easy to build a series of new cars for private owners based on those ten prototypes; such a model would certainly have been competitive in the new group of homologated sports cars created by the CSI for 1966, and for which the six-cylinder engined 904 would have been eligible, if only 50 units had been made. For the following reasons, however, it was decided to build an entirely new car:

Generally speaking the glass fibre body of the Type 904 had proved successful. Due to the production methods, however (resin was sprayed on to the glass fibre) the weight of the body differed notably from car to car, with the result that there were rather large differences in the torsional rigidity of the various cars produced. In many cases, corrosion of the pressed steel frame could not be readily detected and was difficult to eliminate as the body could not be removed. Hence the decision to go back to a tubular space frame that would be wholly responsible for the car's stiffness, and to cover it with a very light plastic body giving the car its shape. The resin was also to be applied by hand rather than by spraying it on to the glass fibre. Consequently the part played by the body in the stiffness of the Carrera 6 was considerably less than in the 904. The lower weight of the new car was mainly attained by the use of a very light body.

It is a rule at Porsche that a customer who acquires an expensive competition car should expect it to remain competitive for at least two seasons without any major modifications. In view of the interest shown by Ferrari in the 2-litre class, this might not have been the case with a six-cylinder 904.

The new car was to have a lower air drag than the 904 which had not been tried in the wind tunnel and the shape of which was also known to produce considerable lift over the front axle.

The centre of gravity was to be lowered by accommodating the fuel as low as possible; it was also to be kept as central as possible in the car, in order to avoid variations in the weight distribution during the course of a race.

Only 50 cars were to be produced to satisfy the new homologation requirements and for such a small number a pressed steel frame was not necessarily much cheaper than a space frame.

And finally the Porsche engineers are such perfectionists that they hate to produce a new car if they know they could make a better one.

Another of the many considerations which clinched the decision was that a production racing model, representing the latest line of thought of the factory, could serve as a base for factory-entered prototypes from which precious experience could be gained for the future.

As already related, the Carrera 6 was developed from the space frame Spyder which made its debut in the Ollon-Villars Hill-Climb of 1965 (fitted with the 2-litre eight-cylinder engine it took second place behind Scarfiotti's Ferrari), and became known under the same project number 906. Neither space frame nor running gear had anything to do with earlier Porsche space frame cars, but the experience gained in the course of the 1965 racing season was apparently used to good effect, the development story of the Carrera 6 being a quick and happy one.

The original space frame hill-climb car (chassis No 906 010) had 13-in diameter wheels which had proved fully adequate and the fact that the Carrera 6 used 15-in wheels caused some surprise. Porsche had many explanations ready, but not the true one: the year before, complete suspension and brake sets had been bought for a second 100 series of 904 models, of which only 20 were actually built. Since the running gear of the 904 had proved quite satisfactory, Dr Porsche insisted that those parts should now be used for the sake of economy. This is the true reason why the Carrera 6 used practically the same running gear as the 904 except for wider wheels. Aluminium brake calipers and rear radius arms were used only on the Carrera 6s fitted with fuel injection and running as prototypes.

Though in some ways the instruction manual still hinted at the use of the Carrera 6 as a road car (it recommends that for racing, the back plates protecting the brake discs should be removed and mentions that in winter, when salt is spread over the roads, brake pad wear is increased) the new car was in fact intended as a pure racing car: the use of road tyres was not even taken into consideration and the fact that the adjustment of valve clearances required the removal of the engine from the chassis would hardly have been acceptable in a car intended for everyday use!

Before the first car, which had underslung side tanks, was assembled, an engine was dropped into the chassis which was then submitted in that form to torsional stiffness tests. The first tests showed the frame to be little stiffer than that of the ultra-light Ollon-Villars Hill-Climb car; in fact it was some two-and-a-half times more flexible than a complete, bodied 904 with six-cylinder engine used for comparative purposes. Adding a pyramid-like tubular reinforcement girder at the back of the frame produced a considerable improvement and this was to become a feature of all Porsche racing models in subsequent years. Another notable improvement was effected by adding a diagonal tube across the engine bay. This tube was bolted on and could be removed for taking the engine out of the frame. These modifications made the frame slightly stiffer than the complete bodied 904/6 thus fulfilling all set requirements. It was even found that the diagonal tube (for which unfortunately there was no room when the eight-cylinder engine was fitted) permitted a saving in weight, as several tubes could be omitted from the rear part of the frame without any significant loss of stiffness.

In order to detect quickly any weak points in the frame, it had become a rule at Porsche, since the six-cylinder was dropped into the 904 at the beginning of 1965, to submit racing cars in the development stage to destruction tests on the proving ground similar to those which normal series production models underwent. As at that time the Porsche proving ground in Weissach was not yet finished, the first trials of the Carrera 6 took place on the Volkswagen proving ground in Wolfs-

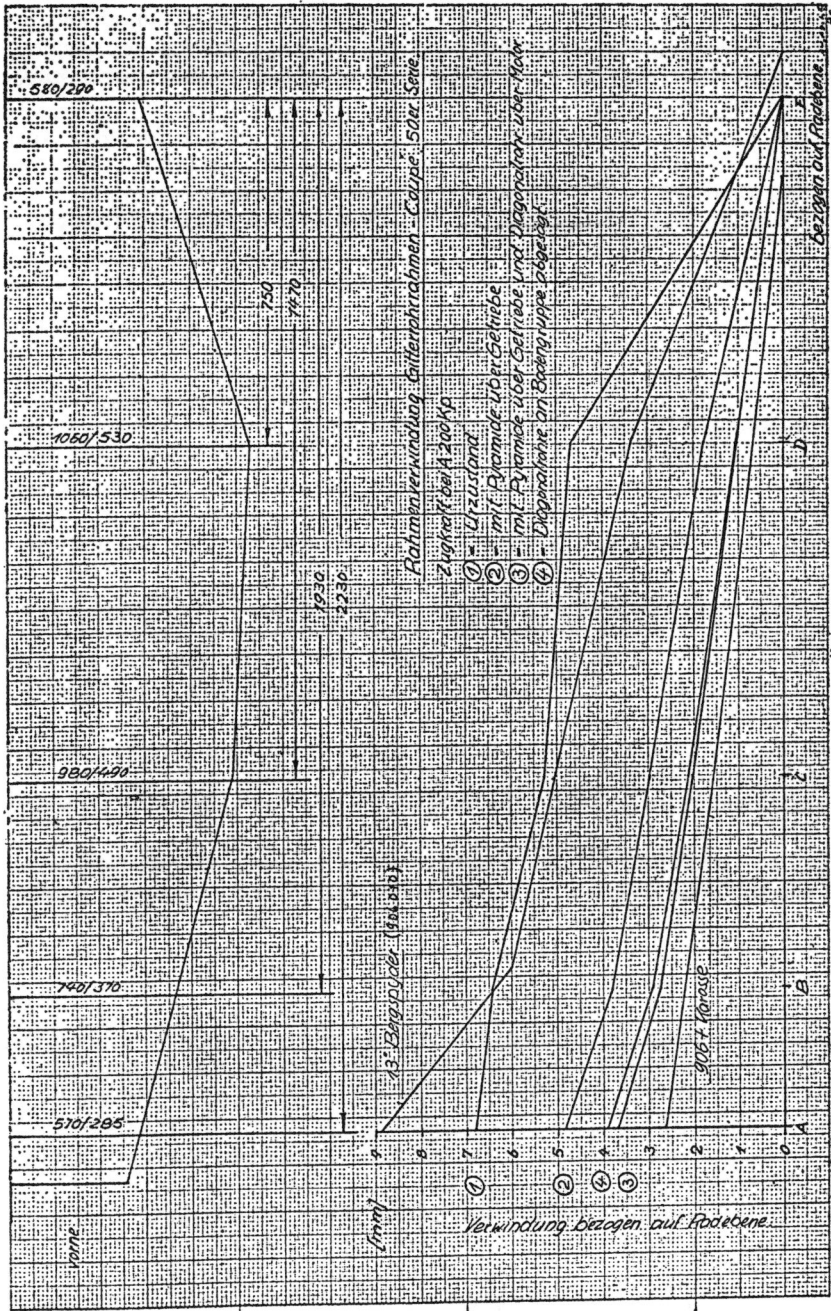

Torsional deformations of the Carrera 6 frame in various experimental and in its final version.
Verwindung bezogen auf Radebene=Torsional deformation in plane of wheel. Rahmenverwindung
Gitterrohrrahmen=Distortion of tubular space frame. Zugkraft bei A 200 kg=Traction at A 200 kg.
1: Original design.
2: With pyramid over gearbox.
3: With pyramid over gearbox and diagonal tube across top of engine bay.
4: Diagonal floor tubes removed.

burg. Among the drivers were Porsche's chassis development engineer Helmut Bott, as well as other engineers and test drivers of the experimental department: Falk, Hannes, Wütherich and Linge. The weather conditions could hardly have been worse. The test report mentions 'ice, locally snow, locally wet with salt'. Later the bulletin mentions a very slippery road due to snow and occasional drifts. The conditions were so bad that for part of the test runs, Dunlop radial snow tyres with spikes had to be used in conjunction with $5\frac{1}{2}$-in wide rims front and rear.

Despite these adverse conditions 690 miles were covered in two days on a circuit comprising the shock absorber test lane, the Pflanzgarten, the test hill, the hump and the asphalt road. Due to the conditions, the speed was rather low: anything between 30 and 45 mph.

For a completely new design the car was remarkably trouble-free. Some of the criticisms made by the drivers and engineers were prompted more by the terrible weather conditions than by any fault of the car itself. The only real faults were in the clutch operating mechanism and in the air duct to the engine blower of which the plastic walls had to be reinforced. The driving position needed some correction and the drivers complained that the high front wings made necessary by the 15-in wheels impaired the visibility on sharp corners. Little could be done about that. Just how much experience in chassis design had been gained, since the 904 was put into production, is shown by the fact that in the course of this first trial, in which the car was driven for nearly 700 miles on the destruction course, no cracks or breakages were detected although the car was meticulously inspected at intervals of about 170 miles during the run. In order to gain further experience the test car was not stripped after the endurance run but, even in the course of further tests, no breakages showed up.

It has been mentioned that the running gear of the Carrera 6 was identical to that of the 904 but in fact there were two notable differences: one was that as a result of the experience gained with the 904 and various development prototypes, all suspension joints were metallic, being either ball joints or needle bearing bushes. Rubber had completely disappeared from the suspension pivots. Ball joints were even used at both ends of the shock absorbers. The second important difference was that, following current practice, considerably wider wheels were used, the rims being 7 in wide at the front and 9 in wide at the rear. They were fitted with 5.50 L-15 and 5.50 M-15 racing tyres, respectively. The same 10-mm thick brake discs were used as for the 904, but the pad surface was larger. Additionally the tandem master-cylinder had been dropped in favour of two separate master-cylinders operated via an adjustable compensating lever. This device made it possible to adjust the proportion of front and rear wheel braking according to the tyres used and to the road conditions. On its first time out in January 1966 the Carrera 6 lapped the Weissach circular pad in 18.62 s. The best time by a series production 904 on Dunlop R7 tyres was 18.86 s.

Basically the Carrera 6 engine, known as Type 901/20, was identical to the production unit of the Porsche 911. The working surface of the aluminium cylinders was chrome plated and there was one chain-operated camshaft per cylinder head. The racing unit differed from the production engine mainly by its camshafts providing a larger valve overlap, larger valves, larger ports, a tuned exhaust system, higher compression and its forged pistons (also used in the 911S). More important, however, was the fact that the racing engine had twin ignition, titanium connecting rods with titanium bolts and a cast magnesium crankcase. The power output was 210 hp at 8,000 rpm with a maximum torque of 146 lb/ft (20 mkg) at 6,000 rpm.

The following table compares the valve gear of the Carrera 6 engine with that of the contemporary 911S.

	Carrera 6	911S
Intake valve diameter/lift	45 mm/12.2 mm	42 mm/11.6 mm
Exhaust valve diameter/lift	39 mm/10.5 mm	38 mm/10.3 mm
Inlet opens/closes	104° btdc/104° abdc	38° btdc/50° abdc
Exhaust opens/closes	100° bbdc/80° atdc	40° bbdc/20° atdc

In principle the transmission was identical to that of the 911 and the 904. It featured separate gear sets which could be chosen individually, four standard sets being offered as for the 904, the car being normally delivered with comparatively wide ratios and a high fifth gear.

The standard sets were as follows:
the production Nürburgring combination;
the hill-climb set;
the set for airfield racing;
the set for fast circuits.

For factory entries in the prototype group the engine was also produced with a Bosch fuel injection system in place of the two triple-choke Weber type 46 IDA 3C carburettors. The injection system raised the power of the 2-litre engine to 220 hp, this being obtained at 8,000 rpm, as for the carburettor engine. The injection plant will be dealt with later.

The shape of the Carrera 6 was dicated entirely by aerodynamic considerations. To start with a 1/5th scale model was tested in a wind tunnel. In its final form it had a drag coefficient Cw=0.235 which, however, was not expected to be reproduced on the full scale car with its various air intakes and exits and the various joints creating local turbulences. In fact, the drag coefficient for the finished car turned out to be about 50 per cent higher. The extensive wind tunnel tests to which the Carrera 6, which had a frontal area of 1.325 m², was submitted were not only aimed at reducing the air drag as much as possible. They also looked at future developments, particularly the influence of front and tail spoilers on lift and downthrust as well as on drag.

(If D is the total car drag, v its velocity, S its frontal area and ρ the air density, the drag coefficient Cw is defined in the usual way by the formula

$$D = CwS \times \tfrac{1}{2}\, \rho\, v^2)$$

The results obtained in the Institute for Motor Vehicle Research of the Technical High School, Stuttgart, were proved by later experiments to be applicable not only to the type of car tested but also to other forms of vehicles. Road tests had shown that apparently a tail spoiler was necessary to get optimum handling and consequently the car went into the tunnel with an 80 mm high spoiler across the tail. The car was then tested in various modified forms and data were obtained on the influence of the modifications on drag, lift and downthrust. The more significant test results are summed up below:

1.   Car as originally intended for production but with 80 mm high spoiler added across the tail: Cw=0.346. Slight lift over front axle, strong downthrust over rear axle.

2.   With tail spoiler and two lateral nose spoilers: Cw=0.351. Slight downthrust over front axle, downthrust over rear axle smaller than for 1.

3.   With tail spoiler and central front spoiler (deflector under the nose): Cw= 0.342. Slight lift over front axle, but less than without spoiler; downthrust on rear axle intermediate between 1 and 2.

4.   Without any spoiler, as originally intended for production: Cw=0.357. Slight lift over front axle, strong lift over rear axle.

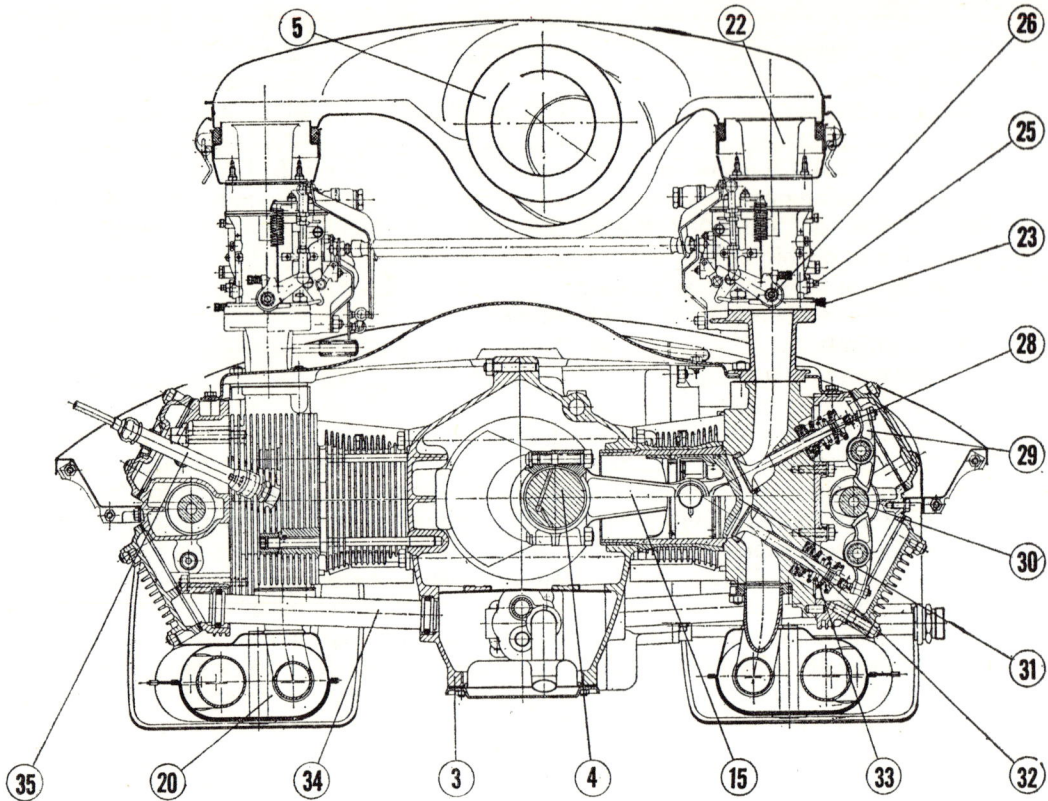

Cross section through engine Type 901 (here 2-litre production unit for car Type 911).

5. Without any spoiler, but with slightly domed disc applied on wheel rim to cover the dished wheel: Cw=0.342.

6. As 5, but with tape covering all joints and all air intakes and outlets blanked off: Cw=0.315.

7. As 6, but with tail spoiler: Cw=0.308.

It should also be mentioned that the car as intended for production, without any spoiler (position 4) and the car fitted with an 80-mm high tail spoiler and two lateral front spoilers (position 2) were submitted to the airstream at an angle to their longitudinal axis, simulating high speed driving under cross wind conditions. These tests proved the car fitted with spoilers to be less sensitive to side winds than without spoilers, the advantage being accentuated by the better adhesion of the spoiler-equipped car.

It may seem surprising that of all combinations tried, the car without any spoiler had the highest air drag. The 80-mm high tail spoiler improved the drag coefficient by approximately 3 per cent, which can probably be attributed to the fact that a tail spoiler creates a ram effect compressing the air flowing over the body's upper surface and keeping the air flow laminar until it reaches a smaller section area. This assumption was confirmed by measurements which proved the air over the rear deck to be at a pressure of 1.5 to 2 ten-thousandths atmosphere above atmospheric pressure.

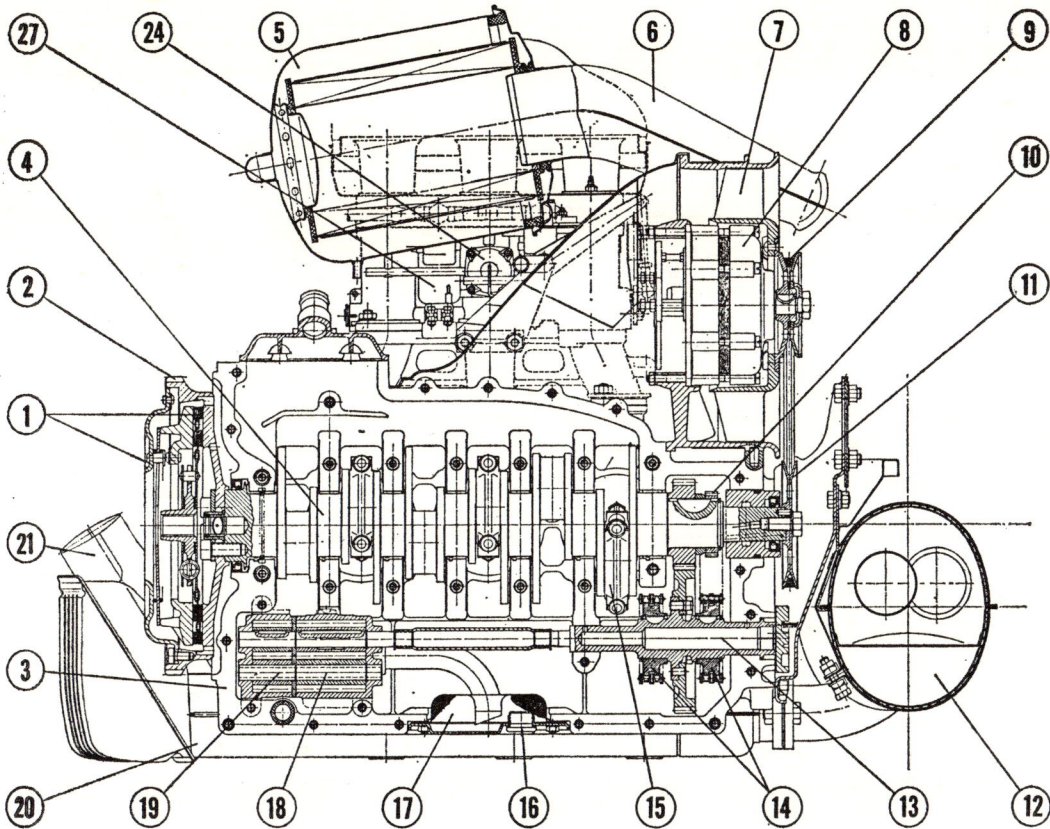

Longitudinal section through the Type 901 engine (here the 911 production engine).

A further slight improvement of the drag factor and a simultaneous reduction of the lift over the front axle was obtained by the use of a central front spoiler. This probably results from the fact that the spoiler deflects the air to the sides and prevents pressure build-up underneath the vehicle. Lateral front spoilers, however, were more efficient in reducing front lift and even produced downthrust, though this was at the cost of a 2.5 per cent increase in drag. In a car capable of some 175 mph, this means a reduction in maximum speed of some 2-3 mph, a comparatively low price to pay for better stability and higher speeds through bends. The tests also showed that front spoilers may be useful for increasing the adhesion of the front wheels, but that this is achieved at the cost of rear wheel adhesion. This finding, which was later confirmed by other tests, is easily explained by the rocking action of the car over the front axle that acts as a fulcrum, tending to lift the car's tail.

Further measurements taken in various zones of the vehicle with alternately open and blanked off air intakes brought interesting results. For instance, the influence of the openings ducting air to the front brakes: at an air stream speed of 93 mph and with discs fitted to the wheels, a vacuum of 5.5 mm water was measured in the wheel arches when the intakes were blanked off, but with intakes open the situation was reversed and a pressure of 9 mm water built up. If the wheel discs were removed, this was reduced to 5.5 mm, hinting at a much increased air flow and better brake cooling.

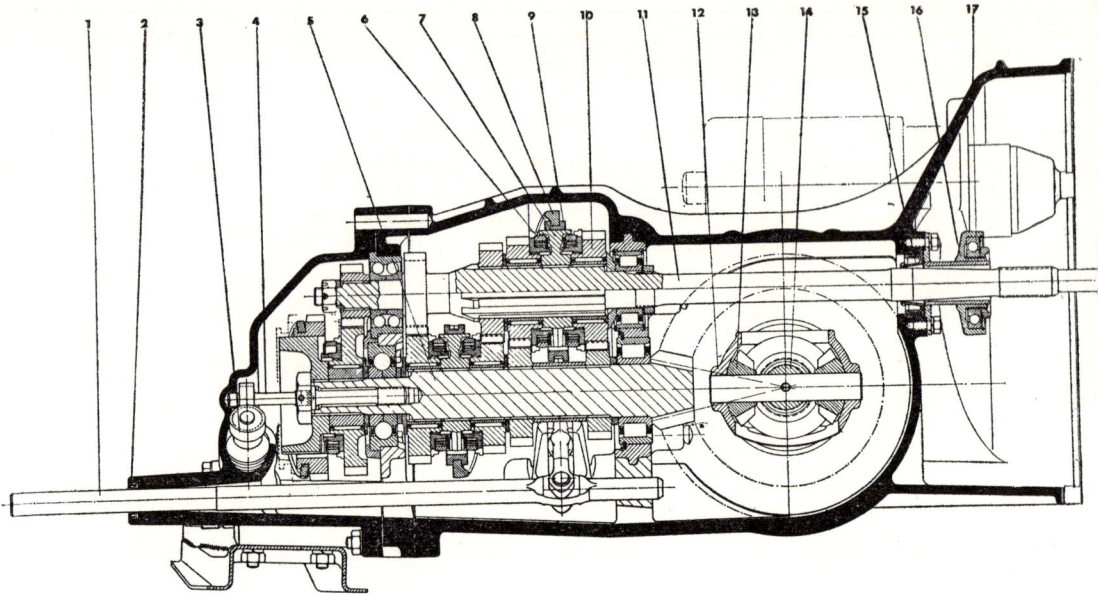

Gearbox Type 822 for 911, 904, 906, 910 and 907 model cars.

Air flow over the rear brakes, fed from an intake at the front end of the rear wings, was less satisfactory. The same intakes also fed the gearbox cooling ducts and their location was apparently excellent as a pressure of 42 mm water was measured at the inlet. Strangely, however, the vacuum measured in the wheel arches was practically not affected at all by blanking off the intakes. Suspecting that most of the cooling air was diverted to the gearbox, the gearbox ducts were closed, but this too was without effect. No explanation was found for this strange phenomenon, which remained the more mysterious for the fact that closing the gearbox cooling ducts or blanking off the air intakes made a significant difference to the vacuum measured in the immediate vicinity of the gearbox: opening the intakes dropped the vacuum from 7.5 mm water to 3.0 mm.

It would be logical to expect a large opening in the rear body panel, as was often seen in contemporary sports racing cars, to increase considerably the air flow through the engine bay under the effect of the vacuum building up behind a car at speed. This was tried on the Carrera 6 with practically no effect on the air pressure in the engine compartment and none on the external air flow.

As a result of these experiments, it was decided to deliver all Carrera 6s with an adjustable rear spoiler and two lateral front spoilers.

In the course of further development testing some doubts arose as to the reliability of the figures obtained for lift and downthrust. These figures can vary considerably with the angle of incidence of the car in the air stream. Consequently new data were obtained six months later, in May 1966, when a production Carrera 6 was tested in the wind tunnel of the Stuttgart Technical High School. Great care was taken this time to ensure that the car could move absolutely freely on its suspension in spite of the small track variations resulting from the suspension geometry. A higher and more realistic air stream speed of 145 mph was also adopted. Though the original test results were generally confirmed, no possibility was found of creating downthrust on both axles simultaneously. The test series was initiated with the car in standard trim with tail and front spoilers. The car had a kerb weight of 608 kg and carried a 72 kg dummy driver. The tanks were full. The test results were as follows:

1.   Standard car with tail and front spoilers:
downthrust on front axle, 90 kg
lift over rear axle, 50 kg
angle of incidence, —1° (rear end lifts).
(the angle of incidence is a result of the front suspension being compressed and the rear suspension being extended by the downthrust and lift respectively).

2.   Car with tail spoiler but no front spoilers:
lift over front axle, 44 kg
lift over rear axle, 2 kg
angle of incidence, +0.4° (car lifts at the front).

3.   Standard car (as under 1) but with no spare wheel in the nose and 25 kg ballast over the rear axle, resulting in an initial angle of incidence of 0.35°:
lift over front axle, 64 kg
downthrust on rear axle, 6 kg
angle of incidence, $0.35° + 0.65° = 1°$.

4.   As under 3 but without tail spoiler:
lift over front axle, 14 kg
lift over rear axle, 110 kg
angle of incidence, $0.35° - 0.6° = -0.25°$.

5.   Car as under 1 but without any spoilers:
lift over front axle, 122 kg
downthrust on rear axle, 6 kg
angle of incidence, +0.86°.

6.   Standard car with front and tail spoilers, but tail spoiler only 50 mm high:
lift over front axle, 29 kg
lift over rear axle, 34 kg
angle of incidence, —0.01°.

These tests showed that it was not possible with the body shape of the Carrera 6 to obtain downthrust simultaneously on the front and rear axles, or even to reach an aerodynamically neutral behaviour, with no lift front and rear. The considerable importance of the static angle of incidence was also confirmed. This is indicated by the comparison between the tests No 1 and No 3 for which the car was externally identical (in standard form) but where test No 3 was carried out with the front-located spare wheel removed and 25 kg ballast over the rear axle, producing a static angle of incidence of 0.35°. As a result of this very small angle, the downthrust of 90 kg on the front axle, which was measured with the angle of incidence zero, was transformed into a lift of 64 kg. Thus the very small static angle of incidence of 0.35° reduced the pressure of the front wheels on the ground by 154 kg. Simultaneously the lift of 50 kg over the rear axle was changed into a downthrust of 6 kg, mainly as a result of the ensuing rocking moment around the front axle.

The great sensitivity of a low drag car to its static angle of incidence is easily explained by the fact that the incidence has a cumulative effect: a very small angle will create lift over the front axle and raise the front of the car, thus increasing the angle of incidence and its effect.

It should be noted that the settings chosen as a result of extensive track testing were apparently the best that could be found as only with the car in its standard form (test No 1 above) is front downthrust obtained together with a significant negative angle of incidence ensuring that when the car is driven over a hump and the front suspension is fully extended, the angle of incidence will not become positive to the extent of becoming dangerous. The 50 kg lift created at a speed of 145 mph over the rear axle is certainly not desirable, but amounting to only about 15 per cent of the total weight borne by the rear wheels, it could still be considered reasonable at the time, though it would be unacceptable today.

Long term research on the Type 906 Carrera 6

While the standard Carrera 6 was being delivered to private customers in its homologated form, the factory proceeded with its development from which the works entries in the prototype group as well as the hill-climb car (generally known as Bergspyder) were to benefit. The development aimed at three main objects:
    saving weight,
    improving the running gear,
    developing the fuel injection system.

Particularly since Ferdinand Piëch became Chief of Development, weight saving has been taken extremely seriously at Porsche. Specially for works entries, when a specific car had to last for only one race before being completely overhauled or even replaced, the possibilities of weight saving were examined to the smallest details. In later years, the policy of building a racing car to last one race only was pushed so far that in all important events the factory competed with only brand-new cars. But things had not yet reached that point at the beginning of 1966.

This weight-saving procedure was carried out with typical German thoroughness. Each development engineer was put in charge of a specific sphere—for instance electrics, brakes, running gear, engine, gearbox and so forth—and asked to examine each single part, down to the smallest, with the aim of reducing its weight, if necessary in co-operation with the sub-contractor responsible for its manufacture. According to the reliability to be expected from the lightened parts, of which the weight was calculated or estimated on the grounds of previous experience, these were classified in four groups:
    suitable for long-distance racing (24 hours)
    suitable for long-distance racing (12 hours)
    suitable for hill-climb car
    suitable for experimental development.

How thoroughly every part was taken into consideration is shown by reports indicating that the windscreen wiper and washer switch, which weighed only 53 gr anyway (less than 2 oz), could be lightened by 7 gr by machining down the large nut securing it to the dashboard; that in the same way 14 gr ($\frac{1}{2}$ oz) could be saved on the ignition switch while 12 gr (less than $\frac{1}{2}$ oz) were saved forthwith by deleting the fuse box cover. In some cases it was found that quite drastic weight savings were possible: for instance 9 kg (and even more if a lighter Motorola alternator was used in place of the Bosch unit) on the electrical parts only of the hill-climb car compared with a long-distance racing car. In later years the alternator was deleted altogether on the Bergspyder.

It was on the running gear, however, that the slimming down action brought the most spectacular results. Investigation showed that, for example, many steel parts of 7.8 specific gravity could be replaced by parts made of aluminium or duralumin (specific gravity 2.7), beryllium (1.85), titanium (4.5), magnesium or even glass fibre (both with a specific gravity of 1.8). It was found that replacing the cast iron brake discs by beryllium discs could cut down their weight from 18.5 to 4.56 kg, this saving being particularly significant as the discs are unsprung parts which should be kept as light as possible in the interests of roadholding, while brake discs also act as undesirable flywheels adversely affecting positive and negative accelerations. Previous tests had indicated that the ultra-light but extremely expensive chrome-plated beryllium brake discs were suitable even for long-distance racing. A notable contribution to the reduction of unsprung weight could also be obtained by the use of titanium front stub axles weighing just over 1 kg, each a saving of 1.55 kg over the equivalent steel part. For the time being, however, they were used only on the Bergspyder.

The conclusion was finally reached that in the case of the Bergspyder, the unsprung part of the brakes could be lightened by a total of no less than 21.2 kg or 62 per cent of the weight of the standard equipment with aluminium brake calipers. Even on the long-distance cars, 17 kg or 50 per cent of the weight could still be saved.

Similar investigations were performed for other parts of the car and it was found that the weight of 76 parts which did not belong either to the engine and transmission unit, or to the chassis frame, or to the body, could be reduced from approximately 91 kg to 50.2 kg, a saving of 40.8 kg and the saving did not always result from the use of different materials. For example, the anti-roll bars could be lightened by about 50 per cent, with no change of stiffness, by the use of a tube instead of a plain bar.

The above weight savings were achieved without recourse to light alloy wheels. As had already been the case with the 904, the Carrera 6 had light alloy rims but the wheel centre was pressed steel. It was calculated that a light alloy centre would save 8.4 kg per pair (this does not include the spare wheel which was already made of light alloy). Pressed alloy wheel centres could be used only for short races, however (hill-climbs and short circuit events), the alloy centre being prone to early fatigue cracks and breakages. Some such pressed alloy wheels were nevertheless ordered for use in short races and duly delivered to the factory. The racing department was not informed of their arrival, however, and only found out when on the 58th lap of the 1966 Spa 1,000 km race Hans Herrmann broke a wheel and crashed at high speed, fortunately without injury. The race crew was very surprised as it had never been intended to use light alloy wheels for such a long and fast race as the Spa event. Only when they were back in Stuttgart was it discovered that when the wheels were delivered, nobody in the stores department noticed that they were not ordinary steel ones and they were mixed with the other spares. The breakage on Herrmann's car did not have any serious consequence but several alloy wheels had been sold to normal customers and nobody knew to whom they had gone. So a crash operation had to be organised to retrieve the wheels before they broke— perhaps with catastrophic consequences—and they were finally all retrieved, one of them from as far afield as Japan!

As already mentioned, the Carrera 6 had practically the same running gear as the 904 except for its wider rims and tyres and for the metallic pivots and joints in the suspension, as tried previously on factory-entered prototypes. There were no major handling problems in the development period which was also helped by the fact that the new car had about the same torsional rigidity as the 904. The six-cylinder engine had proved itself too, experience having been gained by the factory which had run several six-cylinder-engined 904s in various races. After the Carrera 6 had been finalised, however, and most of the production models had been delivered to their customers, development testing was pursued on the circular pad of the Porsche proving ground in Weissach, primarily to gather as much data as possible for future models. Among the data collected on the 190-metre diameter circular pad was the roll angle relative to the lateral force. This was done by photographing the car from the front. From the roll angle the wheel camber angles could be deduced and later used in connection with tyre tests on a roller test bed. Among the data obtained, the lateral acceleration of 0.84 g on wet asphalt using Dunlop R7 Mk 2 Red Spot dry weather tyres is rather remarkable. Another interesting finding is that on a wet track the driver had to reduce the steering lock slightly as the limit of adhesion was approached, indicating that the car was beginning to hang its tail out, while on a dry circuit the steering lock had to be progressively increased up to the limit of adhesion reached at around 1 g lateral acceleration.

Before tyre tests were carried out on the test bed of the Technical High School, Karlsruhe, it had become usual for Porsche to try out several brands of Dunlop tyres (Porsche had a contract with Dunlop) during the practice period preceding all races, but occasionally Goodyear tyres were also tried and quite often turned out to be slightly faster than Dunlops. Following this, the factory decided, some time in 1966, to carry out comparative tests on the Hockenheim circuit for which a works driver who shall be nameless was summoned to the track. He was sent out alternately with various types of Dunlop tyres and comparative Goodyear tyres, times being taken separately for the fast part of the Hockenheim circuit and for the slow and very winding section called the Motodrom. On the latter part, there was very little difference in the times obtained with either make of tyre, but on the fast part the Goodyears were apparently quite unexpectedly slower. This seemed so strange that someone got suspicious and sent an observer out to the fast part of the track, taking great care that the driver shouldn't see him. The mystery was soon explained: each time the car ran on Goodyears, the driver slowed down on the straight. It was a good reminder of the fact that today's drivers are not only interested in the sport but also drive for a living: good contracts are not to be scorned!

Long-tail and flap cars

Further work was devoted to the development of a Carrera 6 derivative particularly suitable for racing on high-speed tracks, such as Le Mans. For this purpose a new, better-streamlined body was designed, mainly differing from the standard body in its longer nose and notably longer and slimmer tail giving a smaller area at the breakaway point, where the air flow becomes turbulent. The first experiments in the wind tunnel were made by fitting a cardboard nose and tail to a standard car. This gave a drag coefficient of 0.306 which in practice was raised to Cw=0.326 because the undershield was deleted in the interests of better gearbox cooling and because little tail spoilers increased the cross section of the breakaway area. Inevitably, the longer body made the car slightly heavier and less manoeuvrable, but the 10-16 mph increase in maximum speed obtained with appropriate gearing proved to be a definite advantage at Le Mans.

In contrast the so-called Carrera 'Flap Car' was of a purely experimental nature. Its aim was to investigate the unfluence of aerodynamics on handling and road-holding. The test car was the Carrera 6 No 906 141 which for many years was used by the factory as a guinea pig. On this occasion, two large and more or less hori-zontal flaps were recessed into the rear body panels and could be raised separately by the driver from inside the car. Several locations were tried for these rear flaps, among which the one illustrated proved to be the most efficient. The car also had standard size lateral front spoilers which were made to pivot so as to reduce their surface or disappear altogether. Their angle of incidence was about 22° and they had a total surface area of 0.019 m² when partially extended and 0.047 m² when fully extended. The two rear flaps were much larger: they had a total surface area of

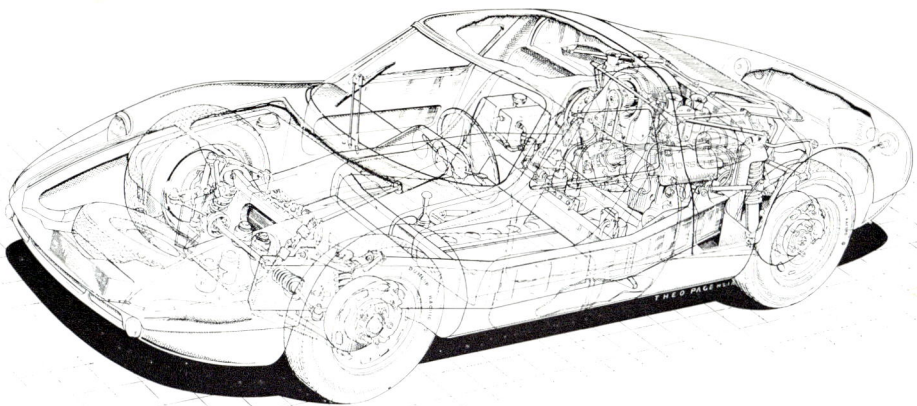

Carrera GTS, Type 904

Technical specification

Engine:	4 stroke flat-four, air-cooled, 4 ohc
Bore:	92 mm
Stroke:	74 mm
Capacity:	1966 cc
Power output (DIN):	180 hp at 7000 rpm
Chassis frame:	Box section pressed steel
Suspension, front and rear:	Transverse wishbones and coil springs
Body:	Glass fibre

Dimensions

Length:	4090 mm
Width:	1540 mm
Height:	1065 mm
Wheelbase:	2300 mm
Track, front:	1314 mm
rear:	1312 mm

Left-hand rear suspension. Note the inner universal joint of a design accommodating both angular and axial movements.

Left-hand front suspension

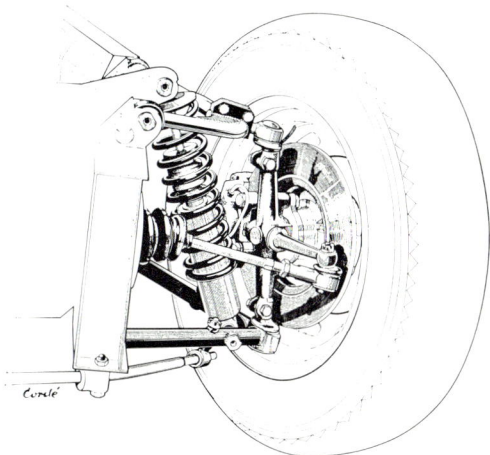

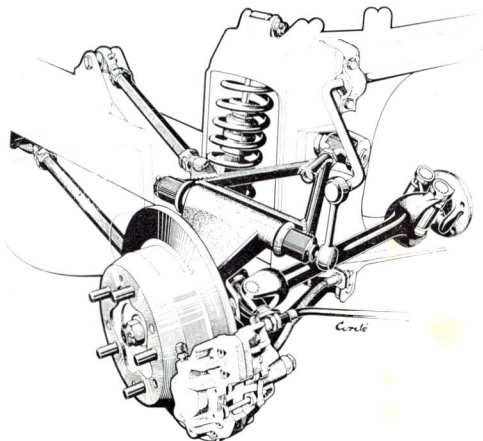

Edgar Barth: he lived for Porsche and twice became European Hill-climb Champion on Porsche cars.

The Kangaroo (906 007), an open-bodied eight-cylinder engined car based on the 904 pressed steel frame. It came second in the 1965 Targa Florio, but its roadholding was unsatisfactory and Mitter (seen driving the car) crashed it in practice for the Nurburgring 1,000 km race.

Rear part of the Ollon-Villars car (906 010). Its tubular space frame is the ancestor of all modern Porsche racing frames. It was devoid of the rear 'pyramid'.

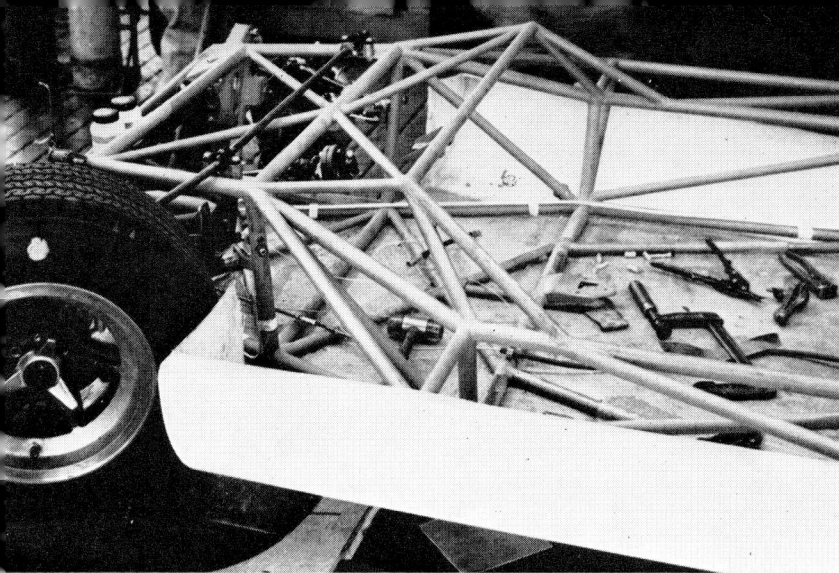

Front part of Ollon-Villars car with Lotus wheels and suspension parts.

Lotus magnesium upright on car 906 010 (Ollon-Villars 1965).

The 906 010 Bergspyder was built in three weeks for the Ollon-Villars hill-climb using Lotus suspension parts. Gerhard Mitter is at the wheel.

Carrera 6 engine (Type 901/20). The disc type oil filter seen next to the flywheel is bolted to the flange used for the oil filter in standard production 911 engines.

Carrera 6 engine (Type 901/20) with diaphragm clutch. The plastic air cowls can be seen.

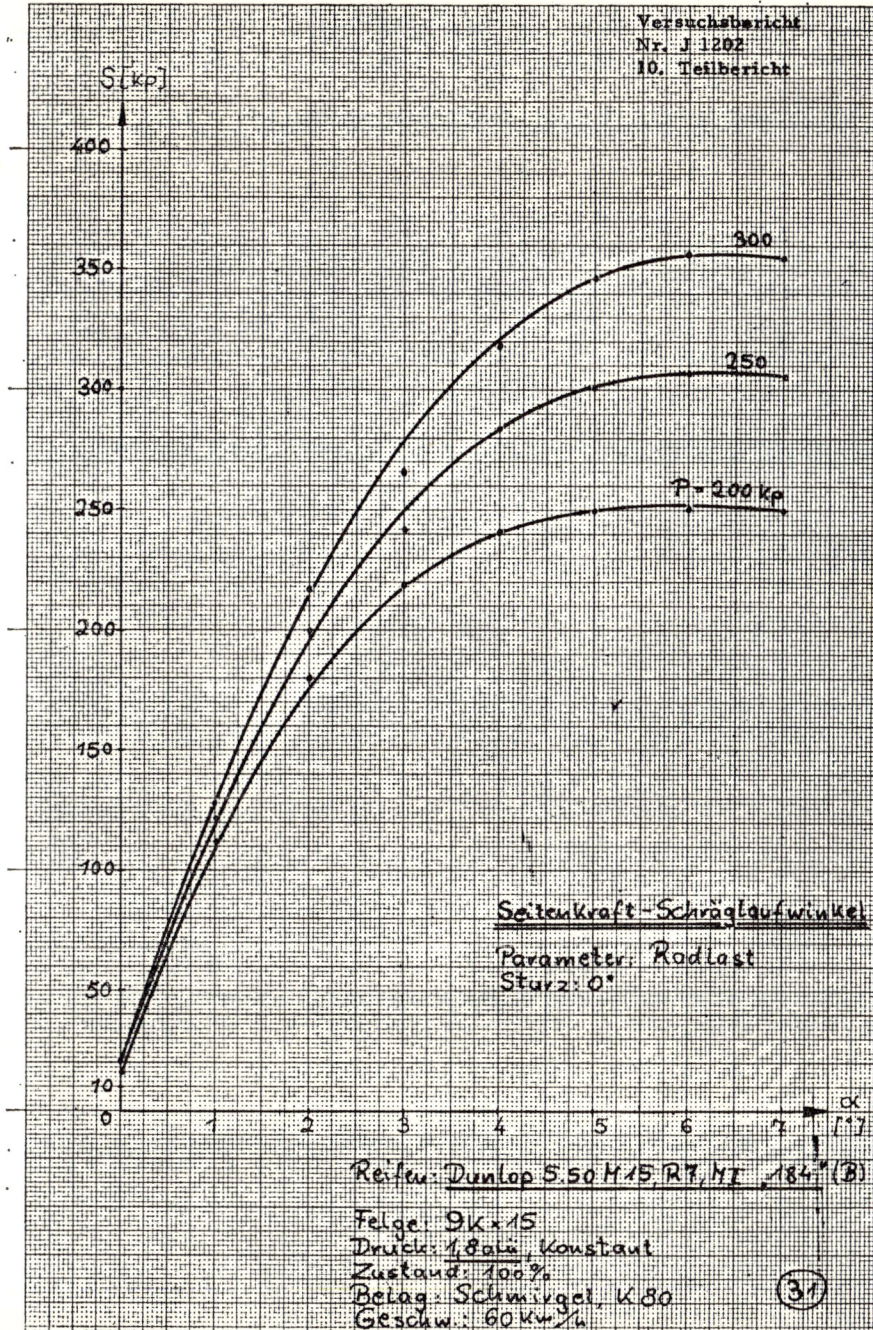

Typical slip angle curves related to the cornering force for three different static wheel loads (200, 250 and 300 kg). Dunlop R7 racing tyres 5.50 M—15 on 9K × 15 rims. Inflation pressure, 26 psi. Speed 60 kph.

c

0.19 m² and could be raised to form an angle of about 30° to the nearly horizontal body surface. The car was first tested on the Grand Prix course at Hockenheim, with Herrmann driving, then in the wind tunnel of the Technical High School, Stuttgart. For the track tests, the usual small multi-coloured rods were attached to the front wishbones and driven through the wings to measure any compression or extension of the front suspension due to aerodynamic forces at speed.

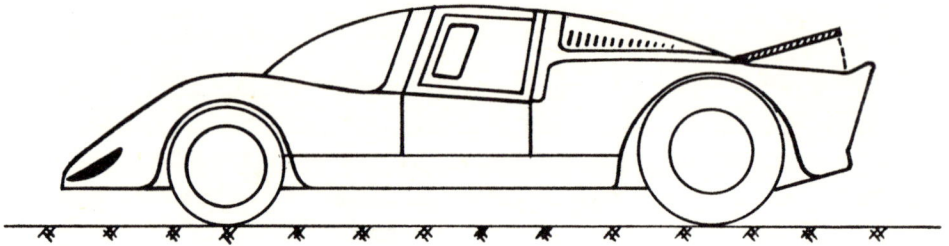

Schematic drawing of Carrera 6 experimental 'Flap' car indicating the position of the mobile front and rear flaps.

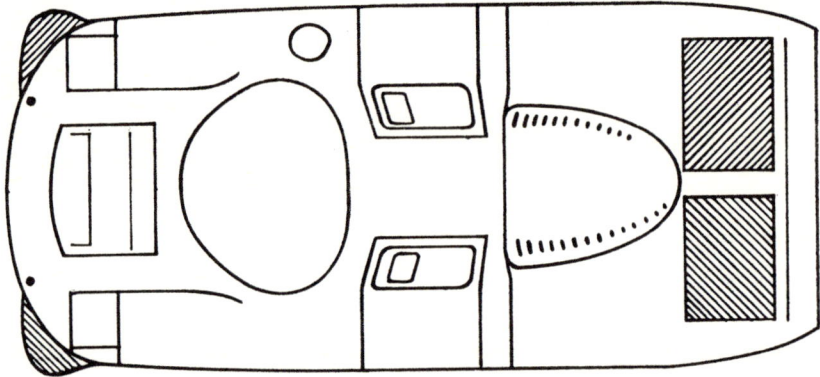

Practically any reasonable combination of front and rear flaps was tried as well as the effect of flaps on one side only. The test series was concluded on the Weissach circular pad in order to understand better the effect of the flaps on cornering speed. Subsequent wind tunnel tests confirmed pretty accurately the findings of the road tests.

Summing up the tests, it was found that the influence of the flaps on cornering speeds was astonishingly small even though the driver who did the testing at Hockenheim insisted that they made a great difference to the behaviour of the vehicle and his findings were confirmed by the circular pad tests where any tendency to oversteer or understeer could be accurately detected by measuring the angle of steering wheel rotation. Even at 75 mph on the circular pad, the influence of the flaps was quite considerable and there is no doubt that their effect was even more noticeable on the fast curves of the Hockenheimring. But it must be remembered that when all flaps were raised which, according to the driver, gave the best cornering behaviour (this was confirmed by the tests on the circular pad), the drag was so high that the engine had no excess power to drive the car through the fast East Curve. This explains why the speed through the curve was no higher than without any aerodynamic aids. The slowest speed through this curve was obtained

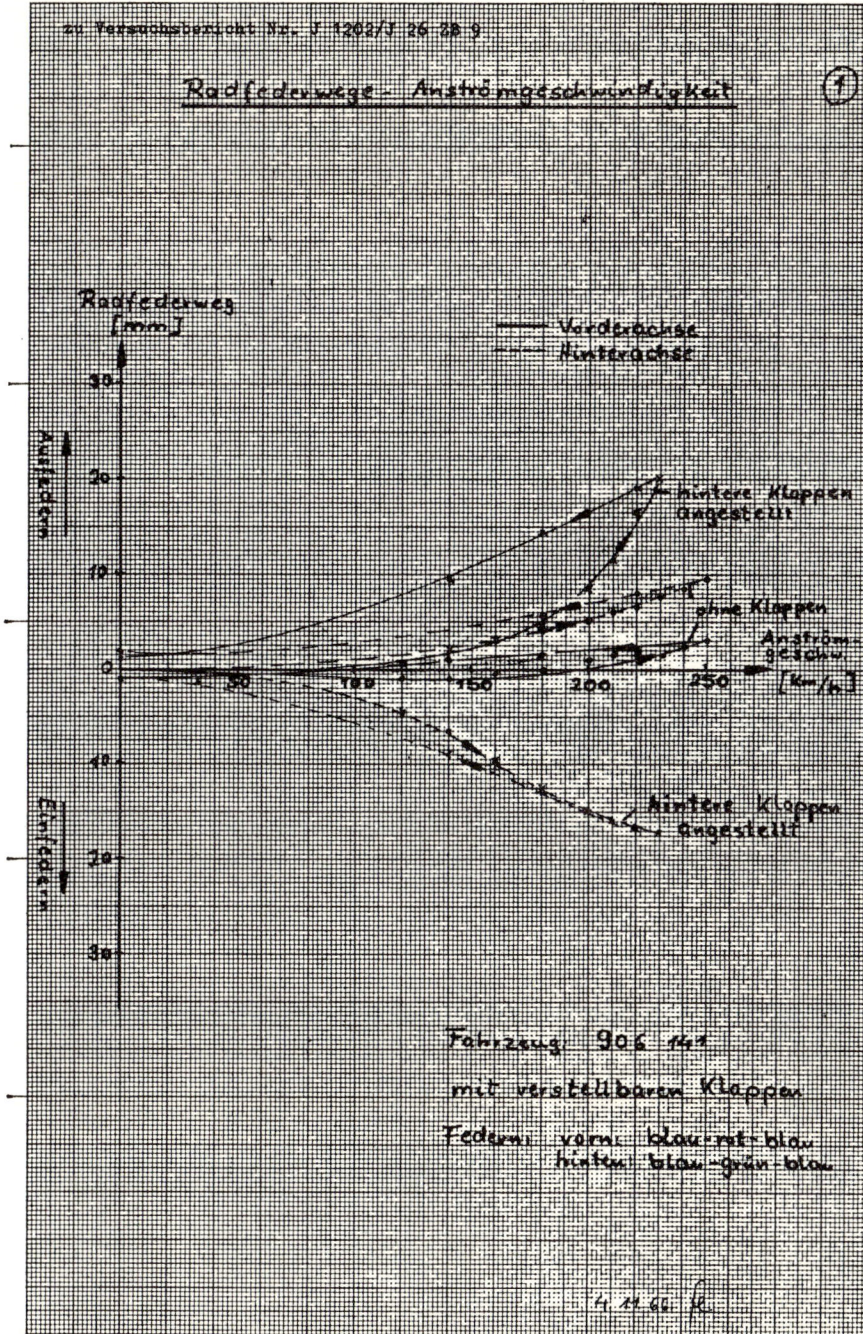

Carrera 6 Flap car. Diagram of front and rear suspension movements in function of the air speed for various positions of the rear flaps. Vorderachse=front axle; Hinterachse=rear axle; Radfederweg= wheel movement; Ausfedern=extension; Einfedern=compression; Hintere Klappen angestellt= rear flaps raised; Ohne Klappen=without flaps.

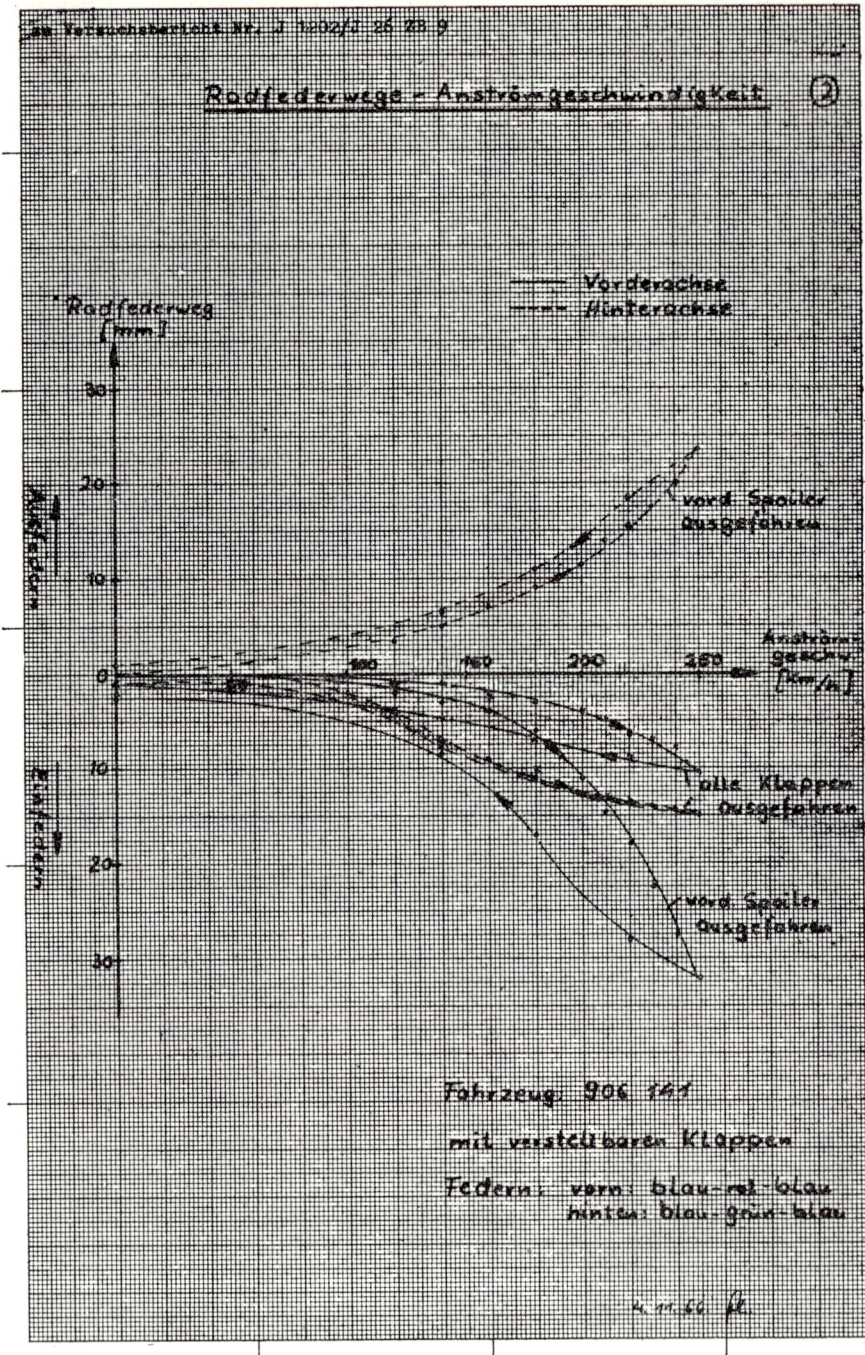

Carrera 6 Flap car. Diagram of front and rear suspension movements in function of the air speed for various positions of front and rear flaps. Vordere Spoiler ausgefahren=front spoilers extended; Alle Klappen ausgefahren=all flaps and spoilers extended. For other translations see page 41.

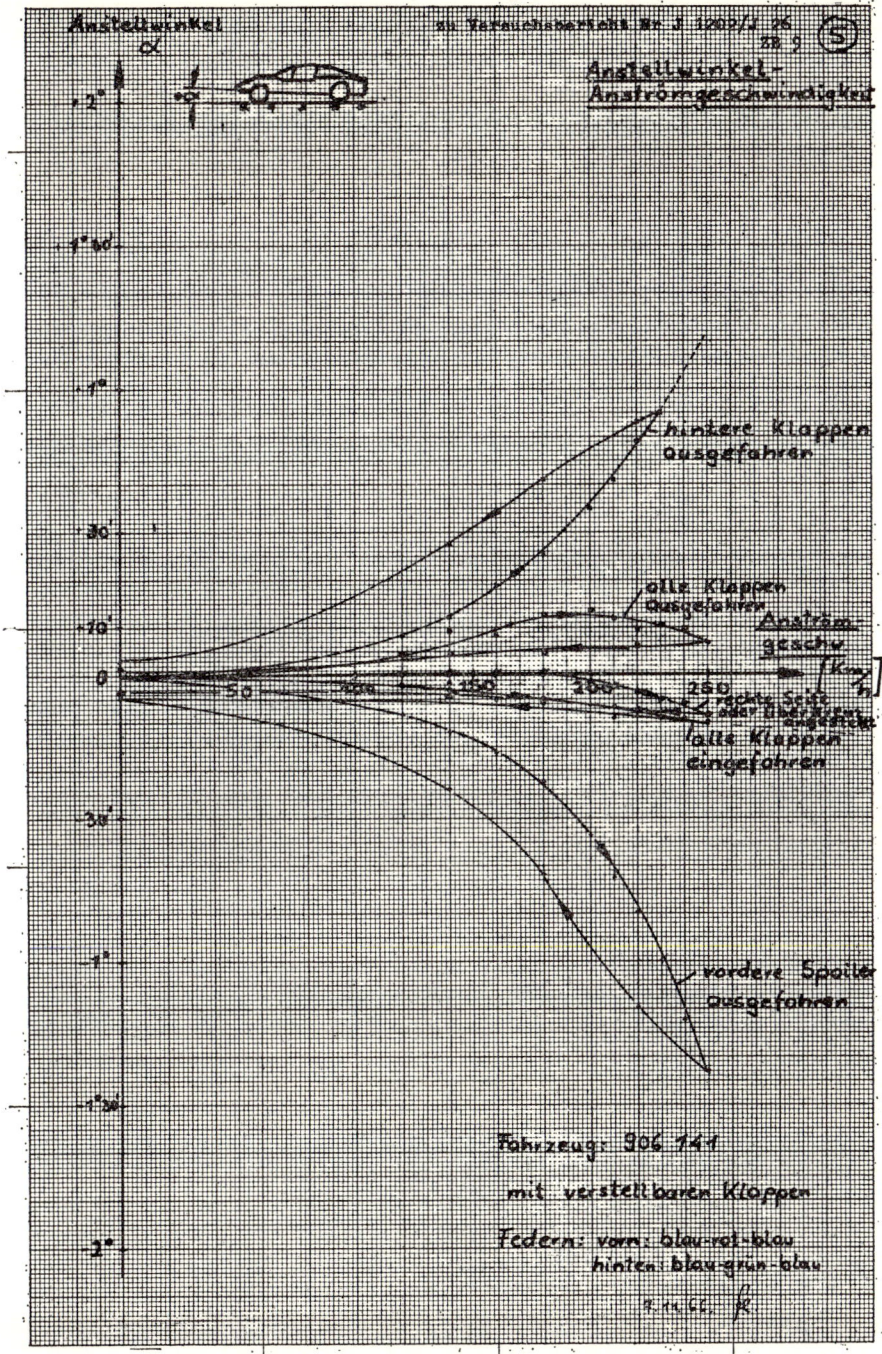

*Carrera 6 Flap car. Diagram showing the angle of attitude in function of the **air speed**.*
Anstellwinkel=angle of attitude. Other translations as pages 41 and 42.

with the front spoilers fully extended and retracted rear flaps (best time about 3 per cent slower, average about 5 per cent slower). Severe understeer induced by raising the rear flaps (increasing rear wheel adhesion) and nearly complete retraction of the front spoilers, gave the lowest lateral acceleration on the circular pad but in practice the car was only insignificantly slower through the East Curve.

These were the results obtained on the Weissach circular pad for the most important combinations:

(a) Without any flaps or spoilers: centripetal acceleration=1.05 g.
(b) Rear flaps raised: centripetal acceleration=1.05 g.
(c) Front spoilers fully extended: centripetal acceleration=1.07 g (car oversteers at the limit).
(d) Front spoilers and rear flaps fully extended: centripetal acceleration=1.11 g.

The circular track tests also confirmed the findings made at Hockenheim, that the cornering power is improved not only by extending all spoilers and flaps, but also by extending them on one side only and that, on whatever side the flaps are in use, it makes very little difference whether the corner is to the right or the left though what little difference there is indicates that it is an advantage if the flaps increase the load on the inside wheels.

On the circular track where the full engine power could not be used, the best times were obtained, as expected, with all spoilers and flaps extended, but at Hockenheim this condition produced the slowest lap times in spite of optimum cornering behaviour. This results from the fact that in practice cornering speed is only little affected by the aerodynamic aids, whereas on the fast Hockenheim track the speed down the two long straights is the deciding factor. This was confirmed by the correspondence of lap times and engine revolutions on the straights. Here, with all flaps retracted, 7,800 rpm were reached while only 7,000 rpm could be obtained with all flaps raised, corresponding to a loss of about 15 mph in maximum speed. Even on the slow and very winding Motodrom course, full use of the flaps did not produce the best lap times, probably because the high drag had an adverse effect on acceleration.

The considerable drag increase caused mainly by the rear flaps was confirmed in the wind tunnel. After covering up the front spoiler recesses with tape, a drag coefficient Cw=0.354 was measured for the actual test car with the flaps lowered. (It should be remembered that the figure for the production Carrera 6 with standard front and tail spoilers was Cw=0.346.) With all flaps fully extended, the coefficient was raised to 0.487 and to 0.464 with the tail flaps alone.

From these tests it was concluded that for a 2-litre car of comparatively limited power output, fixed spoilers no doubt improved the cornering behaviour but reduced straight line performance excessively. This is why some time later mobile flaps were developed which were connected to the rear suspension in such a way that they had only a very small angle of incidence during straight line driving but increased the downthrust as the suspension was extended.

The Hockenheim tests were also used as an opportunity to try a surface oil cooler forming the upper surface of the car's nose. As a cooler it was much inferior to the through-flow cooler normally used: after six laps at Hockenheim the oil temperature rose to 110° C while with the standard cooler it did not exceed 75° C. The use of a surface cooler had been contemplated because it was thought that the aerodynamic drag could be reduced by closing the front air intake required by the through-flow cooler. As, however, the subsequent wind tunnel tests showed that practically nothing was gained by blanking off the intake, the surface cooler was soon forgotten.

Wind tunnel tests centring around the long-tail car hinted at another possibility of reducing the drag by some 3 per cent when it was found that the drag coefficient of 0.326 rose to 0.334 when the engine was running and expelling its cooling air underneath the car. This was avoided by appropriately ducting the cooling air towards the back of the car and thus avoiding any disturbance of the air flowing around the vehicle.

3

Development of the six- and eight-cylinder engines

ALTOGETHER 65 UNITS of the tubular frame Type 906 were made. Fifty-two of them were standard Carrera 6s, nine were prototypes using a fuel injection version of the six-cylinder engine, and four were eight-cylinder prototypes with a capacity of 2.2 litres. The various means of weight saving which had been investigated were never applied in their entirety to the 906, but some of the solutions recommended were tried on cars running in the prototype group, as, for example, the chrome-plated beryllium brake discs. The most important difference between the homologated sports racing cars and the prototypes was the engine.

Power and torque curves of engine Type 901/21.

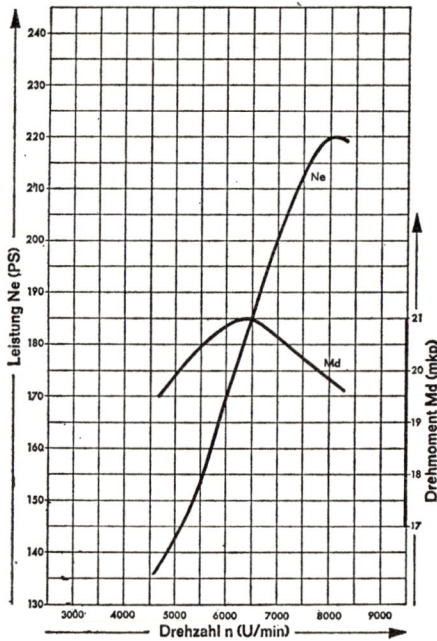

Power and torque curves of engine Type 901/20

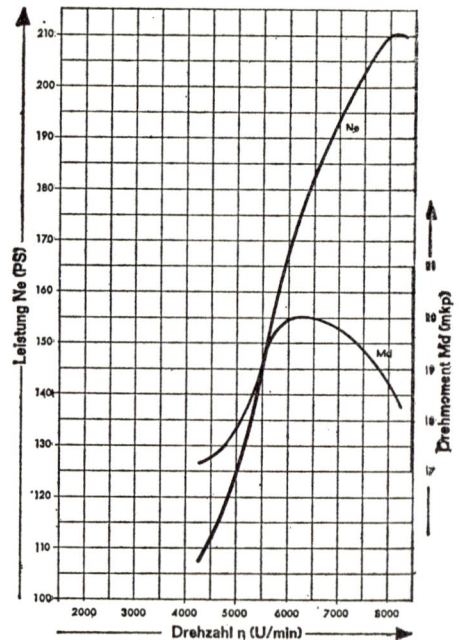

Leistung=power Drehmoment=torque Drehzahl=rpm.

The six-cylinder prototype used an engine (Type 901/21) fed by a Bosch fuel injection system instead of the two Weber triple-choke carburettors of the Type 901/20 engine. The fuel injection plant consisted mainly of an electric centrifugal pump which fed the fuel to a six-plunger injection pump. This was driven through a cog belt from the rear of the right-hand camshaft and fed the injectors located aft of the throttle slides under a pressure of 260 psi. As usual in racing injection systems, the slide replaced the more common butterfly throttles in this installation. The fuel was metered mechanically by means of a cam incorporated in the injection pump. Even with the slide in the closed position, the pump continued to inject the fuel normally required at idling. In later installations the two-dimensional metering cam was replaced by a three-dimensional cam taking account of engine speed through a centrifugal governor which notably reduced the fuel consumption. In this installation, the fuel supply to the injectors was stopped completely on the overrun as long as the engine was running at over 4,000 rpm. This enabled the injectors to be relocated at the top of the intake trumpets, upstream of the throttle slide, resulting in a more homogeneous mixture, and preventing fuel from accumulating above the slides on the overrun, which would have caused the engine to be fed with too rich a mixture when the throttles were re-opened. The 10.3:1 compression ratio was maintained for the fuel injection engine, but the output was raised from 210 to 220 hp at the same rate of 8,000 rpm, while the maximum torque was increased from 146 lb/ft at 6,000 rpm to 153 lb/ft at 6,400 rpm. These correspond to mean effective pressures of 181 lb/sq in and 190 lb/sq in respectively.

The first track tests with the injection engine took place in March 1966 at Hockenheim. There were no improvements in lap times compared with the carburettor engine but the fuel consumption was reduced and the engine was more flexible. The 911 production fuel injection unit was later developed from the racing engine.

In contrast to the six-cylinder engine, the eight-cylinder was designed purely for racing. Its origins go back to the time when Porsche decided to take part in Formula 1 racing, when engines were limited to a capacity of 1,500 cc unsupercharged. At the

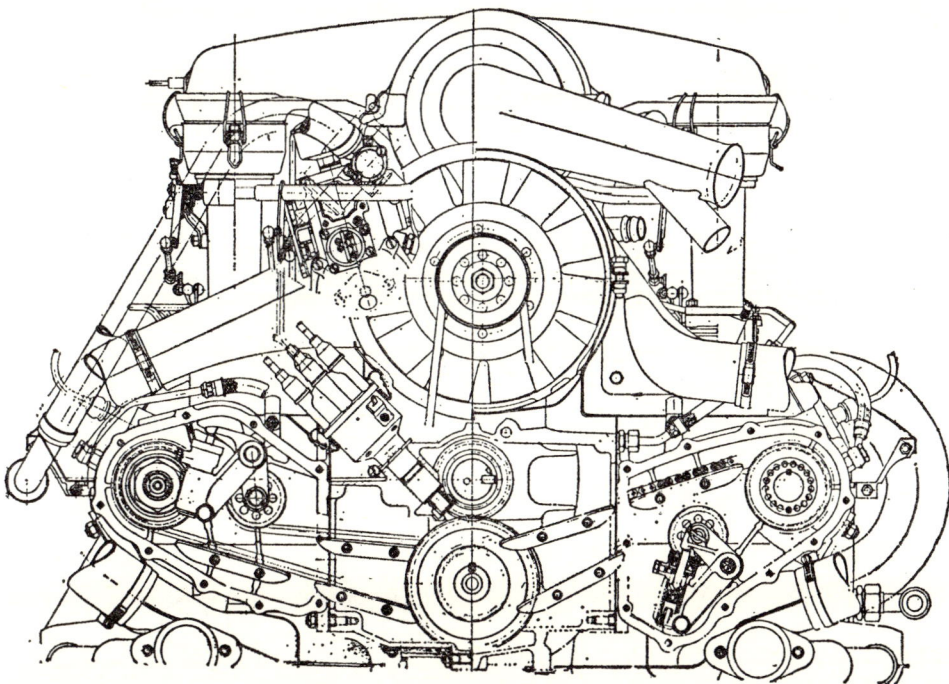

Cross section of engine Type 901 showing the camshaft drive.

time when this formula came into force, Porsche already had a 1,500 cc racing engine: the four-cylinder Carrera racing unit. But it could hardly be expected to produce more than 175 hp, even when developed to the very limits of its possibilities. It was consequently decided to design an entirely new eight-cylinder Formula 1 engine, the dimensions of which would be chosen so that it could also be enlarged to 2 litres for sports and prototype racing. The two versions were, in fact, developed simultaneously and the 2-litre was used for the first time in the 1962 Targa Florio. It had the same stroke of 54.5 mm as the 1,500 cc Grand Prix engine, but its bore was increased from 66 to 76 mm.

The very short stroke was chosen because it would allow the engine to run at 11,000 rpm at a piston speed of around 3,600 ft min, considered to be the limit of acceptability (to start with the target was 10,000 rpm), and because this resulted in a shorter crankshaft. In this connection it should be remembered that, with opposed cylinders, the minimum overall length of the engine depends not on the length of the cylinder blocks but on the length of the crankshaft. The shorter the stroke, the shorter the crankshaft can be made as its strength and rigidity depend to a large extent on the overlap between the crankpins and the journals, and the larger the overlap, the thinner the flanges can be kept. Another advantage of a very short stroke for a flat engine is that the connecting rods can be kept shorter, thus reducing the overall width of the unit. The large bore also permitted the use of very large diameter valves.

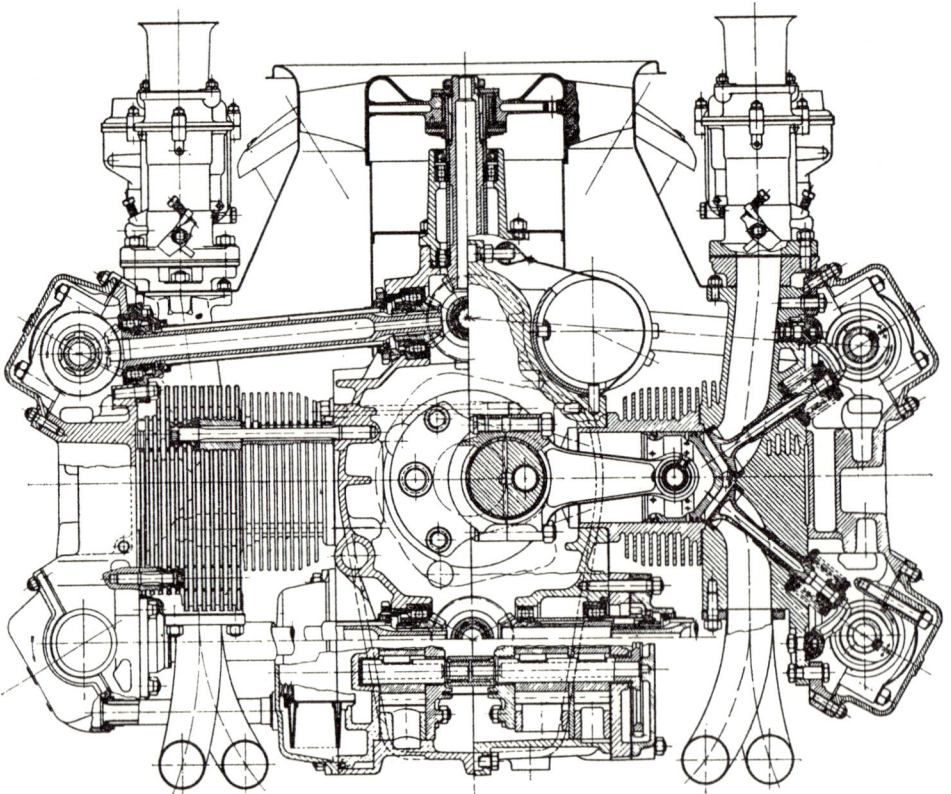

Cross section of engine Type 771 eight-cylinder (2-litre).

The choice of a flat engine for this entirely new unit was not only a question of tradition and previous experience, for it also had the advantage of slightly lowering the centre of gravity of the car. As the complication of this engine, known as Type 753 in 1.5-litre form and 771 in 2-litre form, indicates, nothing was spared to make it as efficient as possible. The four camshafts were hollow to save weight. They were driven from two gear-driven shafts, running parallel to the crankshaft, by four cross shafts having bevel gears at each end. The longitudinal shafts were used to drive a plastic axial fan running at 9,200 rpm (at 10,000 rpm engine speed), at which speed it fed the engine with 1,400 litres of cooling air per second; they also drove the twin ignition system and the three pumps of the dry sump lubrication system. This comprised one scavenge pump for the sump, one pump scavenging the cam boxes and one pressure feed pump. All were of the gear pattern. The lubrication system was remarkable in that the nine plain main bearings were fed in the usual way from a longitudinal gallery drilled in the crankcase, and the big end bearings (also plain) were supplied with oil, fed axially into the crankshaft at the front end of the engine, the shaft being drilled through its entire length to ensure the supply of oil to the crankpins. This method made unnecessary the circumferential groove with which the main bearings must be provided if they have to ensure the constant flow of oil to the big end bearings. Doing without the groove makes possible a reduction in the width of the bearings, without any reduction in bearing area, thus reducing the length of the crankshaft and, at the same time, increasing its torsional rigidity. This method of lubricating the crankshaft journals proved so successful that it was later also applied to the eight- and twelve-cylinder engines used in the Types 908 and 917. The Type 771 eight-cylinder engine, designed to the highest standards of efficiency, was so complicated that it took a racing mechanic 220 working hours on average to put it together, while assembling a six-cylinder 901 series engine, as used in the standard Carrera 6, took only 14-16 hours!

In the course of 1962, the steel connecting rods of the eight-cylinder engine were

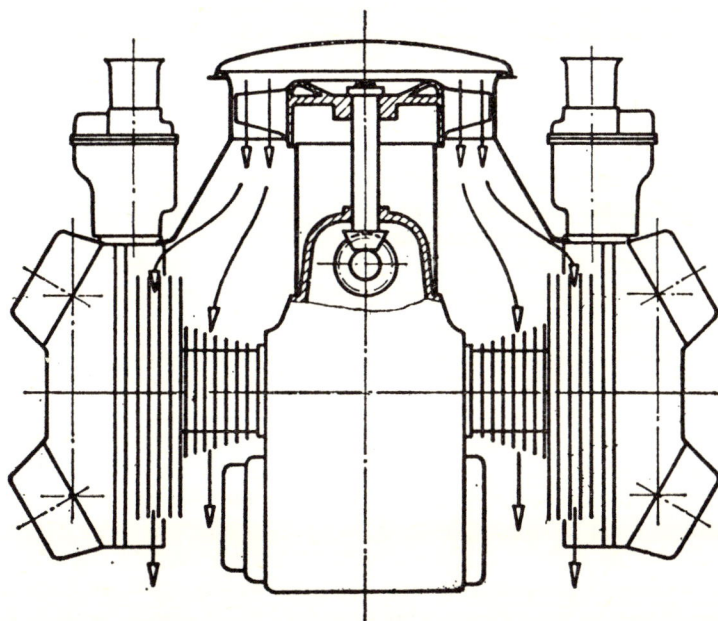

Cooling, engine 771 eight-cylinder.

replaced by 30 per cent lighter titanium rods making it possible to reduce the diameter of the crankshaft journals and also to reduce the oil supply to them. This combined operation increased the power output of the engine by no less than 12 hp.

Despite the extensive use of high tensile and light alloys (titanium for the connecting rods, magnesium for the crankcase, camboxes and all covers, aluminium for the cylinder heads and the internally chrome-plated cylinders and their cooling fins—the so-called chromal cylinders) this complicated engine was not by any means light: it weighed 155 and 160 kg (340 and 350 lb) respectively in 1.5- and 2-litre forms which, for the 2-litre in its original form, with 240 hp and carburettors, corresponds to a specific output of 0.67 kg/hp (1.48 lb/hp). This is certainly quite heavy if compared with the later eight-cylinder Type 908, as used in 1969, which produced 350 hp for only 178 kg (393 lb), a specific weight of 0.51 kg/hp (1.13 lb/hp).

Both in 1.5- and 2-litre forms, the eight cylinder engine was fed by four twin-choke Weber downdraught carburettors. The 2-litre was first used in the Type 718 Spyder. Then it was used for prototype versions of the 904, driving through a five-speed gearbox of 911 origin instead of the old six-speed gearbox. It also propelled Edgar Barth to two titles as European Hill-climb Champion in 1963 and 1964 and was also used by Gerhard Mitter—in this case with fuel injection—when he won the European Hill-climb Championship for three years in succession, from 1966 to 1968.

When it was used in the space frame 906, the eight-cylinder engine was set higher targets: it was to make Porsche works entries competitive with the fastest machines the opposition could muster, not only in the Targa Florio, where manoeuvrability is more important than sheer power, but also in other, faster races. As, with this engine, the ambitions went beyond a class win, the cylinder bore was increased from 76 to 80 mm to bring the total capacity up to 2.2 litres and the carburettors were replaced by a Bosch fuel injection system. Except for the fact that the pump had eight plungers instead of six, this installation was identical to that of the six-cylinder engine. The injection pump, driven from the left inlet camshaft via a cog belt, underwent the same development as that of the six-cylinder engine: in 1967, the two dimensional metering cam was replaced by a three dimensional space cam regulating the quantity of fuel injected not only as a function of the throttle opening, but also as a function of the engine speed. For the reasons already given, this made it possible to relocate the injectors at the top of the intake trumpets, providing the engine with a more homogeneous mixture.

In this form, the power output was raised by some 35 hp to 275 hp, of which 15 were a result of the increased capacity and 20 came from the fuel injection and larger valve overlap.

Despite all racing successes, some doubts were expressed in technical circles at the time as to the suitability of the air cooling which seemed to be part of Porsche's technical religion. It was suggested that precious horsepower was being wasted not only because of the power absorbed by the cooling fan, but also because the specific output had to be kept down in the interests of reliability. Nobody in fact suspected how little power was actually absorbed by the cooling fan: at 8,900 rpm, at which the engine produced its maximum power, initially only 9 hp were absorbed, rising to 12 hp after some modifications had been adopted to improve the cooling efficiency. In this connection, it must be remembered that an aircooled engine requires much less air flow than a corresponding water-cooled engine, because the heat exchange is much quicker with a temperature differential (the difference

Typ 771-2,2 Ltr. Motorleistung Ne

V_H = 2196 cm³
D = 80 mm
s = 54,6 mm

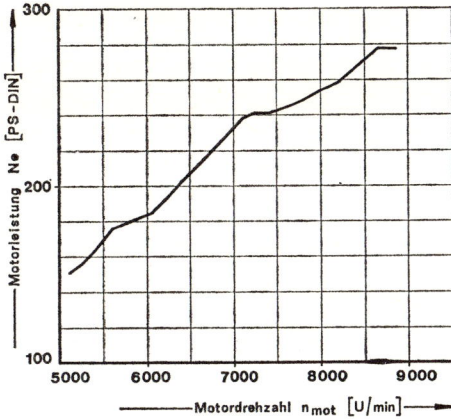

Typ 771-2 Ltr. Motorleistüng Ne

V_H = 1982 cm³
D = 76 mm
s = 54,6 mm

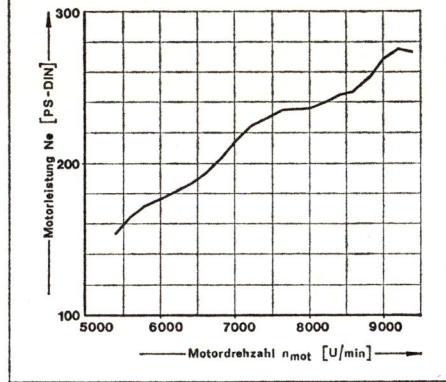

Power curve of Type 771 2.2-litre, fuel injection, eight-cylinder engine as used for long distance racing in cars Type 910 and 907. Maximum bmep 193 lb/sq in at 7,000 rpm. Maximum torque 170 lb/ft at 7,000 rpm.

Power curve of Type 771 2-litre, eight-cylinder fuel injection engine as used for Bergspyders Types 906, 910 and 909. Maximum bmep 195 lb/sq in at 7,100 rpm. Maximum torque 156 lb/ft at 7,100 rpm.

between the cooling fin temperature and the air temperature) of around 280° C, than when it does not exceed some 80° C, which would apply to the air flowing through a radiator in which the coolant temperature does not exceed 100° C. At speeds of the 170 mph order, the 12 hp required by the cooling blower are much less than the power absorbed by the drag created by the air flowing through a water radiator. Disregarding the power absorbed by the blower, the output of the engine becomes 287 hp, a specific power of 130 hp/litre which certainly does not compare badly with the specific output of other contemporary engines. If anything, it indicates that the air cooling did not call for any sacrifice of engine efficiency. For hill-climbs, in which the capacity limit was set at 2 litres and the event was short, the 771 engine retained its original 2-litre capacity but with fuel injection, and by 1967 its specific power output reached 136 hp/litre (without blower, 142 hp/ litre) : it produced 272 hp at 9,000 rpm.

Unfortunately, the fuel injection 2.2-litre eight-cylinder, as used in the Type 906 in 1966 and in the Type 910 the following year, was far less reliable than the much simpler, but not so powerful six-cylinder.

A larger oil pressure pump and the previously mentioned improvements to the cooling system (which cost 3 hp) were not satisfactory remedies, the main offender being the attachment of the flywheel to the crankshaft (if we may call the very light dished wheel driving the diaphragm clutch a 'flywheel'). This was driven by a Hirth dog coupling which was taken from the old Grand Prix engine and was just too weak for the much higher torque developed by the current 2.2-litre, fuel injected power plant. No quick remedy was found to this problem, and finally the decision was taken in 1967 to redesign both the crankshaft and the flywheel using a straight-forward flange attachment and additionally to provide the crankshaft with a torsional vibration damper. Unfortunately, long delivery times delayed the introduction of the new part until 1968, when the 2.2-litre, which was progressively being replaced by the new 3-litre engine, had become Porsche's most reliable racing engine. This, however, has no bearing on the development story of the 906.

4

Hill-climb and experimental cars
leading up to the Type 910

AS ALREADY MENTIONED, a long development period was not required to make the Carrera 6, and its derivatives running as works prototypes, an extremely successful model. This is not surprising, however, when one remembers that between the beginning of the 904 production, in the first weeks of 1964, and the completion of the first Carrera 6, nearly two years later, the Porsche racing and experimental department (which form a single unit at Porsche) had been relentlessly at work improving the chassis of the 904 and developing it to take more powerful six- and eight-cylinder engines, as well as investigating new possibilities in chassis design. As early as July 1964, only a few weeks after the last 904 had been delivered, a car of this type ran with an eight-cylinder Type 771 engine in the 12-Hour race at Reims (which it did not finish owing to gearbox failure).

That the eight-cylinder 904/8 appeared, even before a six-cylinder version was seen, is easily explained by the fact that the eight-cylinder engine had already been used successfully in previous years and had attained a certain maturity, while the racing derivative of the Type 911 six - cylinder unit was still being developed. The first time a six-cylinder engined 904 appeared (we shall call the six- and eight-cylinder derivatives of the 904, 904/6 and 904/8 respectively for easier identification) was in the Paris 1,000 km race in October in which the eight-cylinder version scored its first success: victory in the 2-litre class and third place overall.

Much care was dedicated to the development of the 904/6, because at this stage it had already been decided that the 904's successor would use the six-cylinder engine. Before the Paris 1,000 km race, the car had undergone tests on the Porsche circular track in Weissach as well as on the Nürburgring and at Hockenheim. The main object of these tests was to optimise the suspension settings for use on the road, as well as on the race track, and to find out the best location for the air intakes to get the highest possible pressure around the carburettors and the highest possible flow of air to cool the engine, the transmission and the brakes. In spite of the much higher power output of the six-cylinder engine compared with the four-cylinder (210 as against about 180), the same rims (5 in wide at the front and 6 in wide at the rear) were used, and the comparatively low standard of the contemporary racing tyres is reflected by the fact that the best time recorded round the Hockenheim track on racing tyres (1 m 47.2 s) was only 2.8 s faster than the best time obtained on 60 per cent worn radial road tyres. It should, however, be pointed out that practically new, just rubbed-in radial tyres were notably slower because of the lesser rigidity of the thick tread.

It is also notable that the lap times obtained by the test engineers on the southern loop of the Nürburgring on Dunlop R6 D 12 racing tyres were practically the same for both the racing and the higher rally settings of the suspension: test engineer Bott did his best lap with the racing settings while test engineer Falk did his best on the rally settings. They both agreed, however, that there was little to choose between the two, and this certainly reflects a well-chosen suspension geometry. As a result of the pressure and temperature checks made in the engine room compartment, the air inlets and outlets in the rear part of the body were relocated, and the car was then entered for the Paris race. But one defect could not be cured before the race: the throttle response on the floatless Solex carburettors was very poor below 4,000 rpm and above this the power came in suddenly, making driving on wet roads particularly difficult. A partial remedy was found by inclining the tube scavenging the constant level chamber, but only a change from Solex to Weber carburettors, on the occasion of the Targa Florio in May 1965, gave fully satisfactory results.

A gearbox failure was the reason for the retirement of the six-cylinder car in the Paris race. This was not altogether unexpected in view of the high gearbox oil temperatures registered at the time of the test runs. This problem was one of the main objects of further development test runs in the course of which a different front suspension geometry was also tried. The castor angle was increased from 7° to 15°, with no variation when the suspension was compressed (in the standard car, the castor was slightly reduced on bump in order to defeat the excessively quick steering response and to combat oversteer). The aim of this new geometry was to reduce understeer on sharp bends. This was to be obtained by the fact that, due to the large castor angle, the negative camber on the outer front wheel is notably increased when lock is applied and is decreased or becomes positive on the inside wheel, with a resultant reduction in slip angle. Against all expectations, the increased castor angle did not make the steering much heavier, but it reacted fiercely to even quite small movements of the steering wheel particularly on poorly surfaced bends and when the driver had to make quick steering corrections. The tests were thus soon abandoned and pressure of time prevented further tests with a 10° castor angle.

Experiments with the same object of reducing understeer on sharp corners were resumed four years later, this time with a front suspension geometry producing considerable castor variations with suspension movement, but, as related later, they were again unsuccessful. On the same occasion, efforts to reduce the gearbox oil temperature led to the use of larger diameter ducts, though the reduction they achieved of 7-8° C was not very convincing.

As early as September 1964, the first prototype 904/6 lapped Porsche's circular test track at Weissach in 19.24 s, corresponding to a lateral acceleration of 1.045 g, 5.5 per cent higher than the figure reached one year earlier in the course of the development tests of the 904.

The 904 was by no means a particularly light car. It was essentially meant to be robust and durable and even with the six- or eight-cylinder engine, it was not particularly suitable for short hill-climb races, even though private owners driving the standard version were practically unbeatable in the 2-litre GT class. The factory, however, was more interested in overall victories and in the European Mountain Championship based on a point scoring system. The Championship was restricted to cars up to 2 litres and was the only one ruled by the CSI in which the cars from Zuffenhausen stood a fair chance of success.

By 1964, the old eight-cylinder Porsche Spyder with which Edgar Barth had become European Hill-climb Champion the previous year had become pretty obsolete, but the development of the new sports racing car had taken too much time to allow the development engineers to dedicate themselves seriously to developing a special hill-climb car. So, for 1964 it was decided to buy a British Elva

The Carrera 6 had a good shape. Its drag coefficient was approximately 0.36.

In its final form the Carrera 6 was fitted with front spoilers which improved its high speed stability without increasing the drag.

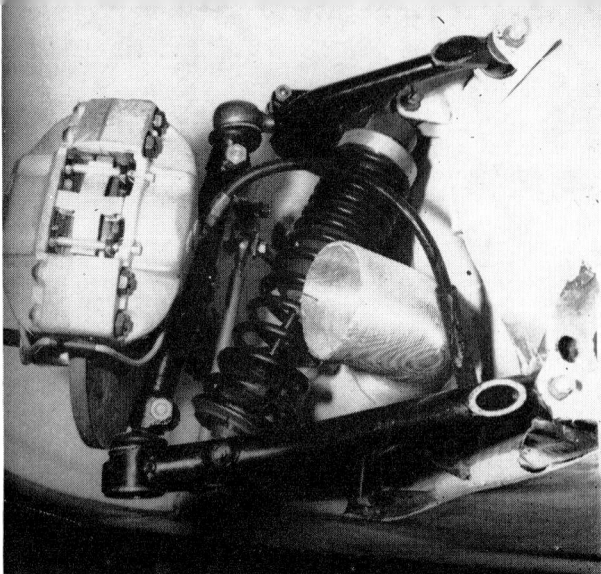

Front suspension of Carrera 6, seen from the rear. Wishbones and uprights are made of steel. The spring has a progressive rate and the concentric shock absorber incorporates an auxiliary rubber spring also used as a suspension stop.

Carrera 6 (906) rear end. Most suspension parts of the 906 were identical to those of the Type 904.

This view clearly shows the rear pyramid of the Carrera 6 space frame and the hoses directing cooling air to the rear brakes.

Above: The 910 was the first Porsche using magnesium wheels, except for the Ollon-Villars car. This example has a slightly raised roof line to accommodate a tall driver. This was found to actually reduce the air drag slightly.

Type 910 front suspension seen from the front. The progressive rate spring and the auxiliary rubber spring on the shock absorber piston can clearly be seen. Also note the light alloy upright and the wrap-round cooling air duct for the brake disc.

Two-litre Type 901/21 engine with Bosch fuel injection and mechanical control of the injection pump output. The pump is mounted longitudinally. The injectors are downstream of the throttle slide. This type of engine delivered 220 hp in the Type 906 and 910 cars.

Below: Two-litre engine Type 901/21 fitted to one of the long-tail 907s for the Le Mans race 1967. In this car the output of the fuel injection pump is governed by a space cam in function of the throttle opening and engine speed. Space dictates the transverse mounting of the pump, driven by a pair of bevel wheels.

chassis (Elva had previously bought 15 Porsche four-cylinder racing engines) and to drop the eight-cylinder engine into it. The resultant Elva-Porsche weighed only 1,100 lb, some 380 lb less than the eight-cylinder 904/8 coupé, and it was intended not only to uphold Porsche prestige in international hill-climbs but also to provide a useful comparison with the Porsche products. The Elva-Porsche was driven to victory by Edgar Barth in the Rossfeld international hill-climb in 1964.

But in later events, Barth, who was to become hill-climb champion for the second time running, elected to drive the old eight-cylinder Porsche Spyder rather than the Elva which was used only occasionally, as in the Trento-Bondone race in which it took fourth place driven by Herbert Müller, while Barth won all of the first six Championship races, each time beating the existing record. It is only fair to mention, however, that the only serious opposition that year came from the 2-litre Abarth-Simcas, scantily modified GT cars which were much too heavy to be really suitable for hill-climbing. His second consecutive title of European Hill-climb Champion was a fitting end to Barth's career for only a few months later he died from an incurable illness.

The course of events took a serious turn in 1965, however. Not only had the Abarths become faster but, worse still, the European Hill-climb Champion of 1962, Ludovico Scarfiotti, reappeared with an overwhelmingly fast V6 Dino Ferrari and clinched the title, even though he had not taken part in the first two runs of the Championship series. For Porsche this was a real blow as an entirely new, lighter car had been prepared for 1965 in the light of previous experience. This new model was based on a 904 chassis, but was fitted with the eight-cylinder engine and had an open body. Weighing 570 kg (1,240 lb), it was heavier than the Elva but still some 120 kg (265 lb) lighter than a 904/8 coupé. Elegance was not its forte and it soon became known as the 'Kangaroo' among factory people. The car, chassis No 906 007, had the front suspension wishbones mounted on needle bearings, to produce more exact location and to reduce uncontrolled resilience and friction. Later, needle bearings were also incorporated in the rear upright pivots. Apparently these measures were intended partly to compensate for the lack of stiffness in the car which, at the beginning of its career, used a non-reinforced 904-type chassis frame in conjunction with an open body providing practically no additional rigidity. The first tests of the 'Kangaroo' took place on the Weissach steering pad on April 14 1965, first using $5\frac{1}{2}$-in wide rims at the front and 6-in rims at the rear, then 6-in rims at the front and 7-in rims at the rear, which proved to be the better combination on which the final suspension settings were obtained. Less than four weeks later, this car was driven by Colin Davis and Gerhard Mitter into second place in the Targa Florio, behind Bandini and Vaccarella's 3.3-litre Ferrari. A few days later, Mitter crashed it in practice for the Nürburgring 1,000 km race and it was rebuilt with a reinforced frame. After this it took Mitter to a victory in the Rossfeld hill-climb, in which he preceded Herbert Müller (904) and Tony Fischhaber (Elva-Porsche eight-cylinder). This was the end of its official career but for a long time it was used as a guinea pig for various developments. In the meantime, what had been learned from the 'Kangaroo' was incorporated in two new, much better looking Bergspyders, Nos 906 008 (Fischhaber) and 906 009 (Mitter). These cars also had a needle bearing suspension front and rear and the Unibal-pivoted rear radius arms were made of aluminium tubes. For the first time in the history of works-entered racing cars, these Porsches were painted white instead of silver. This apparently did not bring them particular luck because at their first appearance, in the Trento-Bondone hill-climb, the new cars were beaten, not only by Scarfiotti driving a brand new works Ferrari on its first outing, but also by Hans Herrmann's

D

Abarth which had already won the Mont Ventoux hill-climb, beating Mitter's six-cylinder engined 904 coupé. Thus Mitter and Fischhaber had to be content with third and fourth places respectively. At Sestriere, Mitter was again beaten by Scarfiotti, and Fischhaber demolished 904 008 against a tree. The replacement car, which strangely bore the number 904 004, went to Mitter who won the Solitude race with it, but when it came to the hill-climb championship, it was again beaten by Scarfiotti's Ferrari in the Schauinsland event. To get more immediate response, this new hill-climb car had, for the first time, metallic ball-jointed shock absorber and anti-roll bar attachments and, also for the first time adjustable anti-roll bars were used. The adjustment was performed in the usual way by modifying the leverage applied to the bars.

By that time, however, defeat did not come as a surprise. Comparative tests on the southern loop of the Nürburgring, of which a section was used in the opposite direction to the normal one to form what amounted to a hill-climb course, had shown that even with its reinforced 904-type chassis, the open hill-climb car (in this case 906 007) had inferior handling when compared with the Elva-Porsche and with an eight-cylinder 904 type coupé. Certainly the 'Kangaroo' had obtained the best result of the Porsche entries in the Targa Florio, but Bonnier, who was originally supposed to drive it, refused it because of its bad handling after he had tried it in practice. The hill-climb tests performed on the Nürburgring confirmed this, the 'Kangaroo' being only insignificantly faster than the 120 kg (260 lb) heavier coupé whose engine was notably down on power after having run in the Nürburgring 1,000 km race. Comparative times were 1 m 29.9 s for the coupé and 1 m 29.6 s for the Spyder while the Elva did 1 m 29.8 s. All cars used the same type of Dunlop racing tyres on 6-in wide rims at the front and 7-in rims at the rear.

Just how important handling is was shown by an experiment in which the coupé was loaded with 50 kg lead ballast attached to the floor, lowering the centre of gravity. The four runs it did with this equipment were all faster than the best the car could do without the ballast and three times in succession it did the absolute best time of 1 m 29.3 s, despite its inferior engine. Gerhard Mitter, who drove the test cars, confirmed that the coupé was the best handling car of the lot and, in his opinion, the 'Kangaroo' was the worst: it required extreme concentration to keep it on the road, he commented, especially on bumpy sections. Of the Elva he said, 'It runs straighter and is not so sensitive to bumps, but its roadholding isn't much better than the "Kangaroo's" '.

A defeat being expected, several timing wizards were summoned to the Schauinsland hill-climb in order to find out in which type of section the Porsches lost ground to the opposition—mainly Ferrari. Their finding was that the Ferrari was faster mainly in slow corners and accelerating out of slow corners. In fast curves Scarfiotti was, if anything, slightly slower than Mitter but he was faster in winding sections with a bad surface. This hinted at excessive unsprung weight on the Porsche and also excessive total weight.

Another conclusion could be drawn from those tests: the trials on the circular track were no doubt excellent for setting up a car for optimum cornering on a smooth surface, but gave little indication of the roadholding abilities of a car in actual racing conditions where it must contend with humps, dips and rough surfaces and is submitted to heavy acceleration and braking forces. This is borne out by the fact that the 'Kangaroo' had gone very well on the circular track: before it was sent to the Targa Florio on 6-in rims at the front and 7-in rims at the rear it had lapped the steering pad in 19.12 s, corresponding to 1.063 g (0.12 s quicker than the best time recorded six months earlier by a 904/6 with 1-in narrower rims front and rear);

and in August the same year, with 9-in wide rims fitted at the rear, the 'Kangaroo' was the first car to break the 19 s barrier. Its best time of 18.92 s (using Dunlop R7 Yellow Spot all-weather racing tyres) was equivalent to a lateral acceleration of 1.083 g.

The same car was used two days later for the first experiments with front and rear spoilers to increase tyre grip aerodynamically. These measures immediately dropped the time to 18.52 s, a lateral acceleration of 1.14 g. This test series was later continued on the Hockenheim track with various types of cars, in connection with tyre tests.

As has already been mentioned, the Bergspyder, No 906 004, entrusted to Gerhard Mitter in the course of the 1965 season, had been fitted with metallic shock absorber and anti-roll bar attachments in an effort to compensate in part for the lack of rigidity of the chassis by a quicker response to the suspension movements. Comparative tests with the 'Kangaroo' on the Hockenheimring confirmed the validity of this solution: the new car definitely handled better and it later got down to the remarkable time of 17.84 s (equivalent to 1.22 g) without any aerodynamic aids on the Weissach circular track. But already, after the Cesana-Sestriere hill-climb, the Porsche engineers had come to the conclusion that only a completely new car with a very light but very rigid chassis frame had a chance of beating the Ferrari. The last three events of the Championship series had still to be run and, as Scarfiotti had not taken part in the first two, Mitter still had a chance of winning the Championship if he was given a competitive car. It was not before the beginning of August, however, that this conclusion was reached; the factory was about to close down for holidays and nothing could prevent Scarfiotti beating Mitter once again at the Schauinsland hill-climb on August 8.

The next event was to take place on August 29, on the Ollon-Villars course. Just four weeks were left before the start of practice and in this time a completely new car was to be built. Bulk and weight considerations dictated the use of 13-in diameter light alloy wheels. As it was impossible to get these parts in time in the holiday period, the German Grand Prix was taken as an opportunity to buy a complete set of wheels, stub axles, uprights, brakes and brake discs which Colin Chapman had brought along as spares for his Grand Prix cars. Thus the legend was created that the new Porsche hill-climb car had Lotus suspension, which was only partially true as the wishbones and radius rods were of Porsche manufacture and design and the suspension geometry was Porsche's own.

Immediately after the German Grand Prix, on August 5, the engineers got down to work at their drawing boards. On August 25, exactly 20 days later, the new car turned in its first laps on the circular track in Weissach, getting down to the excellent lap time of 17.86 s. There was no doubt, however, that a completely new car with an entirely new chassis and running gear, using smaller 13-in diameter wheels with wider rims than before (8 in at the front, 9½ in at the rear) and tyres which were an unknown quantity, could not be set up optimally within a few hours. Pressure of time had dictated the use of the same springs and the same damper settings as for the previous Bergspyder, and there was no possibility of experimenting with different suspension geometries which had to remain as originally designed. The only changes that could be made were to substitute the slightly shortened front springs, giving an insufficient bump travel, with standard Spyder springs, trying out various anti-roll bars and their settings.

For this new car (chassis No 906 010) Porsche had gone back to a tubular space frame to obtain minimum weight in conjunction with a very light open body. The wheelbase was increased from 2.30 m to 2.38 m and the track of 1.43 m front and rear was 10 to 12 cm (according to the width of the wheels used) wider than on the coupés and Spyders of 904 origin. The reason for the longer wheelbase was the layout of the rear suspension where the wishbones and radius arms were pivoted around an axis parallel to the centre line of the car, which meant that the front anchorage points of the radius arms were well within the framework. The wheelbase had to be lengthened accordingly, otherwise the rather wide flat engine would have been in the way of the radius arms. An alternative would have been to move the driver's seat forward, but at that time it was feared that some difficulties might ensue for the driver.

The entirely new, open glass fibre body was of course kept as light as possible. It served only as a cover for the chassis and no stresses were fed into it. Even the engine had been further developed by a new exhaust system raising the power output to about 245 hp, an increase of 5 hp, but in practice Mitter decided to go back to the old exhaust which gave the engine better flexibility. Little more than the gearbox and the steering gear were taken over unmodified from the old model.

'Look at my wheels!' said Colin Chapman when he first saw the new 530 kg (1,170 lb) car coming to the starting line. It was about 50 kg (110 lb) lighter and much stiffer than the previous 904 based hill-climb car and the effect was immediately obvious. As a precaution, the old car had also been taken along to Villars and was used by Mitter for most of the practice runs. The new car at once proved to be much faster due to its lighter weight and better handling and road-holding, enabling Mitter to get within a fraction of a second of Scarfiotti's best practice time. Apparently, however, Scarfiotti still had something to spare and in the actual climb he was about $2\frac{1}{2}$ s faster than Mitter in both heats, finally clinching the title of European Hill-climb Champion by a margin of 5.2 s. Perhaps the march of events could have been reversed if higher authorities had not imposed their veto on Sunday work which the workers of the racing division, who had very little sleep in those days anyway, were quite willing to accept. A suggestion by Mitter that the engineers and mechanics should transfer on weekends to his own workshops, located in the immediate vicinity of the factory, could not be put into practice.

Even if the new car had not won, the future certainly looked brighter. Everyone knew that a completely new car needed more than a few hours' development and if, even in this condition, it had come so near to matching the Ferrari, the hopes of making it a real winner were high. The last race of the season for the European Hill-climb Championship was to take place on September 19 on the Gaisberg near Salzburg. Technically Mitter still had a chance of becoming Champion, but only if he won and Scarfiotti did not finish or did not come at all. Neither of these possibilities could be seriously contemplated as Scarfiotti would probably not take any risk and just try to finish, but even so no chance was missed of making the new car as competitive as possible. It was sent on a three-day testing session to the Nürburgring, together with the old pressed steel frame Spyder (on this occasion with a six-cylinder engine). As expected, the new car was far from mature. Among other things, it was found that the front suspension was compressed up to the bump stops under severe braking, which made the car very unstable; that Dunlop R6 (Yellow Spot) tyres were much more suitable than the R7 tyres on which all previous testing had been done and which were used for the Ollon-Villars hill-climb, and that the 30' rear negative camber was insufficient. Much better handling was obtained by increasing it to 2°. It was also found that there was too much braking on the rear and that the tyre pressures could with advantage be reduced from 26 to 23 psi.

The car was also tried with different half shafts, those using solid needle bearing universals being replaced by shafts incorporating rubber Giubo doughnuts which according to Mitter, made the car react much more smoothly on opening or shutting the throttle in curves. Earlier tests with the 'Kangaroo' on the Nürburgring had already indicated that doughnut half shafts definitely produced faster times. This was a pleasant surprise anyway, as they reduce the stress on the transmission. After all these modifications had been incorporated, Mitter went around the southern loop of the Nürburgring in 2 m 16.7 s. On the mountain course (part of the southern loop in the reverse direction) he did 1 m 24.3 s, 2.8 s faster than the previous best time obtained with the older pressed steel frame Spyder, while the northern loop of the Ring was lapped in 8 m 42.2 s.

Finally, spoilers were added to the car, first at the front and then front and rear (the latter, a very large one, 1 m wide and about 12 cm high—more than 3 ft and $4\frac{1}{2}$ in respectively) which made the car much more stable on humps. With the spoilers, Mitter reduced his time for the southern loop to 2 m 15.8 s and did a lap of the northern loop in 8 m 41.8 s, adding that he had made less effort to get down to that time, than when he did 8 m 42.2 s without spoilers. The enormous progress that had been achieved compared with the pressed steel frame Bergspyder is emphasised by the comparison with the best times achieved by the latter: 2m 20.5 s for the southern loop and 9 m 16.0 s for the northern loop of the Nürburgring.

The old pressed steel frame 'Kangaroo', now fitted with a six-cylinder engine, had been taken along to the Nürburgring, together with the new car, in order to finalise its suspension settings with the new engine. It was to take part in the Gaisberg hill-climb, driven by Herbert Müller. This entry, which was known to have no chance of success, was part of the development programme of the Carrera 6, which was to use the same engine and running gear in a car of approximately the same weight.

Unfortunately, the Gaisberg hill-climb did not provide a direct comparison between the now more thoroughly developed Spyder and Scarfiotti's Ferrari. After the GT cars had gone up the hill, thick fog drastically reduced the visibility for the sports and prototype cars, preventing Mitter from achieving better than fourth place, behind three 904s driven by Michel Weber, Sepp Greger and Rolf Stommelen. And although Mitter beat Scarfiotti's Ferrari, it would be unfair to draw any conclusions, as the Italian had no reason whatsoever to risk anything under the bad conditions which prevailed.

At the end of the season, the new Bergspyder had another occasion to make news, when Porsche's 54-year old Competitions Manager, Huschke von Hanstein, climbed into the cockpit and rounded off his racing career by taking two world records (a quarter mile and 500 m) and three new international records. By deleting the alternator and the rear brakes and using a motorcycle battery, the weight of the car had been reduced to 485 kg (1,060 lb) for the occasion. In spite of a damp track, he covered the quarter-mile, from a standing start, in 11.892 s while the 500 m were covered in 13.557 s. Only 22.212 s were taken to cover a kilometre from a standing start, which was a new 2-litre Class record. It is notable that after 500 m the speed had reached 200 kph and the car rushed through the end of the kilometre at 240 kph (150 mph). Only a few days later, these records were broken by Carlo Abarth himself in one of his 2-litre cars, but it must be added that Abarth benefited from a perfectly dry road and that he drove a single-seater car which was much lighter than the compulsory all-enveloping two-seater body of a hill-climb car.

After the end of the racing season, some further development tests were made on the air pressure around the engine air intakes both when the cover over the passenger seat was in use and when it was removed. Lap times around Hockenheim showed that a smooth air flow over the body surface (with the passenger seat covered) had an adverse effect on engine performance because it created a higher vacuum on the upper rear deck surface. For comparison purposes, the car was then taken to the Weissach circular track, set up in the same way as it was for the Nürburgring tests and a record time of 17.72 s was immediately registered. These pad tests confirmed that the newer Dunlop R7 tyres were not as efficient as the earlier R6 tyres, but a new improved R7 and a slightly softer front anti-roll bar setting, slightly reducing the understeer, produced a new absolute record of 17.52 s, a lateral acceleration of 1.265 g.

If the Ollon-Villars Spyder, as it soon became known in factory jargon, was unable to save Porsche from defeat in the 1965 European Hill-climb Championship, it was nevertheless one of the most important racing cars built up to that time in Zuffenhausen. It was a design exercise from which the running gear of the 910 and all following Porsche racing cars was developed, and it was the ancestor of all the ultra-light hill-climb cars built by Porsche in the following years, on which innumerable weight saving techniques were tried out, some of them later to be adopted for the long distance racing cars. Following new FIA regulations, the original Ollon-Villars car was modified to take a removable top and with Mitter at the wheel it won very event for which it was entered in 1966: the Rossfeld, Mont Ventoux, Trento-Bondone, Cesana-Sestriere and Gaisberg hill-climbs.

5

Racing the Carrera 6 and its prototype derivatives

THE BAD CLIMATIC CONDITIONS in which the Carrera 6 was developed had made it impossible to find out the best settings for the running gear. It will be remembered that an earlier chapter mentioned that part of the destruction tests on the Volkswagen proving ground had to be carried out with snow tyres and spikes! In January 1966, however, the circular track in Weissach was free and dry with 10° C frost, but the testers were unlucky; after the car had done ten laps and before any alternative settings had been tried, the engine of the test car began to make noises that dictated an immediate stop. A subsequent check on the oil tank design showed that under the high lateral acceleration reached on the track, the surface of the oil was inclined at such an angle that the oil pump in the engine sucked in air instead of oil.

When the test was stopped, the best lap time (obtained on the last lap) was 18.62 s. In his report on the test run, experimental engineer Peter Falk who drove the car (he is Weissach's acknowledged circular track champion, even faster than the professional racing drivers) expressed the opinion that, after slight attention to the tyre pressures and anti-roll bar settings, he could have come down to a time of around 18.2 s. For comparison, here are the best times obtained up to then for various types of cars, all on Dunlop R7 Yellow Spot racing tyres:

904 coupé (standard)	18.86 s
904 Spyder (front 7-in, rear 9-in rims)	17.84 s
Ollon-Villars Bergspyder (906 010)	17.52 s

Time had become pretty short before the cars had to be sent off to the Daytona 24-Hour race and, as the short test on the circular pad had shown the new car to be fairly neutral and easy to drive, no further tests were done. The oil tank was redesigned and after a new engine had been dropped into the test car (No 906 017), it was shipped to the States together with two series production 904 coupés. This maiden race was a tremendous success for the brand new car, driven by Hans Herrmann and Herbert Linge, which ran like clockwork to take sixth place overall at an average speed of 100 mph, leading home the two works-entered 904s. The three Porsches were preceded only by cars of more than twice and even three times their capacity: three 7-litre Fords headed by the race winners Ken Miles and Lloyd Ruby, one 4.4-litre Ferrari and another Ford 7-litre. Under the new FIA ruling, the 904s now ran as sports cars and won the sports group outright (beating all the Ferrari 275 LMs), while the Carrera 6 was still entered in the prototype class pending the completion of the 50 units required for homologation as a sports car.

A similar success was scored in the Sebring 12-Hour race, one month later, when a works-entered Carrera 6 driven by Herrmann, Buzzetta and Mitter finished fourth overall, behind three Ford prototypes, and left the 2-litre Dino Ferrari, driven by Bandini and Scarfiotti, three laps behind. An over-revved engine caused the retirement, in the seventh hour, of the second works-entered Carrera 6, but similar models driven by private owners finished sixth and eighth while a private 904 was driven into seventh place and won the 2-litre sports car class.

Outright win in the Targa Florio

The first big European race in which the Carrera 6 was entered was the Targa Florio which took place in May 1966 over the traditional 45-mile-long Sicilian mountain course. On this occasion, five cars were prepared by the factory, four of them to be run as works entries and one to be entrusted to the Swiss Scuderia Filippinetti for drivers Willy Mairesse and Herbert Müller. In view of the peculiar character of the Targa, a small party was sent to Sicily in April for a short, unofficial practice session on open roads. There followed tyre and shock absorber testing on the Nürburgring, comparative tests being made with Koni and Bilstein dampers. The choice finally went to the Bilsteins which gave an improvement of approximately 3 s on the southern loop of the Nürburgring.

All cars sent out to Sicily had a series production chassis and body and used Textar 1431G brake pads. Two of the cars also had the standard six-cylinder carburettor engine and ran in the sports car group in which they were now homologated. They were driven by Mairesse/Müller (No 906 128) and Pucci/Arena (No 906 141). The other three cars were entered as prototypes. On two of them the only non-standard item was the fuel injection, and they were fitted with a slightly lower fourth gear, presumably only because the drivers preferred it that way. They were entrusted to Herrmann/Glemser (No 906 111) and Mitter/Bonnier (No 906 143). The fifth car (No 906 142), driven by Klass and Colin Davis, was fitted with an eight-cylinder carburettor engine, for the first time in 2.2-litre form. This car had slightly wider ratios in its five-speed gearbox.

In addition, two practice cars were taken along to Sicily, one being the Daytona car (No 906 017) now fitted with an injection engine, and the old 906 001, a 904 coupé with a six-cylinder carburettor engine. There is only one day of official practice on closed roads preceding the Targa Florio. In view of the length of the course and of the hundreds of bends to be remembered, most of the drivers need to practise for a much longer period and many can be seen going round and round the circuit in fast cars many days before the official practice day. This was certainly the case for the Porsche drivers who took the practice cars around on the open roads for many more miles than the race itself covers. This provides quite good endurance testing, especially as the road surface is very rough, and a half shaft broke on two of the cars. In the case of the 904/6 the shaft was an obsolete plain one, while the up-to-date hollow shaft which broke on the Carrera 6 had had a long and hard life, having done the Daytona 24 hours, tests with the first injection engine at Hockenheim and the Targa Florio pre-practice in April which, among other things, served to decide the gear ratios to be used. The Carrera also had two minor accidents, and in addition the transverse chassis tube below the gearbox broke, later experience showing this to be a weak point on the car.

Practice on the open road indicated that the brake pads would last through the race and that an average fuel consumption of 6 mpg would necessitate two refuelling stops. These would have to be scheduled in such a way that all cars would not have to stop simultaneously at the pits or at the auxiliary depot installed half way round the course. In order to obtain more information on tyre wear, it was decided that for the official practice, in which every driver would do one lap with his actual race car, the various cars should be fitted with different types of tyres. The two standard Carrera 6s and the eight-cylinder were sent out on Dunlop R7 Green Spot (dry weather) tyres; the other two injection cars went out on R7 Yellow Spot (universal) tyres and R7 White Spot (rain) tyres.

Good weather conditions prevailed during practice in which Günther Klass did the absolute best time in 39 m 05 s in the eight-cylinder, beating Vaccarella's time in the 4-litre Ferrari P3 by 2 s and Scarfiotti's time in the 2-litre Ferrari Dino by 5 s. The Pucci/Arena carburettor six-cylinder did not practice as for some unaccountable reason water had found its way into the fuel tank.

The tyre checks after practice showed that at least one tyre change would be necessary, except for six-cylinder cars on Green Spot (dry weather) tyres. The day before the race was very wet and race day weather was uncertain so the choice of tyres became very much a gamble and finally the Pucci/Arena six-cylinder carburettor car started on dry weather tyres, the eight-cylinder on intermediates and the other three cars on rain tyres. The first lap of the race confirmed that official practice times in the Targa are not necessarily a reliable measure of driver ability and car performance. Experienced drivers often refrain from taking any risk with the race car on their single practice lap and now Vaccarella and Mitter showed what they were really up to: the 4-litre Ferrari led the 2-litre Porsche by a margin of only 5 s but Scarfiotti's 2-litre Dino was already 34 s behind the Porsche. Mairesse was fourth and Klass, who had apparently exercised some caution on the partially wet course, was fifth.

At the end of lap 2, Mitter led Vaccarella while Klass had overtaken Mairesse and Scarfiotti. It was a hotly contested race and after rain had set in again, the two Ferraris, now driven by Bandini (4-litre) and Parkes (Dino) were in the lead at the end of five laps. But soon Parkes crashed his Dino, Glemser did the same with his Porsche and Bandini ran into some difficulty so that, going into the seventh lap, the Porsches of Klass and Mitter were in front again. On corrected time, Mitter was nearly 2 m behind Klass, but on the road they were only 5 s apart. Klass was a fast and ambitious new boy in the Porsche team and Mitter, the acknowledged number one, saw a possible rival in him. Having the more powerful car, Klass was not prepared to surrender, but Mitter wouldn't let him go. So the inevitable happened: Mitter went off the road and tore the front and rear suspensions right off.

But on the same lap Bandini went off too, so that again Porsches occupied the first two places. This was just as well as in the eighth of the ten laps making up the race distance, a rear wishbone broke on Klass's car, presumably due to a defective weld. So finally Mairesse and Müller won on the standard production Carrera 6, leaving Guichet and Baghetti's Dino Ferrari well behind, closely followed by the other standard Carrera 6 of Pucci and Arena.

The fuel consumption and brake pad and tyre wear reflected the way the cars had been driven in the race; the Hockenheim tests which had shown the six-cylinder fuel injection engine to be slightly more economical than the carburettor engine were not confirmed in the race where the injection cars returned a ten per cent higher consumption.

The fastest lap was done by Gerhard Mitter in 40 m 19 s. This compares with 40 m 45 s for Vaccarella (Ferrari 4-litre), Klass 41 m 02 s, Scarfiotti (Dino 2-litre) 41 m 18 s and Mairesse 41 m 23 s. In the rain the fastest driver was Glemser (45 m 34 s) but he later crashed. He was followed by Müller (46 m 10 s) and Parkes (Dino) (46 m 23 s), but he, too, later crashed.

The 1966 ADAC 1,000 km race on the Nürburgring

After the Porsche team had scored so many successes abroad, the ADAC 1,000 km race on their own German ground brought them bitter disappointment. Preliminary tests were done on the Nürburgring with the object of trying out the various Dunlop, Goodyear and Firestone tyres on a Carrera 6 experimentally equipped with Bosch transistor ignition and a lightweight Motorola alternator. On that occasion, the Goodyear tyres proved to be fastest, but not to the extent of persuading Porsche to break their contract with Dunlop whose R7 Yellow Spot tyres were chosen for the race. For this, the following five cars were prepared:

One Carrera 6, No 906 108, running as a sports car, with a standard carburettor engine but specially equipped with a lighter Motorola alternator and transistor ignition. Previous tests had shown this to combat plug fouling successfully, though it brought no advantage in power. This was the car previously used for tyre tests on the Ring and, for experimental reasons, it retained the engine and the accessories used for the test runs. It was driven in the race by Jean-Pierre Beltoise and Peter Nöcker.

Three 906 prototypes with fuel injection engines and standard ignition and alternator; the drivers were:

906 128 (Targa winner): Bondurant/Hawkins
906 141 (third in Targa): Klass/Schütz
906 154 (new car): Herrmann/Glemser

One 906 prototype No 906 142 with 2.2-litre eight-cylinder carburettor engine. This, another Targa Florio car, was driven by Rindt/Vaccerella.

Tyres were all 5.50-15 at the front and 6.00 M-15 at the rear except for the sports car which, for gearing reasons, used 5.50 L-15 at the front and 5.50 M-15 at the rear.

Only two of the fuel injection six-cylinders used the same gear sets. Between the other cars there were slight variations and the lowest gearing was used on the eight-cylinder in accordance with its higher revving ability, as well as on one of the injection six-cylinders (906 154).

During official practice, the eight-cylinder was tried on Goodyear tyres with gear ratios suitable for their slightly smaller radius. Thus equipped, and despite a broken anti-roll bar, Rindt was 4 s faster than on Dunlop tyres, which confirmed the results of the preliminary tests. Surprisingly, however, the eight-cylinder was not materially faster than the injection six-cylinders (on Dunlops, Rindt was only 6 s faster than Herrmann on the six-cylinder) which may also be due to the fact that in practice the eight-cylinder still used the Targa engine which was replaced only for the race. On car 906 154 the engine was also replaced as a precautionary measure, the original engine having been over-revved in practice.

Quick and consistent as they were, the Porsche practice times were bettered by the 8 m 31.9 s clocked by John Surtees on the 4-litre Ferrari and by the 8 m 35.4 s recorded by the surprising American Chaparral, using a 5.3-litre Chevrolet engine with semi-automatic transmission, which was coaxed round the circuit by Phil Hill. Third best was Rindt, heading the Porsche team, whose times were as follows:

906 142 (eight-cylinder)	Rindt (Goodyear)	8 m 44 s
	Rindt (Dunlop)	8 m 48 s
	Vaccarella	8 m 58 s
	Bondurant	8 m 52 s
906 154 (six-cylinder injection)	Herrmann	8 m 54 s
	Glemser	9 m 02 s

906 141 (six-cylinder injection)	Klass	8 m 57 s
	Schütz	8 m 54 s
906 128 (six-cylinder injection)	Bondurant	8 m 56 s
	Nöcker	9 m 19 s
906 108 (six-cylinder carburettor)	Beltoise	9 m 21 s
	Hawkins	9 m 05 s

Small differences between practice times are no reflection on driver ability, as many drivers may only do a few laps and could have been baulked more than their team-mates. Only Beltoise and Nöcker were notably slower than the others, Beltoise because he had never driven on the Ring before and Nöcker probably because he was out of practice. Consequently it was decided to pair these two drivers for the race and to let Hawkins co-drive with Bondurant on the six-cylinder injection car. Due to a previous accident, Mitter was not available for this race.

Right from the start, Porsche's hopes went up in smoke. Clutch lining smoke that is, for Rindt burned the eight-cylinder's clutch at the start and soon had to contend with more and more severe clutch slip until he stopped to have the clutch adjusted after the seventh of the 44 laps. This, however, was only the beginning, for on the 25th lap a lever broke in the throttle linkage, requiring a nine-minute stop in the pits; then Vaccarella made a small excursion off the road and damaged the right-hand fuel tank which had to be checked for leaks. Finally the car had to retire because the transverse tube of the frame had broken under the gearbox, a trouble also experienced by a private Carrera 6 during practice. Glemser crashed when in third place and Klass retired when a half shaft broke so that only two of the works cars finished the race: 906 128 with Bondurant/Hawkins in fourth place behind the winning Chaparral and two Dino Ferraris, and 906 108 driven by Beltoise and Nöcker in 11th place.

After the race, it was calculated that, as expected, all the cars could have covered the distance without changing either the tyres or the brake pads. The highest pad wear of 6.9 mm/1,000 km (0.43 in/1,000 miles) was measured on the rear brakes of the eight-cylinder. The fuel consumption confirmed the practice findings and once again the carburettor car was the most economical, having achieved 9.6 mpg. The fuel injection six-cylinders did 8.3 mpg but were admittedly driven faster. Oil consumption ran fairly high at anything between 560 and 350 mpg, the lowest consumption being registered by the six-cylinder carburettor car whose engine had already done 750 miles at racing speeds before the start. It was not a happy race for Porsche, but it led to an important decision. Both the half shaft failure on Klass's car and the chassis failure on the eight-cylinder could be traced to material fatigue. It was therefore decided that, as far as possible, from then on all important races would be contested with brand new cars.

The 1966 Le Mans 24-Hour race

The decision to enter only brand new cars for important events was nearly put into effect two weeks later, on the occasion of the Le Mans 24-Hour race. In fact, this was only by chance as by that time the 906 production had already run out. A few examples had, however, been kept aside and slightly modified to take the long-tail body described in an earlier chapter. This type of body, which also had a longer nose than the standard model, had been developed specially for the Le Mans race in which it is very important to obtain the highest possible speed on the 3.5-mile long Mulsanne straight. Except for the wind tunnel tests already described, for which cardboard extensions had been adapted to fit a standard car, the long-tail model remained an unknown quantity up to the beginning of the official practice at Le Mans. A hurriedly prepared car had been brought along to the track for the preliminary practice sessions in April, but the makeshift tail extension attached fell off before any data could be obtained. In the wind tunnel, a drag coefficient of Cw=0.306 had been measured for the long-tail car with an undershield and no rear spoilers. For Le Mans the undershield was removed for better cooling, and experience dictated the use of two small rear spoilers which slightly increased the cross section where the air flow broke away. Subsequent wind tunnel tests indicated that the real drag coefficient of the Le Mans car, as raced, was Cw=0.326, comparing with Cw=0.346 for a standard Carrera 6.

Five cars were entered for Le Mans, of which two were standard carburettor Carrera 6s running in the sports car group. One of these, 906 143, to be driven by Klass and Stommelen, was the only team car that was not brand new. The other sports car, 906 155, was entrusted to the American/Swedish pair Gregg/Axelsson.

The other three team cars, 906 151, 152 and 153 were all long-tail models with fuel injection and transistor ignition. In addition to supplementary lights, all cars were fitted with a 700 watt alternator instead of the 490 watt unit, and the long-tail cars also had a supplementary battery. No eight-cylinder engine was used for this race, as it was not considered sufficiently reliable. With full tanks holding 22 gallons (100 litres) of fuel, to comply with the regulations, the long-tail cars weighed 712 kg (1,570 lb) on the scrutineers' scales, that is roughly 22 kg (48 lb) more than the Carrera 6s. As an additional precaution, all five cars were fitted with the heavier but stronger Nadella plain half shafts with needle roller universals instead of the more usual tubular shafts.

The gear ratios used for the race are interesting because they reflect the higher speeds reached by the long-tail cars. They were as follows (in every case in connection with a 7:31 final drive):

Carrera 6—15:36, 19:32, 22:29, 25:26, 27:24;

Long-tail—16:36, 19:32, 23:29, 26:26, 28:23.

The even faster 29:23 fifth gear originally intended for the long-tail cars proved to be slightly optimistic and was replaced after the first practice.

Practice was completely trouble-free for the standard Carrera 6s, which reached 8,100 rpm on the straight, but the long-tail cars were unstable at speed due to a strong tendency for the tail to lift. Adding a full-width Carrera 6 type rear spoiler turned the high negative angle of incidence into a large positive one, dangerously reducing front wheel adhesion. Experiments led to the adoption of two small front spoilers and two small tail spoilers, resulting in satisfactory stability. Originally, the long-tail cars had a shield under the engine and their wheels were covered by discs intended to reduce the turbulence created by the dished wheels. After experiments with and without these, neither was used for the race. The wheel discs brought an advantage of approximately 2 mph on the straight, but it was feared they might come off during the race, while the undershield made no measurable difference to speed, but increased the gearbox oil temperature by some 15° C.

Several types of tyres were tried on the Carrera 6 driven by Günther Klass. These trials showed that the new Dunlop CR 70 Red Spot tyres, featuring a new, flatter tread, were faster than the usual R7 Green Spot tyres (best lap in 3 m 56.6 s as against 3 m 58.0 s), while Goodyears were slightly faster still (3 m 55.8 s). Unfortunately the long-tail car's narrower wheel arches did not permit the use of the new CR 70 tyres, but in the end this proved to be of no importance as, because of the uncertain weather before the race, all cars started on R7 Yellow Spot tyres. Given equal tyres, the fastest long-tail car (Siffert driving) was 6 s faster than the fastest standard Carrera 6 (Klass driving). Both during practice and in the race, the long-tail cars also proved to be notably more economical than the Carrera 6s which used more fuel than expected, Klass only just reaching the pits with a spluttering engine after 25 laps. Though the carburettor engine was now known to be more economical in itself, the Carrera 6s averaged 9.7 mpg during the race while the long-tail cars did 11 mpg. The higher stress on the engine in the standard car is also reflected by the oil consumption figures: the Carrera 6s did only 500 and 580 miles on a gallon of oil whereas the long-tail cars averaged between 700 and 1,300 mpg.

The race was run mostly in rain and no brake pads had to be changed. Up to the 23rd hour, only one unforeseen pit stop was registered: when the rev counter on Stommelen's car (906 143) had to be changed. Unfortunately a connecting rod broke on the Gregg/Axelsson car little more than one hour before the finish.

For Porsche this Le Mans race was a real triumph: four of the five works cars finished, preceded only by 7-litre Fords, and took first, second and fourth places on Index. The team was headed by the three long-tail cars with Jo Siffert and Colin Davis one lap in front of Herrmann and Linge and another lap in front of DeKlerk/Schütz, while the Klass/Stommelen Carrera 6 won the sports car group outright.

Grosser Preis von Hockenheim

This rather unimportant race at Hockenheim, on August 14 1966, was the last race of the year to see official Porsche entries. It was mostly interesting for the test runs organised by Porsche, before official practice began, which gave a further opportunity to compare the performance of the long-tail and the short-tail cars. To get a really accurate comparison, a new six-cylinder injection engine was put into the long-tail car 906 152 exactly as it ran at Le Mans, except for the fact that the gearing most appropriate for Hockenheim was used. Lap times were obtained and both the engine and the rev counter were immediately transferred to one of the Le Mans Carrera 6s (906 143), which in turn was optimally geared for Hockenheim before the final lap times were obtained. The only difference between the two cars, except for the body, that could have had an influence on lap times, was the tyres, because the rear wheel arches of the long-tail car would take only 5.50 M-15 tyres whereas the Carrera 6 used the 6.00 M-15 size giving slightly better handling.

Additionally, beryllium brake discs (weighing only one quarter as much as cast iron discs) were tried for the first time on the short-tail car in conjunction with Ferodo DS 11 brake pads. This combination gave satisfactory results but had a higher rate of wear than the Textar 1431 G linings on cast iron discs (0.32 in as against 0.19 in per 1,000 miles). Textar linings on berrylium discs were said to bind, however, and to have a tendency to pull irregularly.

For both the long-tail and the short-tail cars, the gearing was chosen to allow the engine to run up to 8,200 rpm (on the same rev counter) which in theory corresponds to a speed of 161 mph for the long-tail car and 154 mph for the short-tail car, both being pessimistic figures not taking into consideration the growth of the tyres at speed. The best lap times obtained by Hans Herrmann were as follows:

	Long	Short
Dunlop R7 Yellow Spot	2 m 09.4 s	2 m 10.2 s
Dunlop R7 White Spot	2 m 08.9 s	2 m 09.6 s
Dunlop CR 70 Red Spot	2 m 09.0 s	2 m 08.9 s

According to Herrmann, the very slightly better time obtained with the short-tail car on Dunlop CR 70 tyres called for a lot of effort and in spite of the better handling provided by the larger rear tyres on the short-tail car, it was decided to use three long-tail cars for the race. They were all fitted with aluminium brake calipers and beryllium brake discs and finished first, second and third; as the works cars had no serious opposition, the drivers were given a free race and Mitter won both heats at an average of approximately 118.5 mph for just over 500 km, while Klass did the fastest lap in 2 m 05.22 s, an average of approximately 121 mph. Schütz and Koch driving privately-entered Carrera 6s followed the works cars to the finish.

6

The development of the 910

EVEN AT THE TIME when the Carrera 6 was designed, the Porsche engineers were convinced that 13-in wheels and tyres offered decisive advantages over the 15-in wheels they used, if only because they were lighter and smaller. Another advantage was that, being used for most Formula 1 cars, the 13-in tyres were technically more advanced. This is why, as soon as the decision had been taken to design a new car for the Ollon-Villars hill-climb of 1965, a set of 13-in wheels and attendant suspension parts was bought from Lotus on the occasion of the German Grand Prix. This hill-climb car (906 010) was one of the most important of all Porsche racing cars as its tubular space frame formed the basis of the Carrera 6 frame (to which, following a decision of Dr Porsche, 904 type running gear was attached) and further development culminated in the 910, which used 13-in wheels and running gear developed from that of the Bergspyder. It also became the guinea pig on which lightweight techniques were developed, culminating at the end of 1968 in a 382 kg (850 lb) 2-litre eight-cylinder car and also resulted in considerable weight savings on the long distance cars.

After the 1965 season, the Ollon-Villars Bergspyder was modified to comply with revised CSI regulations: it was fitted with a high windscreen to form a coupé of which the top could be removed if necessary. With this car Gerhard Mitter reigned supreme over European hill-climbs in 1966, winning at Rossfeld, Mont Ventoux, Trento-Bondone and Cesana-Sestriere, the last two with the fuel injection system adapted to the eight-cylinder engine. The next event, at Schauinsland, gave him the European Championship, but in this case he drove a completely new car: 910 002, the second of the new 910 series, a direct development of the Ollon-Villars car. Both at Rossfeld and Schauinsland, the Porsche beat the 1965 Champion Scarfiotti driving a works Dino Ferrari which in 1966 was entered only in a few chosen events. The last event of the Ollon-Villars car was the 1966 Gaisberg hill-climb which it won after Mitter had crashed the 910 in practice.

In general design the 910 was quite similar to the 906 010 Bergspyder but in the interests of lower weight and better manoeuvrability the wheelbase had been brought back to the traditional Porsche figure of 2,300 mm used for all Porsche racing cars from the 904 to the 917 inclusive. To achieve this, the front pivots of the rear suspension radius rods were moved outwards. Following the observation of a Carrera 6 being driven around the circular track, when roll angles were registered, the suspension was designed in such a way that in no case would the outside wheels assume a positive camber angle due to body roll, while roll itself and weight transfer were reduced by a 93 mm increase in the front track, compared with the Carrera 6. The front track was now up to 1.43 m, as in the Ollon-Villars Bergspyder, while the rear track remained practically unchanged at 1.40 m, mainly in the interests of better streamlining.

As was the Bergspyder, the 910 was designed to take 13-in wheels with 8-in wide rims at the front and 9.5-in rims at the rear. The Carrera 6 composite wheels with a steel disc and alloy rims were discarded in favour of much lighter cast magnesium wheels. For long-distance racing it was important that wheels could be changed as quickly as possible, and for a long time Porsche pit crews had been using a compressed-air tool which screwed up all five nuts together. But even then the nuts had to be started on their threads by hand, so this was still not the ideal solution. The old Rudge hub being much too heavy, a new centre-lock system was evolved, incorporating four driving studs and a light alloy central lock nut which could be screwed on or off with the aid of a compressed-air tool. This central-locking system was to be used for all later Porsche racing cars and was also extensively copied.

In the design stage, great care had been taken to ensure that the diagonal tube across the engine bay, which had been shown to improve notably the torsional stiffness of the Carrera 6 chassis, could now be used with the eight-cylinder engine. Torsional stiffness tests performed after the completion of the first 910 hill-climb car showed this to be slightly stiffer than the Carrera 6 frame. The torsional stiffness was obtained by clamping the frame at the attachment points of the rear suspension units, while at the front, it was twisted in the plane of the suspension units. In order to obtain comparative figures for various chassis, the torsional stiffness is expressed by the formula

$$S = \frac{TL}{\theta} \text{ (ft}^2 \text{ lb)}$$

in which T is the torque applied in the longitudinal axis of the frame, L the wheelbase and θ the twist angle. From this we obtain

$$\frac{S}{L} = \frac{T}{\theta} \text{ (lb ft/radian)}$$

giving the torque required to twist a chassis of a given wheelbase one radian. Converting this into torque per degree of twist, this gives the following comparative figures:

	Torsional stiffness
Formula V Beach Car frame	284 lb ft/deg
Elva frame (Elva-Porsche hill-climb car)	568 lb ft/deg
Ollon-Villars space frame car 906 010	680 lb ft/deg
904 pressed steel frame (without body)	725 lb ft/deg
Lotus 23B frame	870 lb ft/deg
906 (Carrera 6) space frame	1,400 lb ft/deg
910 space frame (without body)	1,750 lb ft/deg
904 pressed steel frame, reinforced for Bergspyder	2,240 lb ft/deg

It should, however, be noted that due to the wider track of the 910 compared with the 906, the effective torsional deflection of the 910 frame, measured at the wheels, is approximately the same as for the 906. On the same occasion, the deflections of the transverse wishbones and longitudinal radius arms of the front and rear suspensions were measured for the highest forces produced under extreme conditions of braking, accelerating and cornering. In every case these were less than 1 mm. In order to save weight, chassis tubes were used as oil pipes connecting the engine to the front oil cooler.

As part of the development tests of the 910, the front and rear wheel travels were recorded both with the car travelling in circles and being driven on a sharp zig-zag course, the car No 910 001 (of which the frame had been submitted to the torsional

Gearbox as used in cars 960, 910 and 907. The housing is a magnesium casting and the general design is similar to the transmission fitted to the production 911 until 1971.

907 long-tail car for Le Mans 1967. The scoops at the rear direct air to the transmission.

907 long-tail car in 1967 form. This car had the lowest drag coefficient of all racing Porsches.

The Type 907 was the first Porsche racing car with right-hand drive in consideration of the fact that most races are run clockwise.

Rear suspension of Type 907 with progressive rate springs and infinitely adjustable anti-roll bar. A ventilated brake disc is used. The 910 suspension was practically identical to this.

907 long-tail cars took the first three places in the 1968 Daytona 24-hour race. The front end had been modified from the previous year with a lower oil cooler air intake, the air being ducted from the cooler to the upper surface of the car's nose to reduce front lift.

Type 907 short-tail coupe 1968. The narrower superstructure reduces the frontal area compared with the 910.

908 short-tail car with pivoted rear flaps at the start of a race at Hockenheim in 1968.

1969 Type 908 engine with room and weight saving Bosch two row injection pump. Note the diaphragm spring clutch.

908 with 1968 type six-speed gearbox and rear-mounted clutch. Note the older type in-line injection pump.

stiffness tests) being used on this occasion. The data obtained were used as a basis for static tests in which forces were applied to the centre of gravity. They led to the following conclusions:

The centre of gravity (with a full tank and a 75 kg driver) is 420 mm (16.5 in) above ground level. The front/rear weight distribution is 44/56.

For 1.12 g lateral acceleration, the roll angle of the car is 3° to 4° of which about 25 per cent is accounted for by the variation of the rolling radius of the tyre due to the weight transfer. On a sharp zig-zag course, the roll angle increases by another 1.5° to 2°, which on the 910 brings the front and rear hollow rubber auxiliary springs into action.

In spite of a suspension geometry providing for increasing negative camber as the suspension is compressed, the roll angle is the overriding factor. In spite of the designed static negative camber of 1° 30' at the front and 3° at the rear, the outside wheels can still assume positive camber under extreme cornering conditions. This led to a modified rear suspension geometry giving a sharper rise of the negative camber as the suspension was compressed, introduced with car No 910 013. With this suspension, the camber change between full rebound and full bump was $7\frac{1}{2}°$ instead of 2° 10'. At the front, the camber variation of $2\frac{1}{2}°$ remained unchanged.

The travels measured for the front and rear suspension indicated that as the car was driven round the circular track with a lateral acceleration of 1.12 g, the car structure was twisted by approximately 1°. On a sharp zig-zag course, this is increased to approximately 1.5°. These figures correspond to a torsional rigidity of approximately 60,000 kgm², a figure nearly twice as high as for the bare chassis frame.

These tests were to dictate the suspension and tyre philosophy adopted by Porsche in the following years, up to the time when the use of very wide and flat tyres became imperative to transmit the power of enormously powerful engines. For the Porsche racing department, handling on the Nürburgring, reflected in the lap times, has always been the final test of a racing car. No doubt this is a very severe test, and if a car passes it satisfactorily, it will also handle well on most other circuits, especially on the Targa Florio course, one of the Porsche favourites. As the Nürburgring is rather rough and bumpy (it was completely resurfaced in 1970, but is still bumpier than most, with several places where the cars take off at high speed) it requires a comparatively soft suspension with long travel. If, with such a suspension, the outer wheels are not to assume positive camber, the static negative camber must be rather large and the geometry of the suspension must be such that the negative camber is considerably increased as the suspension is compressed. These conditions are hardly compatible with the current very wide and flat-treaded tyres because the camber changes reduce the contact surface, create local over-loading and over-heating leading to reduced grip and possible disintegration of the tread. If, however, the suspension geometry provides for only small variations in camber, with minimal static camber, then the camber of the outside wheels changes to positive when the car rolls under the cornering forces being set up. This is doubly undesirable, as positive camber in itself reduces the cornering power and with wide flat-treaded tyres, the contact area is also decreased causing a further loss in cornering power. This is why, as long as increased engine power did not make it imperative, Porsche were reluctant to follow the trend towards very wide and very flat-treaded tyres; they rather stuck to comparatively narrow tyres with a somewhat rounded tread profile which would accommodate considerable camber variations without significant changes of road contact area and without creating high local loads.

E

As the 910 was originally to be used for hill-climbs, the first car was built with an eight-cylinder engine. The hill-climb Championship of 1966 being for sports prototypes up to 2 litres, for which a minimum weight of 575 kg (1,270 lb) without fuel was prescribed, this is exactly how much it weighed when it first turned its wheels on the Weissach circular track on July 2 1966. With 'steering-pad champion' development engineer Falk at the wheel, a best lap time of 18.0 s was obtained, after the anti-roll bars had been suitably adjusted, on Dunlop R7 White Spot rain tyres. This was no record, but the car was said to be an easy one to drive. In fact the 910 is reputed to be the best handling racing Porsche ever made. Three days later, the car was taken to Hockenheim and driven by Hans Herrmann on the mountain course on a wet day. On the same occasion, the hill-climb car 906 010 was tried out by Gerhard Mitter, for the first time with an eight-cylinder fuel injection engine which was praised for its flexibility. It was nevertheless Hans Herrmann with the new 910 who (twice) achieved the best time of 50.3 s, while Mitter, who was usually at least as fast as Herrmann, could not better 50.4 s with the hill-climb car on identical tyres. In its first actual event, however, the Trento-Bondone hill-climb, the 910 of Hans Herrmann was beaten into second place by Mitter's fuel injection car.

As the 910 was to be used for hill-climbs before it competed in long-distance races, it was used as a guinea pig for trying out several weight saving ideas. Among other things, it was fitted with titanium front stub axles and the half shafts had Giubo (rubber) universals at their inner end, to accommodate both angular and axial movements. These had previously been proved to make the cars both smoother and quicker to drive. For reliability reasons, however, these rubber universals were not used in long races. Later, when the lighter six-cylinder engine was used in the 910 for long-distance racing, some of the lightweight features had to go, otherwise the car would have been lighter than the prescribed 575 kg.

Though the second car of the 910 series clinched the European Hill-climb Championship for Mitter, most of the 910 development was done later. For this, the car was fitted with a six-cylinder fuel injection engine, identical to those used in Carrera 6 prototypes, as this was to be used for all long-distance races. The rubber-driven half shafts were replaced by all-metallic Nadella half shafts, of which the needle bearing universals had a titanium spider. To start with, the car (No 910 002) was taken to the destruction course of the Volkswagen proving ground as had now become normal practice during the development period of any new Porsche competition car. Before the destruction tests began, the car had done approximately 200 km (125 miles) of test runs and hill-climb races. The tests were interrupted after 777 km (483 miles) when an important frame tube broke.

In the first part of the tests, the following parts broke:

The 6/32 final drive bevel gears used experimentally. These gears lasted only 42 miles and it was decided not to develop them any further.

Both light alloy rear uprights (on the right-hand side twice). A modification was put in hand.

The gearbox supports on the frame. Here too a modification was put in hand.

The thread of the ball at the outer end of the upper right suspension wishbone. It was decided that the ball would be welded to the wishbone. Previous tests had already indicated this modification to be desirable in the interests of a greater rigidity.

The chassis tube supporting the gearbox. It was decided to use a thicker tube in this place.

Additionally several cracks had to be welded in the course of the run. Steel gussets were to be added at those places.

Except for the gearbox supports and the rear uprights, which again broke and for which new reinforcements were planned, all the modifications incorporated as a result of the first trials proved perfectly satisfactory in the course of a second trial on the destruction course in which 1,888 km (1,173 miles) were covered. But trouble was experienced with the straps holding the tanks, with the tanks themselves, and with the door and window frames. Important parts which broke during this second part of the test were the titanium spiders of the half shaft universals (on both sides), which led to the use of larger universals with a steel spider, and a bracket holding a rear radius rod pivot was torn off. This is what put a stop to the trial, but as these parts had stood up to nearly 1,700 miles on the destruction track, they were not modified. They were to prove some of the weakest points of the 910 frame, however.

Meanwhile, the first car of the series, 910 001, was undergoing high speed development tests in Hockenheim. Up to then, the car had only been used for hill-climbs which are short and comparatively slow, and these tests, which were done with the six-cylinder fuel injection engine to be used for long distance racing, were to give more information on air pressure on the various parts of the body, temperatures and spoiler settings.

The body of the 910 had a removable roof section so that the car could be run as an open Spyder or as a coupé. The upper part of the body was cut off just behind the roll bar, but a Perspex fairing (as in the Carrera 6) could be added to prolong the roof line to join the rear deck. The tests were to indicate how the air pressure and temperature were modified around the intake pipes, and in the engine bay, with the roof and the rear fairing fitted and removed, and what their influence was on the car's handling.

The most important findings can be summarised as follows:

Front spoilers are detrimental: with these fitted, the pressure pushing the car's nose down is so high that the wheels foul the wings as soon as the speed exceeds 125 mph!

Even without front spoilers and with the adjustable rear spoiler in the highest position, the car still assumes a negative angle of incidence of 40' at 150 mph with the roof removed.

With identical settings, but with the roof fitted, the angle of incidence becomes 10' positive.

With roof and Perspex rear fairing, the angle of incidence becomes 20' positive.

Without roof but with the plastic fairing, the angle of incidence is 10' negative.

From this it can be concluded that the roof and Perspex fairing both had a considerable influence on the car's handling.

The pressure and temperature checks indicated the conditions to be quite similar to those in the Carrera 6 and not materially modified by fitting or removing the roof and the Perspex fairing. In fact, the 910 was never raced with the latter.

These Hockenheim tests also provided an occasion for testing new Textar TG 22 brake linings which reduced the pedal pressure but proved to have a notably higher wear rate than either Textar 1432 G or Ferodo DS 11. In the course of the tests, a front wheel bearing failed. This was a problem which recurred with the 910 and for which no satisfactory solution could be found for many years. Testing was resumed a few weeks later on the Nürburgring with Hans Herrmann driving, to finalise spring, shock absorber and anti-roll bar settings. The tyres used were Dunlop R7 White Spot 5.50 L-13 at the front and 7.00 L-13 at the rear, running at pressures of 23 and 26 psi front and rear respectively. Initial camber settings were —30' at the front and —2° at the rear.

Initially, the best time obtained on the southern loop of the Nürburgring was 2 m 20.8 s. In order to make the steering lighter, the castor angle was reduced from 7° to 6°, but this proved detrimental to the straight line stability and to the precision with which the driver could keep to his course on fast curves, so finally 6° 30' was chosen as a compromise setting. Further tests led to the adoption of softer front springs and shock absorbers while negative camber was increased front and rear to 1° 30' and 3° respectively. With these settings, Herrmann finally got down to a time of 2 m 16.9 s, a considerable improvement and a time which compares very favourably with that of 2 m 8 s set up by Mitter with the eight-cylinder Ollon-Villars Bergspyder. The —1° 30' and —3° camber settings were to remain standard for the 910.

The test sessions on the Nürburgring were also used to find out, with the help of instruments attached to the shock absorbers, how many times in the course of one lap of the northern loop of the Ring the suspension bumped through to compress the stops incorporated in the spring units. The northern loop not being closed for the occasion, the car was driven comparatively gently (lap time 9 m 14 s), in spite of which the results were quite impressive: at the front, the suspension stops came into action approximately 30 times on compression and 25 times on rebound. At the rear, they came into action approximately 20 times on compression and five times on rebound.

These data were gathered mainly with a view to future designs. Other important findings were that the rubber Giubo half shaft universals stood up very well to the very hard 420-mile test drive and that the Textar TG 22 brake lining which notably reduced the pedal pressure had a rate of wear which unfortunately made it suitable only for hill-climbs and short races.

The test session was interrupted when a titanium front stub axle broke, and closer investigation again revealed that the failure was caused by the development of excessive heat and seizure of the bearing.

Following this second case of titanium stub axle failure, a test rig was made up to investigate in the laboratory whether the bearing failure, that ultimately caused the breakage of the shaft, had anything to do with the fact that the latter was made of titanium. The car was set up with its front wheels on rollers and the front weighted with 160 kg (355 lb) ballast to simulate the weight transfer under severe braking. A titanium stub axle was fitted on the right-hand side and a steel stub axle on the left-hand side and on both sides there were pick-ups registering the temperatures of the brake disc and at the bearing adjustment nut. The rollers were rotated to simulate a speed of approximately 106 mph and the brakes were blower-cooled. Under these conditions, the brakes were operating in a sequence corresponding to their use on the Hockenheim course, making quite sure that the brake disc temperature did not exceed the figure reached in actual racing.

This test showed that with the grease currently used, the outer wheel bearing on the titanium stub axle actually reached a much higher temperature than on the steel stub axle: 400° C on titanium and 180° C on steel. The reason for this is, of course, that the heat conductivity of titanium is notably less than that of steel. The use of ET 300 Molykote grease provided a satisfactory solution, but for safety it was decided that only steel stub axles would, in future, be used for long distance racing.

As already mentioned, the 910 was first used for hill-climbing. This is a category of racing in which the air drag is relatively unimportant and due to pressure of time, the body shape, though based on previous experience, was never tested in the wind tunnel, not even as a scale model. The sharply sloping front end, however, indicates that this was not just a styling exercise, while the front-hinged rear part over the

engine compartment which had to be held open by a stay, was much less conveni-
ent than the rear-hinged Carrera rear deck, but this too had its reason: both Mitter
and van Lennep had been injured at Spa in Carrera 6s when the rear part of the body
flew open after a hasty pit stop, when the locking system had not been properly
secured. For a similar reason, the 910 had front-hinged doors which were heavier
and less practical than the 906 gull-wing doors, but the designers hadn't forgotten
that on the occasion of a press demonstration (of all things), an improperly locked
gull-wing door flew open and was torn away from the car!

Before the 910 was entered for long-distance races, its designers wanted to
know if its form was actually as efficient as they hoped; could it be improved, and
what was the influence of spoilers, removable top and removable Perspex fairing
on the air drag and aerodynamic lift? As the angle of incidence was known to have a
considerable bearing on the air flow, the suspension movements were accurately
measured at an air speed of 156 mph and, in order to obviate any oscillation, the
car was held in a corresponding position for every particular test. Here is a summary
of the most important data obtained:

(a)   Without roof, without rear Perspex fairing, without front spoilers—
Angle of incidence —1° 25';
$C_w=0.438$.

(b)   As (a), but with front spoilers (as used by Mitter for hill-climb racing)—
Angle of incidence —2° 5';
$C_w=0.440$.

(c)   With roof, without rear Perspex fairing, without front spoilers—
Angle of incidence —15';
$C_w=0.354$.

(d)   With roof, with rear Perspex fairing, without front spoilers—
Angle of incidence +20';
$C_w= 0.350$.

(e)   As (d), but with long tail and undertray under the engine bay—
Angle of incidence —35';
$C_w=0.307$.

An interesting additional experiment consisted of measuring the drag with the
front and rear wheels spinning, but surprisingly this had no effect on the drag factor.
Neither did this materially change the air pressure inside the wheel arches.

The drag data obtained indicate that with comparable equipment, the 910 had a
slightly worse drag coefficient than the Carrera 6, these being 0.350 and 0.342
respectively. To compensate for this it had a slightly smaller frontal area $F=1.319$ m²
instead of 1.325 m² so that the product F x C_w was practically identical for both cars:
906, F x $C_w=0.459$; 910, F x $C_w=0.461$.

Further drag tests were made later to find the influence of various details. In order
to eliminate incidental effects, the various joints at the doors, the lids and so on were
covered with tape. In this state, the car tested, fitted with a roof but without the rear
plastic fairing, had a drag coefficient of $C_w=0.342$ (instead of 0.354 as obtained
in the first test). The use of faired rear-view mirrors and the removal of the windscreen wiper did not make any measurable difference, but the following steps
produced a significant reduction of the drag:

The initial drag coefficient being $C_w=0.342$,

$C_w=0.328$ was obtained by blanking off the front intakes leading air to the oil
cooler and the brakes;

$C_w=0.315$ was obtained by additionally fitting an underpan;

$Cw=0.307$ was obtained by additionally cutting and blanking off the air scoops for rear brake ventilation.

The car was also tried with the top removed, but even with a smaller windscreen, a smaller roll bar and blanked off rear brake air scoops, the drag coefficient was considerably worse than for the closed car and, even though the frontal area was notably reduced (by approximately 11 per cent), the product F x Cw was still higher than for the closed car, indicating a higher total air drag. The influence of the angle of incidence was also measured on the Spyder, when it was found that with a positive angle of only $\frac{3}{4}°$ (car raised by 30 mm or 1.2 in at the front axle), the drag was increased by 5.5 per cent.

In order to make more room for tall drivers, a more bulbous roof was developed and was shown to reduce the drag coefficient slightly.

The Type 910 made an excellent debut in long-distance racing when Herrmann/ Siffert finished fourth to three 4-litre Ferraris in the Daytona 24-Hour race and two cars driven by Mitter/Patrick and Herrmann/Siffert finished third and fourth in the Sebring 12-Hour race, behind two 7-litre Fords. Development was nevertheless continued with the European season in view, and further tests were made at Hockenheim. One of these tests confirmed previous Carrera 6 tests, indicating that while the six-cylinder fuel injection engine did not make the car any faster in maximum speed than the carburettor engine, it was more flexible.

On the circular track at Weissach, comparative tests were made matching Firestone and Goodyear tyres against the latest Dunlops. There were no significant differences in tyre temperatures, but both in the current sizes 5.00 L-13 front and 7.00 L-13 rear and in the new flatter sizes 5.25 M-13 front and 6.00/12.00-13 rear (in all cases mixture 184) the Dunlops gave better results than their American competitors. With all tyres several anti-roll bar and camber settings were tried, and, in all cases, the best results were obtained with the largest negative settings tried, —1° 30' front and —3° rear, which had already been adopted as standard settings for the Type 910. With test engineer Peter Falk at the wheel, the fastest times for the various tyres tested were as follows:

Firestone Indy	18.16 s=1.178 g
Goodyear (dry road rubber but rain tread pattern)	17.88 s=1.214 g
Dunlop (M 184) 5.50 L-13/7.00 L-13	17.60 s=1.253 g
Dunlop (M 184) 5.25 M-13/6.00/12.00-13	17.50 s=1.268 g

The fastest time of 17.50 s obtained on the new Dunlop tyres just broke the existing skid pan record held by the 906 010 Bergspyder on the older Dunlop tyres.

Though, following the decision of the Porsche management to use only new cars for all important races, the 910 was built in large numbers, it was never intended to build 50 of them before the start of the European racing season of 1967, so that it could be homologated as a sports car. The Carrera 6 was only one year old and had no serious competitors in the 2-litre sports car class, so the factory would certainly not have made itself very popular with Carrera 6 owners who had paid around 50,000 DM for their car, if after only one year they had brought out a new and more efficient model to beat them. With due consideration to this problem, the 910 was only run as a factory entry in the prototype group. Altogether 28 units were made and, as for 1968 the number required for homologation as a sports car was reduced from 50 to 25 units, it could then be homologated as a sports car. Most of the factory cars, of which many had been raced only once, were completely re-built to new condition and sold to private owners.

7

The 910 in long-distance racing

AS IN THE YEAR 1966 the European Hill-climb Championship was limited to prototypes for which a minimum weight was required (575 kg [1,270 lb] for 2-litre cars, the upper limit for the championship) the hill-climb version of the 910 was designed down to that weight limit, which did not require any radical weight saving solutions. Light metal was obviously extensively used, not only for the various housings of engine and power train, but also for running gear parts, brake calipers, steering box and so forth. The use of titanium parts in the chassis was not absolutely necessary in order to get down to the weight limit, although the eight-cylinder engine used for hill-climbing was comparatively heavy. Consequently, no major modifications were necessary to make the car suitable for long-distance racing, once the few local reinforcements, which the destruction tests had shown to be necessary, had been incorporated into the design. And as the six-cylinder engine to be used for long-distance racing weighed about 20 kg (44 lb) less than the eight-cylinder, a good margin was left for adaptations such as the use of Nadella hollow half shafts with metallic universals and splines to accommodate length variations instead of Giubo rubber universals, additional ducts for brake cooling, supplementary head-lights and so forth.

Daytona Intercontinental (1967)

When a 910 (chassis No 910 003) was first entered for the Daytona Inter-continental 24-Hour race, the only experience behind it was a few hill-climbs and the destruction tests on the Volkswagen proving ground. During practice for the race it was necessary to raise the car on its suspension to prevent the tyres from making contact with the wings when on the banking. Tests were also made with and without the top and the Perspex rear fairing, following which it was decided to run with the top and without the fairing, as this combination had produced the fastest lap times. Goodyear tyres were tried but the results were not as good as with Dunlops. As the engine felt rather indifferent, it was changed before the third practice and with the appropriate gearing, the car, to be driven in the race by Herrmann and Siffert, did its best practice lap in 2 m 05.0 s.

In view of the comparatively limited experience of the new car, the other two factory entries were fuel injected Carrera 6s driven by Mitter/Rindt and Schütz/van Lennep/Stommelen. The Mitter/Rindt car ran on Goodyear tyres on which it had done a practice lap in 2 m 04.9 s, the lower profile American tyres (5.25/9.50-15 front and 5.50/9.75-15 rear) having proved to be slightly faster than the Dunlops. This is easily explained by the fact that for some time Dunlop tyres of 15-in diameter had seen very little development. Surprisingly, the only car which reached the finish was the new 910. A sticking throttle slide caused Schütz to over-rev his engine badly (9,600 rpm) in the 19th lap which was probably the reason for the later engine failure. Mitter stopped twice at the beginning of the race to have out-of-balance tyres changed. As this still did not solve the problem, a set of tyres that had been used in practice was fitted and proved successful. Thus another lesson was learned the hard way: in the future, all fitted tyres likely to be used during the race would be tried for at least one lap during the practice period. After these pit stops, the Carrera 6 was driven faster than the 910, but in the seventh hour, Mitter crashed it when he was baulked by another car.

In spite of some ignition difficulties due to oil getting into the distributor which then had to be changed, the 910 was placed fourth in this 24-Hour race, behind three 4-litre Ferraris. It took, of course, first place in the 2-litre class, but though the result could hardly have been better, there was some disappointment in the Porsche camp, as testified by the internal race report: 'The performance of the 910 did not quite come up to expectations. For two different engines, Herrmann reported insufficient power. In his opinion the two Carrera 6s were faster both in acceleration and maximum speed.'

This was confirmed when after the race the Carrera 6 driven by Schütz was fitted with the engine from Mitter's crashed car and was 3 to 4 s a lap faster than the 910. On the same occasion, Firestone Indy tyres were for the first time faster on a Carrera 6 than either Dunlops or Goodyears. Unfortunately they could not be tried on the 910 due to lack of time. These tests confirmed that part-worn tyres with a sculptured tread (as were all racing tyres of the period) are faster than new, only just run-in tyres of which the deeper tread pattern is less rigid and consequently produces lower cornering forces.

Sebring 12-Hour race (1967)

Nothing wrong could be found with the engine of the 910 used in the Daytona race when it was taken for tests to the Hockenheim track. But, after only four laps a piston failed and the engine was replaced by a spare one which reached 700 rpm more on the straight, so it can be assumed that the Daytona engine was really not up to par. This was confirmed as soon as practice for the Sebring 12-Hour race began: under similar conditions (full tank, new tyres and brake linings) the two works 910s (chassis Nos 004 and 005) driven by Siffert and Mitter, lapped in 3 m 01.0 s and 3 m 01.1 s respectively, while the two works Carrera 6s (Nos 906 159 and 160) did 3 m 03.8 s (Buzzetta) and 3 m 06.2 s (Schütz).

How much lighter the 910 was than the 906 is shown by the weights obtained at the factory before the cars were sent to America. The 910s weighed 574 and 570 kg, that is, less than the minimum prescribed weight (which was brought up to the limit by filling up with more oil), while the two 906s weighed 618 and 620 kg despite the use of several non-standard titanium and magnesium parts.

The 910s ran in closed form, without spoiler and all cars used Dunlop tyres of 184 mixture. As usual the brake pads were Textar 1431 G. In practice the fuel consumption fell within the very narrow 8.0 to 8.2 mpg bracket for all cars.

The best Porsche practice time was done by the privately-entered 906 with Charlie Kolb at the helm: he did 2 m 58.8 s with a nearly empty tank. No other 2-litre car got down to under 3 m. Zeccoli did 3 m 00.6 s with the 2-litre Alfa Romeo 33 and the best Ferrari Dino time was 3 m 02.4 s by Casoni. The absolute fastest practice time was done by Bruce McLaren driving a 7-litre Ford Mk. IV in 2 m 48.0 s, while Phil Hill did 2 m 50.6 s with the 7-litre Chaparral-Chevrolet.

In the race, however, Patrick, Mitter's American co-driver in the 910, took the lead in the 2-litre class on the third lap and Porsches were never headed again in the class. All Alfas and Dinos retired without having put up real opposition. Two of the 7-litre American cars survived the race so that in the end, the Mitter/Patrick 910 finished third, only 52 miles behind the winning Ford of Andretti/McLaren and on the same lap as the second Ford driven by A. J. Foyt and Lloyd Ruby. The only work done to the car in the course of the 12-Hour race was to change tyres and brake linings, as scheduled, which cost $6\frac{1}{2}$ minutes. The other 910 driven by Siffert and Herrmann took fourth place. In this case, the mechanics took only 5 m 10 s to change the tyres and the brake linings, but a small collision cost the car ten minutes to change a headlight, and it had to stop twice briefly to repair a tail light. The Gregg/Buzzetta 906 finished seventh after having to be repaired following a minor crash. It lost sixth place towards the end of the race because of worn brakes, when it was overtaken by the privately-owned long-tail car driven by Spoerry and Steinemann. The fourth works entry had to retire on the 55th lap after colliding with a dog.

Monza 1,000 km race (April 25 1967)

In view of the forthcoming 1,000 km race, a 910 with a six-cylinder fuel injection engine (No 910 006) was sent to Monza a few weeks before the race for tyre and brake lining tests with Gerhard Mitter as driver. To start with, the car had to be raised on its suspension with the aid of large washers inserted under the springs and hollow rubber auxiliary springs were added to prevent the tyres from fouling the wings on the very bumpy banking. For the tyre tests, the anti-roll bars were adjusted by suitably moving the connecting link on the anti-roll bar lever, while two different gearboxes were used to suit the tyres' rolling radius.

For tyres having a rolling radius of 330 to 340 mm the following ratios were used: 15:36, 19:32, 23:29, 25:26, 27:25 with crown wheel and pinion 7:31. For tyres with a rolling radius of 316 mm the ratios were: 16:36, 20:31, 23:28, 26:26, 28:24 with crown wheel and pinion 7:31.

Dunlop, Firestone and Goodyear tyres of various types and dimensions were tried, the times being taken for the entire course (including the two bankings) as well as for the road course alone.

In the course of a first test series with tyre sizes normally used for the 910, the Dunlop 184 mixture was the fastest and also gave the easiest handling. Lap times were 3 m 11.4 s for the full course and 1 m 41.9 s for the road course, the time for the full course being 6 to 7.5 s quicker than on corresponding Firestone and Goodyear tyres respectively. All these tests were done with the roof removed. A second series of tests was made with the cockpit closed, which necessitated a different setting of the front anti-roll bar, due to the reduced front aerodynamic downthrust. In this state, the time for the full course was reduced by nearly 2 s to 3 m 09.5 s (road course 1 m 40.6 s) using the same Dunlop tyres as before. In both cases, the engine reached 7,900 rpm in fifth gear, indicating that maximum speed was not increased and that the faster times resulted mainly from the much better handling in fast curves, which was confirmed by Mitter. On the following day, testing was resumed with the higher geared gearbox and tyres with a lower profile ratio and larger contact area. To start with, Dunlop tyres, mixture 184, were tried but instead of the usual dimensions 5.50 L-13 front and 7.00 L-13 rear, the dimensions 5.25 M-13 front and 6.00/12.00-13 rear were used. After several anti-roll bar settings had been tried and the rear tyre pressure had been reduced from 26 to 23 psi, a time (with roof) of 3 m 11.9 s (road course 1 m 41.7 s) was obtained. A fairly neutral handling could not be obtained, however, the car understeering in slow corners and oversteering in fast bends.

As the Dunlop and Firestone technicians suggested that the rear negative camber of —3° was too much for the flat tread of these wide tyres, it was reduced to —20'. With this setting, the tendency to oversteer could not be cured either by altering the anti-roll bar settings or by modifying the tyre pressures. The straight line stability was slightly better, but the car was difficult to drive around corners and the tail tended to break away very suddenly. The negative camber was then increased to —1° 30', but even with this setting, the back tended to break away uncontrollably. The lap time of 3 m 11.9 s was the same, however, as with the standard setting of —3° camber. Later tests indicate that the slower times obtained with the wider and flatter-treaded tyres must partly be attributed to the fact that the $9\frac{1}{2}$-in wide rims were not wide enough for the tyre dimension used.

Firestone low profile tyres of 5.00/9.50-13 front and 6.00/12.00-13 rear led to excessive oversteer. Perhaps this could have been suppressed by reducing the negative camber of the front wheels but, due to pressure of time, this was not tried and again 3° rear negative camber gave the best results, as summed up below:

Firestone Indy 5.50/9.50-13 front, 6.50/11.50-13 rear, gearbox for large rolling radius with modified fifth gear (26:25), with roof:

Rear camber —1° 30', full lap 3 m 14.5 s, road course 1 m 43.6 s

Rear camber —3°, full lap 3 m 12.8 s, road course 1 m 42.6 s

Dunlop 184: 5.50 L-13 front, 7.00 L-13 rear:

Rear camber —3°, full lap 3 m 09.4 s, road course 1 m 40.7 s

Dunlop 184: 5.25 M-13 front, 7.00 L-13 rear:

Rear camber —3°, full lap 3 m 08.6 s, road course 1 m 39.7 s.

Tests with this last combination showed that the car was slightly faster with the wider 5.25 M-13 front tyres than with the narrower 5.50 L-13 usually fitted, primarily because the braking distances are slightly reduced. These tyres also provided very good handling and Herrmann, who arrived in Monza towards the end of the tests, got down to 3 m 08.2 s on his fourth lap.

The object of the brake lining tests was to compare various Ferodo linings with the usual Textar 1431 G. These tests were done on the fastest Dunlop tyre combination using the wider 5.25 M-13 front tyres. The Textar linings were found to give the best and smoothest braking and they were chosen for the forthcoming 1,000 km race through which they would probably last in spite of their rather high rate of wear.

For the race cars 910 008 and 910 009 were used, driven respectively by Mitter/ Rindt and by Siffert/Herrmann. Both used a six-cylinder fuel injection engine and were fitted with Dunlop tyres 5.25 M-13 front and 7.00 L-13 rear, mixture 184 and pressure 31.5 psi front and rear.

The best practice times for the two works cars were as follows:

901 009	Herrmann	3 m 07.0 s	} distance covered 244 miles
	Siffert	3 m 08.0 s	
910 008	Mitter	3 m 09.0 s	} distance covered 188 miles
	Rindt	3 m 10.9 s	

In both cars, the engine reached 8,200 to 8,300 rpm on the 26:25 fifth gear with the usual crown wheel and pinion combination of 7:31.

Other important practice times were:

Chaparral 2F (7-litre)	2 m 53.8 s (Phil Hill)
Ferrari P4 (4-litre)	2 m 54.1 s (Bandini)
Ford-Mirage (5.7-litre)	3 m 01.1 s (Ickx)
Ferrari Dino (2-litre)	3 m 08.8 s (Klass)
Porsche Carrera 6	3 m 12.7 s (Driver not known)

In the 100-lap race, the works Dino stopped, after only 15 laps, with engine troubles. Later the Chaparral, Rodriguez' Ferrari P4 and Ickx' Mirage also fell by the wayside. As the race proceeded, the works Porsches became progressively faster, probably because the engines were getting looser, and reached 8,500 to 8,600 rpm in fifth gear. They were running fourth and fifth behind the three Ferraris when Vaccarella lost time due to a minor crash, but two laps before the end, a front wheel bearing failed on Siffert's car and Vaccarella just snatched fourth place in the last 50 yards before the finish. The two Porsches thus finished third and fifth, the Mitter/Rindt car having lost four laps to the victorious Bandini/Amon Ferrari.

Tyres were not changed during the race but the left rear tyre was worn through by the end. The fuel consumption was 9 mpg for the Mitter/ Rindt car and 9.4 mpg for the Herrmann/Siffert car. The oil consumption was 470 and 560 mpg respectively.

Spa 1,000 km race (May 7 1967)

There is little to be said about the following long-distance races for which the 91n was entered. The cars remained substantially unchanged; only the gear ratio's spring height, suspension bump stops and body equipment were modified to suit any particular circuit.

On the very fast Spa circuit, additional 911-type suspension rubber stops were necessary to prevent the wheels from fouling the wings in the very fast, slightly undulating bends. For aerodynamic reasons, the cars had their roofs fitted which the drivers certainly appreciated as, after two dry practice days, the race was contested in pouring rain. Except for different gearing (a slightly higher 27:25 fifth gear was used with intermediates to suit) the settings and the equipment were the same as for Monza but, on the Herrmann/Siffert car, the castor angle was increased by 30' in the interests of straight line stability. The cars used were:

910 005 (Mitter/Koch)
910 007 (Siffert/Herrmann)
Best practice times:

910 005	Mitter	3 m 59.0 s	distance covered 334 miles
	Koch	4 m 00.2 s	
910 007	Herrmann	3 m 59.5 s	distance covered 280 miles
	Siffert	3 m 54.3 s	

On such a fast course, which the Chaparral lapped at 147 mph, the 2-litre cars were at a considerable disadvantage. Of the fastest cars, the Phil Hill/Mike Spence 7-litre Chaparral did 3 m 35.6 s, the Ickx/Rees 5.7-litre Ford-Mirage did 3 m 39.0 s and the Parkes/Scarfiotti 4-litre Ferrari did 3 m 39.1 s.

On the wet track, however, only Ickx and Paul Hawkins (Lola-Chevrolet) were able to use over 400 hp to good effect while Siffert and Herrmann drove their 910 almost as if the track had been dry. They were rewarded with a quite unexpected second place overall behind the Mirage. None of the works Porsches made a unscheduled pit stop and Koch/Mitter finished seventh, four laps behind the winners.

Triumph in the Targa Florio (May 14 1967)

For Porsche, the Targa Florio has always been of particular importance because manoeuvrability is at least as important as sheer power on the winding Sicilian mountain course. Six cars, all 910s, were prepared for the race. Three had the usual 2-litre six-cylinder fuel injection engine and three were fitted with the 2.2-litre eight-cylinder engine. This was the first time fuel injection was used for the 2.2-litre eight-cylinder. In contrast with the 2-litre eight-cylinder hill-climb car, the fuel metering was performed (as described in an earlier chapter) by means of a space cam sensitive to both throttle opening and engine speed, instead of being a function of the throttle opening only, the main advantage of the new cam being a lower fuel consumption.

As the 45-mile-long mountain course takes a lot of learning and the roads are closed for only one day (on the Friday before the race) for official practice, all drivers have to be on the spot several days in advance and the Porsche crew did no less than 85 laps unofficial practice on open roads, driving two Porsche 911s and one 910 (the 910 003 Daytona car). An additional preliminary practice session had already taken place some weeks before, using a 910, which not only allowed the drivers to learn the course, but also helped in the choice of gear ratios, suspension settings and so forth. Altogether, Colin Davis and Stommelen completed no less than 31 laps before the official practice day, while Biscaldi did only six. The 910 practice car that had come straight from the Daytona 24-Hour race, did no less than 29 laps of the destructive course (about 1,310 miles) with no trouble other than breaking the bracket of the upper rear radius arm pivot on both sides. It will be remembered that the tests on the destruction course of the Volkswagen proving ground had already shown this to be the weakest point of the 910 chassis.

The following cars were used for the race:

Three identical eight-cylinders—
910 024 (Stommelen/Hawkins)
910 025 (Mitter/Davis)
910 012 (Herrmann/Siffert)

Because of the rough roads, these cars were raised on their suspension by washers inserted under the springs and were additionally fitted with hollow rubber bump springs as used in the production Type 911. All cars were closed and used Textar 1431 G brake pads in their standard ATE brakes. Dunlop tyres were used as at Monza but were inflated to 23 and 26 psi front and rear respectively.

In view of the higher power of the 2.2-litre engine, reinforced Nadella half shafts were fitted after the official practice.

Three six-cylinders which, except for the gearing and the non-reinforced half shafts, were identical with the eight-cylinder cars—
910 006 (Maglioli/Schütz)
910 015 (Cella/Biscaldi)
910 014 (Neerpasch/Elford)

Only 910 006 was without a roof, presumably because Maglioli and Schütz are both rather tall and felt more comfortable in an open car.

Except for 910 012 and 910 006, all cars had the modified rear suspension giving a larger camber variation, introduced with car No 910 013.

In official practice every Porsche driver did one lap with his race car except Stommelen and Hawkins, whose car broke a half shaft on the first lap. The following are the practice times for the more important types of cars entered for the race:

4-litre Ferrari P4	37 m 12.4 s	(Vaccarella)
	37 m 53.6 s	(Scarfiotti)
2-litre Ferrari Dino	38 m 13.0 s	(Klass)
2-litre Porsche	38 m 34.0 s	(Cella)
7-litre Chaparral	38 m 39.6 s	(Phil Hill)
2.2-litre Porsche	38 m 46.0 s	(Siffert)
2-litre Alfa Romeo 33	38 m 46.4 s	(de Adamich)

Remembering that on the difficult Sicilian mountain course Vaccarella is on his own ground, it is interesting to note how little relation there is between lap times and power. Of the Porsches, a six-cylinder was fastest with Cella driving, followed by Siffert on an eight-cylinder. Then came another six-cylinder (Schütz) followed by another eight-cylinder (Colin Davis). It is also noteworthy that an eight-cylinder 2.2-litre had the lowest fuel consumption in practice: 8.8 mpg for the Mitter/Davis car, whereas the six-cylinder of Cella/Biscaldi had the highest consumption, running at 7.3 mpg, which reflects the lower consumption of the space cam injection system at that time fitted to the eight-cylinders only. Following the half shaft breakage, all the eight-cylinders cars were fitted with reinforced parts which gave no trouble during the race. The gearboxes proved to be rather weak for the fuel injection eight-cylinder engine, however, and that on the Mitter/Davis car had to be changed after practice because a tooth had broken on the second gear set. In the race, gearbox failure caused the retirement of the Siffert/Herrmann car on the last lap, though they still ranked as finishers, one lap behind. Two of the six-cylinders seemed to have particularly good engines as they revved up to 8,550 rpm on the straight. Consequently a slightly higher geared fifth gear (27:25 instead of 26:25) was fitted after practice. Both the engine and the gearbox were changed on the Cella/Biscaldi car, as after difficulties in engaging fourth gear, the engine had been revved up to 9,800 rpm!

Other pre-race work included changing a bent front wishbone on the Maglioli/Schütz car; on all cars the rear window was taken out to keep the cockpit cooler, and all joints between cockpit and engine compartment or oil tank were carefully sealed up. Air intakes and outlets were opened up in the eight-cylinder cars to bring down the oil temperature which had been running at between 105° and 115° C, although with no success. On the eight-cylinders the brakes also proved to be inadequate, while the six-cylinder car driven by Maglioli and Schütz showed abnormal brake lining wear after the official practice. The cure for this was to change the driver shifts: Maglioli took the start and also drove the last three laps so that Schütz, the harder driver, had to do only four laps!

After leading the race for nearly two laps with his Ferrari P4, Vaccarella hit a kerb in the village of Collesano, breaking two wheels, and had to abandon his car just under one of the many *graffiti* 'Viva Vaccarella' to be found all around the course. On the same lap, Klass crashed his fast Dino, and all hopes for a Ferrari win went overboard when the differential broke on the 4-litre P3, driven by Herbert Müller and Jean Guichet, in the course of the seventh of the ten-lap-long race. Meanwhile Mitter had bent the suspension of his eight-cylinder on the second lap and the best placed Porsche of Siffert/Herrmann fell back with gearbox troubles. Two laps before the finish, the only car left to break the Porsche formation, the surprisingly fast 2-litre Alfa Romeo of de Adamich/Rolland broke its front suspension, so that finally three Porsches finished in the first three places, headed by the 2.2-litre of Targa 'new boys' Hawkins and Stommelen, with the two 2-litres of Cella/Biscaldi and Neerpasch/Elford just behind. Porsche also won the GT class with a 911 driven by French journalist Bernard Cahier and the three-times Olympic skiing champion Jean-Claude Killy, taking seventh place overall.

ADAC Nürburgring 1,000 km race (May 28 1967)

The Nürburgring 1,000 km race in Porsche's home country has always been taken very seriously by the company. In order to get additional practice, the Nürburgring was hired for two days during the week preceding the race. The main object of the exercise, in which the two drivers Neerpasch and Herrmann did three laps each before setting out on their 44 laps (1,000 km) drive, was to find out about fuel consumption and tyre and brake pad wear. The car used was 910 005 coming straight from the Spa 1,000 km race (plus 330 practice miles) with the engine untouched. Only the suspension settings and the gear ratios were altered to suit the Ring. The 44 laps were covered in 6 h 43 m 26 s driving time. If 3 m are added for three pit stops, the actual race time still came out at 6 m 40 s less than the existing record, set up by Surtees in a 4-litre Ferrari in 1965.

This preliminary practice was also used to set up the eight-cylinder 910 028 that was to be used in the race and also to choose the appropriate gear ratios. Just before official practice started, the Ring was again hired for three days, in order to give all drivers (except Herrmann and Neerpasch who had done the preliminary testing) the opportunity to try out the track in practice cars.

The race cars were all closed, except the Mitter/Bianchi eight-cylinder and, following the Targa Florio experience, one of the eight-cylinders (the Stommelen/Ahrens car) was experimentally fitted with ventilated front brake discs. Following practice experience, all cars were fitted with a higher rear spoiler, except for the car driven by Neerpasch and Elford who refused to have their car altered in view of the speed penalty involved on the finishing straight by the higher spoiler. The same fifth gear ratio was used with both the six- and eight-cylinder engines, which reached 8,200 and 9,000 rpm respectively on the straight, indicating that the eight-cylinders were approximately 12 mph faster.

The race cars were:
Three eight-cylinder 2.2-litre cars with space cam fuel injection—
910 026 (Siffert/Herrmann);
910 027 (Stommelen/Ahrens) with ventilated front brake discs;
910 028 (Mitter/L. Bianchi) without roof;
Gear ratios—027 and 028: 11:29, 16:30, 20:31, 23:29, 26:26;
Crown wheel and pinion—7:31;
Gear ratios—026: 14:37; 18:32, 21:31, 23:28, 26:26;
Crown wheel and pinion—7:31.
Following the gearbox failures experienced with the eight-cylinder engines in the Targa Florio, all these cars experimentally used Shell 1747 A gearbox oil instead of the usual Castrol R 40 oil.
Three six-cylinder 2-litre fuel injection cars—
910 007 (Schütz/Buzzetta);
910 009 (Neerpasch/Elford) without higher rear spoiler;
910 013 (Koch/Hawkins);
Gear ratios—as 910 026.
All cars were on Dunlop tyres, mixture 184, 5.25 M-13 front and 7.00 L-13 rear with pressures of 28.5 and 31.5 psi respectively. Textar 1431 G brake linings were used on all cars. In practice all six Porsches were among the nine fastest cars, all eight-cylinders being faster than the six-cylinders. Fastest was Siffert in 8 m 41.4 s, headed only by Phil Hill's 7-litre Chaparral 2F in 8 m 31.9 s and Surtees' Lola-Aston Martin 5-litre in 8 m 39.6 s. The only car that split the Porsche formation was the Scarfiotti/Klass 2.4-litre Ferrari which did 8 m 48.5 s, but subsequently the engine blew up and there was no replacement. Fastest non-Porsche 2-litre car was the Alfa Romeo 33 driven by de Adamich/Nanni Galli which did 9 m 09.6 s.

As the Lola challenge never materialised and the Chaparral went out with transmission trouble when leading the race, the Porsches dominated the event from the 12th lap. The eight-cylinders, however, again showed that reliability was not their strong point. Siffert, who had closely chased the Chaparral, went out on the tenth lap with a broken valve and later the Ahrens/Stommelen car retired for the same reason, having lost a lot of time when the cog belt driving the injection pump had to be changed out on the track. The Mitter/Bianchi eight-cylinder car took the lead after the Chaparral had retired and built up a sufficient lead to have the battery changed on the 35th lap, after the alternator had failed, without loosing its place but it finally stopped with a dead battery on the last lap. Thereafter Buzzetta and Koch had a glorious sprint to the finish, won by the former by 0.2 s. Neerpasch and Elford drove the last eight laps with a broken valve spring and finished third, the Bianchi/Mitter eight-cylinder ranking as fourth finisher, one lap behind but still heading the first Alfa Romeo.

Le Mans 24-Hour race (June 10/11 1967)

Of the two 910s entered, 910 016 driven by Stommelen/Neerpasch finished sixth overall. 910 017, driven by Schütz/Buzzetta, retired in the sixth hour due to oil shortage. As this was the first race for which the Type 907 was entered, however, this Le Mans race will be analysed in the chapter dealing with this new type of car.

Circuito del Mugello (July 1967)

The Mugello race is very similar to the Targa Florio. It is run over a 41-mile long mountain course in Tuscany. Consequently a preliminary practice session was organised to give the drivers an opportunity to become familiar with the course, driving on unclosed roads.

For this pre-practice session the following cars were used:

Two cars Type 910-

910 009, six-cylinder, experimentally fitted with a titanium rear coil spring on the right-hand side;

910 026, eight-cylinder, 2.2-litre, experimentally using a new oil cooler and a ventilated oil reservoir.

Five cars Type 911-

One 911R prototype;

One car with a stainless steel body shell;

Two cars with Sportomatic transmission;

One normal production car.

Altogether, 3,300 miles were covered in the course of which both the 910s had gearbox and half shaft failures while a rear radius rod bracket broke on one of them (a well-known 910 weakness).

For the race itself, six cars were used:

Two eight-cylinder 2.2-litre cars with space cam fuel injection, new, larger oil cooler and ventilated oil tank, reinforced Nadella tubular half shafts, ventilated front brake discs to which cooling air was ducted by flexible pipes, and an extra soft rubber universal in the steering column to absorb better the severe kickback caused by the bad road surface.

910 023 (with roof) for Stommelen/Neerpasch;

910 025 (open) for Mitter/Schütz;

Both cars had their rear spoiler raised by 50 mm (2-in).

One perfectly standard closed six-cylinder fuel injection car—

910 016 for Siffert/Herrmann.

Both the six- and eight-cylinder cars used a 25:27 fifth gear ratio, the lower ratios also being the same except for 910 025 which had a higher fourth gear. Shell 1747 A gearbox oil was used throughout and the usual tyres had their pressures lowered to 20 and 23 psi front and rear respectively.

Two Carrera 6s with carburetter engine were entered in the sports car class—
906 156 driven by Koch/Glemser
906 161 driven by Cella/Biscaldi

In addition the experimental 911R No 306 681 was entered as a prototype for Elford and van Lennep. It stood on light alloy wheels $5\frac{1}{2}$ x 15 front and 6 x 15 rear.

Practice showed that the new larger oil cooler and the ventilated oil tank of the eight-cylinder cars were a success, as the oil temperature dropped from 105/115° C to around 95° C while the pressure was raised from 4.5 to 5.5 kg/cm².

Originally the car 910 016 was fitted with a new twin overhead camshaft six-cylinder engine Type 916. With this engine fitted, however, both drivers complained of lack of flexibility, the engine having little torque in the lower ranges and power coming in very suddenly, which made the car difficult to drive on the very winding course. At their request, the Type 916 engine was changed during practice for the usual 901/21 fuel injection six-cylinder (with flat cam metering unit) which made them happy.

The best official practice time was made by Siffert who drove his six-cylinder racing car round the course in 32 m 23 s. All three 910s were faster than the Müller/Casoni 4-litre Ferrari P4 (33 m 41 s) and the Dino which Klass had been driving round in 33 m 58 s before he crashed with fatal results. The best 2-litre Alfa did 34 m 04 s with de Adamich driving.

In the race, the fuel metering rack in the injection pump of Siffert's car seized up, causing the engine to run intermittently. The fastest lap was finally done by Mitter in 31 m 50 s. The Müller/Casoni Ferrari crashed on the first lap so that the two eight-cylinder 910s led the race from start to finish, with the 906 driven by Koch and Glemser in third place, heading de Adamich's Alfa. All Alfas broke down before the end, however, and the Koch/Glemser car stopped with a broken half shaft. The final classification after 330 miles was:

1.	Mitter/Schütz	910/8, average 76.5 mph, time	4 h 18 m 59.0 s
2.	Stommelen/Neerpasch	910/8,	4 h 20 m 49.3 s
3.	Elford/van Lennep	911R,	4 h 41 m 55.1 s
4.	Schlesser/Ligier	Ford Mk 2, 1 lap behind	
5.	Cella/Biscaldi	Carrera 6 (1st in sports car class)	

Brands Hatch Six-Hour race

It was the Six-Hour race on the Brands Hatch track that was to decide if the World Championship was to go to Porsche or to Ferrari. It was certainly a tough issue for 2.2-litre cars to fight out against 4-litres, and Porsche could win the title only if one of their cars finished in front of the first Ferrari. This Siffert and McLaren failed to do by $3\frac{1}{2}$m when they finished third to Chris Amon and Jackie Stewart (Ferrari P4) who were themselves beaten by Phil Hill and Mike Spence (Chaparral).

In view of its importance, five cars were prepared for this race:
Three of them were 2.2-litre eight-cylinders with space cam fuel injection—
907 007 with short-tail body for Neerpasch/Herrmann—weight 612 kg-225 kg on the front axle, 387 kg on the rear axle;
910 027, open body with 35 mm high rear spoiler for Graham Hill/Jochen Rindt—weight 608 kg-241 kg on the front axle, 367 kg on the rear axle;

1969 908 long-tail car. For the Le Mans race the pivoted flaps had to be immobilised.

908 engine with rubber mounted alternator and cooling blower drive by twin V belts. The problem of V belt breakages was finally solved in 1970 when a fluid coupling was incorporated in the blower hub.

To take advantage of modified regulations, the short-tail coupes were replaced for 1969 by the 908/02 Spyders. Mechanically these differed from 1968 models mainly by their new transmission which had five speeds and the clutch between the engine and the gearbox. In the first Spyders made, the rear pyramid was deleted, which led to a series of frame failures in the Sebring 12-hour race.

Porsche 908/02 Spyder, beginning of 1969. The frame has no rear pyramid and the mobile rear flaps are still legal.

Porsche 908/02 Spyder with modified body, called the 'Sole'. The aluminium frame is now reinforced by a rear pyramid. The higher belt line notably reduces the drag and the mobile rear flaps have been deleted to comply with the new CSI rule.

Gerhard Mitter (left) and Udo Schutz, winners of the 1969 Targa Florio. Mitter was killed in the same year in a Formula 2 car.

Left: Typical Targa Florio practice scene, 1969.

Middle: 908/02: gearbox cooling by ducts and additional cowl introduced at the end of 1969 following the bitter Le Mans experience.

Bottom: 908/02 aluminium frame seen from below, with extension behind the rear pyramid to support the tail of the Le Mans 'Sole'.

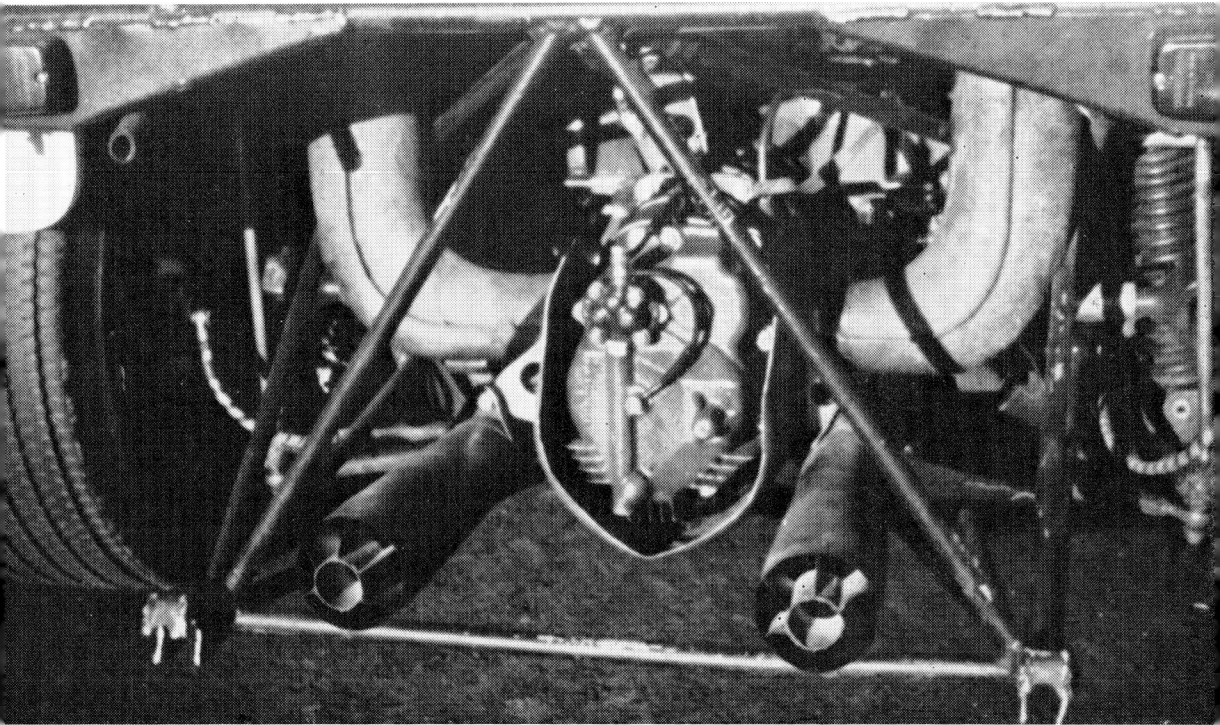

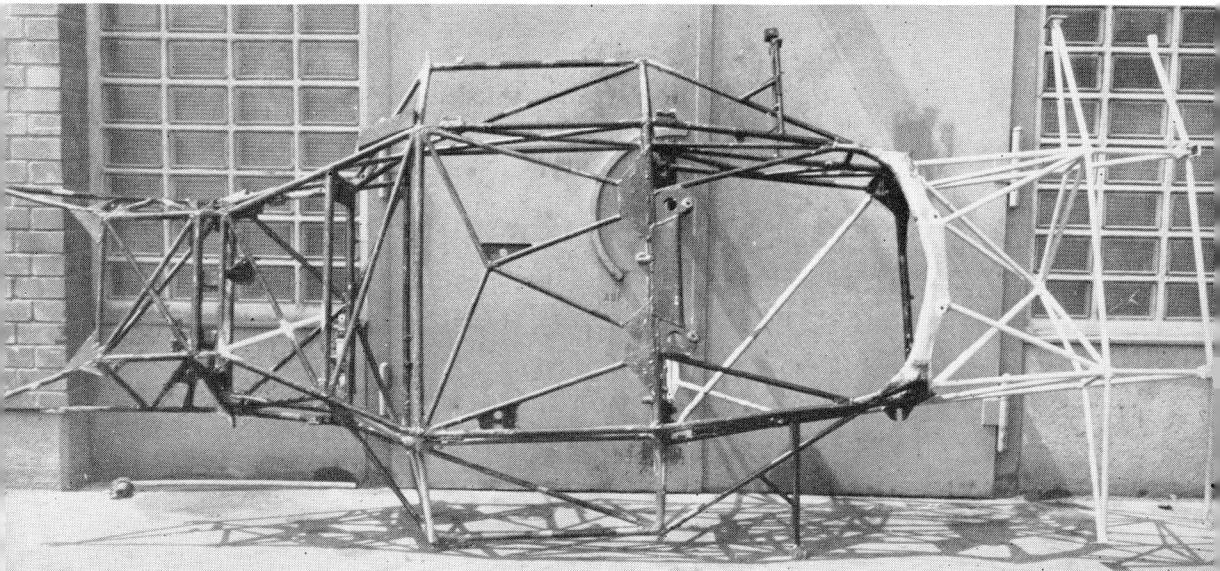

Rear pyramid of 908/02 frame (long-tail
Le Mans 'Sole').

Front view of 908/02 aluminium frame. The
fuel tanks were carried under the lateral
girder structures.

Vic Elford and Dr Ferry Piech, Porsche's
Technical Director until November 1971, at
Le Mans in 1969.

910 028 open, with 35 mm tail spoiler for Siffert/McLaren—weight 602 kg-235 kg on the front axle, 367 kg on the rear axle.
Gear ratios for all eight-cylinder cars:
11 :29, 15 :30, 20 :31, 22 :29, 24 :27 with crown wheel and pinion 7 :31.
Two cars were 2-litre six-cylinders with fuel injection—
910 013, open with tail spoiler for Schütz/Koch;
Weight 595 kg-240 kg on the front axle, 355 kg on the rear axle.
910 017, with roof and tail spoiler for Elford/Bianchi;
Weight 576 kg-228 kg on the front axle, 348 kg on the rear axle.
All six-cylinder cars had the gear ratios:
15 :36, 18 :34, 21 :31, 23 :29, 25 :27 with crown wheel and pinion 7 :31.
All cars, except 910 013, had Type 907 front ventilated brake discs and Type 910 brakes, with quick-change pads at the rear. These were a new development in which only a hinged spring clip had to be released to get access to the pads. 910 013 had brakes with quick-change pads on all wheels. In view of the fact that several of the drivers who were to be brought into the team for the occasion had a Formula One Goodyear contract, the latest Goodyear tyres were tried out at Hockenheim, but no significant difference could be found between these and the latest Dunlops. Consequently the usual Dunlops were used for the race. During practice, Graham Hill asked for the rear wheel camber, the anti-roll bar settings and the tyre pressures to be altered in order to adapt the car to his style of driving. None of these modifications produced faster times, however, and as Siffert was faster with the standard settings, Hill's car was changed back to standard before the race.
After practice, as a precautionary measure, all cars were fitted with new half shafts and the following rev limits were set:
Six-cylinder cars—8,200 rpm; eight-cylinder cars—9,000 rpm.
The difficult Brands Hatch course suited the Porsches very well. The official timekeepers credited both Graham Hill and Siffert with a time of 1 m 38.2 s, the same as Chris Amon's time on the 4-litre P4 Ferrari, but according to Porsche's own timekeeping, Siffert had even done a lap in 1 m 37.0 s. According to official timings, only two Lola-Chevrolets (Hulme/Brabham and Surtees/Hobbs) which had done 1 m 36.6 s, the Phil Hill/Mike Spence 7-litre Chaparral-Chevrolet which had lapped in 1 m 37.4 s, two of the P4 Ferraris under Scarfiotti/Sutcliffe and Hawkins/Williams, both credited with 1 m 37.8 s, had been faster than the two fastest Porsches.
While the fast Lolas did not last the distance, the three Ferraris and the Chaparral did. The latter won but only the Ferrari driven by Chris Amon and Jackie Stewart managed to stay in front of the two fastest Porsches which finished third (Siffert/McLaren) and fourth (Neerpasch/Herrmann), the latter only just beating the Scarfiotti/Sutcliffe Ferrari into fourth place.
The race was an exceptionally hard one and, though practice had indicated that no change of brake pads would be necessary for this Six-Hour race, there had to be renewals on all cars after only four hours. Graham Hill, who right from the start was mixing with the leaders, unfortunately missed a gear after 20 laps, damaging the engine: on his car the brake pads would have lasted only two hours! The Elford/Bianchi car also retired as a consequence of engine trouble.
For the 910, this was to be the last important race as a works car. At the end of the year, the model was homologated as a sports car and most of those made were sold to private customers.

8

The 910 as a hill-climb car

ALTHOUGH LONG-DISTANCE RACING was Porsche's more glamorous field of activity, the development of the 910 in view of its participation in hill-climbs counting towards the European Hill-climb Championship, had even more bearing on the design of future models. In contrast to 1966, the 1967 Mountain Championship was again open to Group 7 (two-seater racing) cars up to 2-litres, with the implication that no minimum weight was imposed. The Championship itself was rather uninteresting as the 2-litre BMW with Apfelbeck radial valve cylinder head, usually driven by Dieter Quester, was not yet fully developed, while Peter Schetty's Abarth was not really competitive. Consequently, Porsche won every single event. There was an intense rivalry between Mitter and Stommelen, however, who so equally shared first and second places (though certainly not of their own volition) that it was Mitter's third place in the Rossfeld race that gave him the title. A Ferrari Dino appeared only once in the Trento-Bondone hill-climb with Scarfiotti driving, and finished second after Stommelen had crashed. This was a considerably lighter car than the previous year's and its V6 engine now had three valves per cylinder.

For the hill-climb series of 1967, Porsche used four different cars. Three of them, 910 030, 910 031 and 910 032 were used only for hill-climbing. Compared with the 910 eight-cylinder prototype, these cars were approximately 100 kg (220 lb) lighter, weighing just over 500 kg (1,100 lb). This drastic weight reduction was obtained by the use of a very thin wall glass fibre body without doors (not required in Group 7), the substitution of a low Perspex windscreen without wiper for the higher laminated glass windscreen compulsory in Group 5, by the use of titanium stub axles, the replacement of the big fuel tank by one containing only 15 litres (3.2 gallons), by deleting the oil cooler and so forth. The fourth car, 910 025, had nominally run in the Targa Florio and won the Mugello race, but had little left in common with it, except for the chassis number. It had the same Group 7 lightweight body with front and rear spoilers as the other three, but for the first time the chassis was made up of aluminium tubes instead of steel tubes. All cars used the 2-litre version of the eight-cylinder engine using a Bosch fuel injection system with space cam controlled metering. The crown wheel and pinion ratio was 6:32 and in the interests of light weight as well as handling, the inner half shaft universals and splines were replaced by Giubo flexible rubber joints.

Otherwise, the cars used for the first two events of the season, 910 030 for Stommelen and 910 031 for Mitter, were fairly standard and even used the normal cast iron brake discs. In Montseny, the usual Dunlop tyres, mixture 184 (inflated to only 19 psi front and 21.5 psi rear) were used and Mitter beat Stommelen into second place. At Rossfeld, however, new, more 'sticky' Dunlop tyres of 970 mixture, especially developed for wet tracks or short races, were used, after having been successfully tried on the southern loop of the Nürburgring during private tests made before the Nürburgring 1,000 km race. The better grip of these tyres did not prevent Mitter from losing time in an off-road excursion, so that he had to be content with third place, behind Stommelen and de Adamich (Alfa Romeo).

It was after the Mont Ventoux hill-climb that the weight-saving campaign began in earnest. Any initiative in this direction was welcomed by the works management, as long as any saving of 1 kg did not cost more than DM.1000 (about £60 per lb). At Mont Ventoux Mitter drove 910 032 with chrome-plated beryllium brake discs and Ferodo DS 11 brake pads, a saving of 14 kg (31 lb), all unsprung into the bargain. It will be remembered that these brakes had been tried on three Carrera 6s entered by the factory for the Hockenheim 500 km race in August 1966. The beryllium disc-equipped car, which weighed only 486 kg (1,070 lb), had been sent to France only as a spare car, but Mitter had to use it in the race without having tried it in practice, because his other car (910 031) had been damaged in an accident on the last practice climb. Mitter nevertheless just beat Quester's BMW by 0.1 s in the approximately 11-minute climb, but finished no less than 27 s behind Stommelen.

In the Trento-Bondone hill-climb, the cars 910 030 and 910 031 were again used, but this time with new lightweight wheels suitable only for hill-climbing. In this case, Stommelen crashed but Mitter beat Scarfiotti's new Ferrari by 12 s. In the next two events, Cesana-Sestriere and Freiburg, Mitter drove 910 031 and Stommelen 910 032, both with cast iron brake discs and Textar linings, the two Porsches taking first and second place in both.

Important new developments were first seen on the occasion of the Ollon-Villars hill-climb at the end of August 1967, for which Mitter had 910 025 and Stommelen 910 030.

910 025, with which Mitter won the event, was particularly interesting. It differed from previous hill-climb cars mainly as follows:

The frame was made of aluminium tubes.

The body had an exceptionally thin skin and cutaway side panels which earned it the nickname 'Miniskirt'.

The steering arms and many of the screws and bolts were made of titanium.

Floating caliper Girling brakes were used all round instead of the usual ATE brakes; they had a titanium caliper saddle and beryllium discs were used with Ferodo DS 11 linings.

The steering rack was made of aluminium.

The engine had been considerably lightened by the extensive use of magnesium castings, of aluminium for various shafts and by plastic air ducting panels.

The 10-litre (2.2-gallon) oil tank and the 15-litre (3.2-gallon) fuel tank were located left and right at the extreme rear of the car in order to improve the adhesion of the driving wheels.

In addition, this car had, in common with its predecessors, titanium front stub axles and rear wheel hubs, as well as lightened wheels. These and other less drastic innovations reduced the weight to 419 kg (925 lb) with a full (10 litres) oil tank. To compensate for the reduction in weight on the front wheels, larger front spoilers were used and the castor angle was increased to 9° 45'. To combat understeer in sharp curves, the negative camber of the rear wheels was reduced from —3° to —2° 30'. This setting was also adopted for the other, slightly heavier car.

This, 910 030, now weighed 461 kg (1,020 lb), 42 kg (95 lb) more than 910 025. It still had a steel frame, normal ATE brakes with cast iron discs and a steel steering rack, but it had been lightened by approximately 40 kg (90 lb) since the beginning of the season, by the systematic use of titanium for screws, steering and suspension parts, a lighter body and lighter wheels. To obtain optimal handling with the lightly loaded front wheels, the weight borne by the two front and the two rear wheels had to be equalised laterally by appropriately setting the anti-roll bar rod lengths with the driver sitting in his car.

In the Gaisberg race, the last in 1967, the cars were exchanged in order to give the two drivers an equal chance of winning the Championship. With the lighter car, Stommelen now managed to beat Mitter, but not, however, to rob him of the title which went to Mitter thanks to his third place in the Rossfeld race : both drivers had scored four wins and three second places.

The remarkable cornering power of these lightweight cars was revealed when one of them was taken for tests on the circular track at the end of 1967. On this occasion, Dunlop tyres, mixture 184, produced a time of 16.80 s on the 190 metre-diameter track, while the higher grip mixture 970 improved this to 16.72 s. This corresponds to the remarkable lateral acceleration of 1.4 g.

In the course of 1967 and in the following year, more and more timings were made on characteristic sections of hill-climb courses and racing circuits. Not only Porsche cars were timed, but also their major opponents, to find out under which conditions —fast curves, slow curves, acceleration from low or from high speeds, braking and so forth—Porsche cars were faster or (which is even more important) slower than the opposition. The timed sections were accurately measured and the speed was obtained at the beginning and at the end of the section, so that the mean acceleration could be calculated. The data thus obtained were fed into a computer which indicated if, on a given course, it was desirable to reduce the air drag even at the cost of increasing the weight, or, on the contrary, to accept an increase in air drag in the interests of better wheel adhesion by fitting appropriate spoilers. From these data it was also possible to calculate the gearbox ratios to be used on a new type of car for a given course, and even to calculate the possible lap time with reasonable accuracy. This was also possible for an unknown course provided a good map was available.

In connection with these calculations, tests were made to obtain information about the conditions prevailing in the course of a racing start and also about the rolling radius of a racing tyre at various speeds. The latter is important since, only if the exact dynamic radius of the tyres is known, can the speed corresponding to the rev counter indication be calculated accurately.

The conditions prevailing during the course of a racing start were obtained with the aid of a radio transmitter connected to antennae set across the road at 0-10-25-45-70-100 metre marks. The car also carried an antenna which produced an impulse every time it passed over one of the transverse wires. The impulses were registered by a chronograph with an accuracy of 1/100 second.

To calculate the dynamic radius of the tyres at various speeds, the number of quarter revolutions was counted over a distance of 100 metres. To achieve this, four magnets were bonded to the periphery of the half shaft flange and as they passed a static winding, they produced impulses which were fed into a counter. The car was then driven over the 100-metre long base at speeds ranging from 50 kph (31 mph) up to maximum speed, the number of quarter revolutions of the wheels being thus counted for various speeds obtained with great accuracy from the times taken by the car to cover the distance.

A standard six-cylinder 910 (910 016) was used, running on the usual Dunlop racing tyres (pressure 26/29 psi) and fitted with the following gear ratios : 14 :37, 17 :34, 20 :31, 22 :29, 25 :27 ; crown wheel and pinion 7 :31. The weight of the vehicle including driver (Herbert Linge) and test equipment was 803 kg (1,770 lb).

The rev limit was reached in first gear at an approximate speed of 85 kph (53 mph). If we accept that between the impulses at the 10, 25 and 45 metre marks (that is before second was selected) the acceleration remained constant (which is not far from true), we obtain, before the gear change, a nearly constant acceleration of just over 0.4 g and the following elapsed times:

0-50 mph: approximately 3.85 s;
0-60 mph: 5.8 s (obtained by extrapolation).

Counting the wheel quarter turns at various speeds indicated that the rolling radius increased by approximately 2.25 per cent from 30 to 125 mph and that the increase was approximately 3.1 per cent at 155 mph. In actual fact, the dynamic increase in rolling radius is probably greater as higher speeds imply a greater driving force which must cause increased tyre slip. The amount of slip cannot be measured separately by the method used, and it is irrelevant anyway for the purpose of correlating car speed with engine speed.

For the 1968 season, the 910 Bergspyder was further developed to become even lighter. Two new cars (910 034 and 910 035) were built with an aluminium frame and the previous year's 910 025 was brought up to latest specification and re-numbered 910 033. In accordance with Porsche's policy of incorporating as many racing developments as possible in the series production models, several developments were aimed at substituting light alloy parts for titanium parts which provide an easy, although expensive, way of saving weight by replacing the steel and iron parts with titanium components of similar size. An example was the titanium brake caliper saddles which were replaced by saddles made of magnesium (cars 910 033 and 034) or aluminium (car 910 035), in all cases in conjunction with beryllium discs. Duralumin steering arms were also used in some cases instead of titanium, but were soon discarded because of their sensitivity to shock.

Weight was also saved by the use of titanium coil springs and shock absorber piston rods. The latter were unsuccessful, however, as they tended to get scored by the seals. Detail investigation went as far as replacing the steel brake pad back plate by one made of titanium, which in theory had the additional advantage of transferring less heat to the pistons and brake fluid.

A further important saving in weight was obtained by deleting the alternator, the battery capacity being sufficient for one climb and there being no reason why the battery shouldn't be changed between two heats. Also silver-plate batteries were used instead of the more usual lead-plate batteries.

In addition to weight saving, two new important developments were incorporated in the Bergspyders for 1968. Two articulated spoilers were added at the back, connected with the supension in such a way that the flaps were raised to create more downthrust when the rear suspension was extended and dropped to a flatter position when the suspension was compressed. This was a practical application of the findings made with the Carrera 6 'Flap Car'. The aim was to keep the rear wheel adhesion as constant as possible and to combat any tendency for the rear to lift by increasing the downthrust. These articulated spoilers were supposed to have a beneficial effect in curves too, as roll caused the outside flap to be raised and the inside flap to be dropped, thus countering roll aerodynamically and reducing the weight transfer which, as is well-known, is detrimental to the cornering power of a vehicle. Later aerodynamic tests, however, were to indicate that the aerodynamic weight transfer thus obtained is negligible.

The front springs were deleted. They were replaced by a Z-shaped torsion bar (similar to the compensating spring used at the rear on late swing axle Volks-wagens) having no roll resistance whatsoever. Front roll resistance was provided only by the adjustable anti-roll bar. This made it possible to modify both the spring stiffness and the roll stiffness quickly and independently of each other by merely modifying the effective length of the Z-bar and anti-roll bar lever arms. The roll stiffness could then be reduced to such an extent as to combat understeer effectively on sharp corners. This revised suspension without any coil springs was even lighter than the previous one and as Mitter's car left the factory for Montseny, it turned the scales at only 382 kg (844 lb) without its spare wheel, but for the race itself the fuel tank had to be reinforced and a heavier battery was used, so its actual racing weight was slightly higher.

In this last stage of development, at the end of the 1968 season, the 910 Berg-spyder weighed in racing trim 410 kg (905 lb), including 10 litres (2.2 gallons) of oil in the tank. Driving one of these cars, Gerhard Mitter became European Hill-climb Champion for the third time, having scored the maximum possible number of points by winning the Group 7 classification in every one of the events counting towards the Championship. His most serious opponent was Dieter Quester who drove the very efficient but still too heavy BMW with Apfelbeck head engine. Unfortunately there were also bad days for the hill-climb cars: one of them was when Lodovico Scarfiotti, who had many times been the greatest rival of the Porsche team and was now driving one of the Stuttgart cars, was killed at Rossfeld, the second Championship climb of the season, when his car 910 035 left the road for reasons which later were never completely explained. Stommelen was hurt in the same event, but his car 910 033 could be repaired for the following races and the driver too was soon mobile again. For the hill-climbs, Dunlop tyres of 970 mixture and R7 tread pattern were used in the usual sizes 5.25 M-13 front and 7.00 L-13 rear, but in view of the light weight of the cars, their pressures were reduced to 15-17 psi front and 21.5-23 psi rear. The engine still produced 272 bph DIN at 9,000 rpm and had a compression ratio of 10.4 :1. Occasionally too, a new exhaust system feeding into a large single exhaust pipe was used to save weight.

Type 909: the unfinished symphony

Despite every effort to improve its handling, the 910 Bergspyder had become a difficult car. With the driver on board, the front wheels carried only about 135 kg (297 lb) from which some 85 kg (188 lb) must be deducted under full acceleration. Based on the lessons learned with the 910, a new car was designed and built in the course of the 1968 season. It was named 909 and entered for the penultimate race of the season, the Gaisberg hill-climb, driven by Stommelen after Mitter had refused it. The weight saving techniques applied to the new car were the same as for the 910 from which the 909 differed mainly by having its five-speed gearbox between the engine and the differential instead of overhung. Consequently the engine and the driver's seat were moved forward to a point where the pedals were overhanging the front wheel centre line. This was helped by moving the front wheels rearwards by 3.6 cm (1.42 in) so that the wheelbase was reduced from the traditional 2.30 m (90-in) to 2.264 m (88.6-in). The increased proportion of the weight carried by the front wheels was intended to improve handling and was taken care of by normal spring units in which the coil springs were made of titanium.

Like the 907, which meanwhile had been developed, the 909 had right-hand steering (possibly in view of later use on circuits) and a Goodrich 'Space Saver' was used as a spare tyre (still required in 1968 for Group 7 cars) and located in the nose. To compensate for the reduced weight on the driving wheels, much wider tyres were used : 6.00/12.00-13 on 12-in wide rims at the rear and 4.75/10.00-13 on the usual 8-in wide rims at the front, and because of the much flatter and wider tread, the negative camber was reduced to —45' front and rear. Articulated rear spoilers were of course used, as before.

More weight was saved by replacing both the fuel tank and the electric pump by a special pressurised tank. This took the form of a titanium sphere containing an artificial rubber bulb filled with fuel. The fuel was put under pressure by filling the space between the sphere and the bulb with nitrogen at a maximum pressure of 215 psi.

Although the car was tried briefly at Hockenheim before being taken to Gaisberg, it was still far from being fully developed and also still heavier than the 910. With ten litres of oil in the tank, it turned the scales at 430 kg (955 lb).

In practice, both cars were said, by their drivers Mitter (909 001) and Stommelen (909 002), to be very unstable on the undulating road, while the engines were not clean in the higher revolution ranges. Mitter also thought the car to be erratic at the limit and decided to use the 910 for the event itself, but Stommelen said it felt rather safer and chose the new car into which the engine from Mitter's 909 was dropped. But this engine, too, ran irregularly in the higher ranges and a leaner injection pump setting used for the second run made things even worse. It was suspected that the comparatively high pressure under which the fuel was fed to the pump might have been responsible for the trouble, but as tests could not be completed before the next event at Mont Ventoux, the car was sent there with a normal electric fuel pump fitted. With this, the engine ran impeccably and driving 909 001 Stommelen finished only 5.5 s behind Mitter who won, driving 910 035, in the new record time of 10 m 12.1 s.

Though the 909 only had a very short career and did not bring Porsche any victories, it is an important link in the story of racing Porsches for it served as a development prototype for the ultra-light 908/03 Porsche 3-litre prototype of 1970.

9

From Type 910 to Type 907

THERE IS NO fundamental difference between the Type 907 and the Type 910 from which it was developed. Consequently the 907 has a rather short development history. It will be remembered that the 910 was originally developed as a successor to the Ollon-Villars hill-climb car 906 010 which used Lotus suspension parts, and that no time was wasted trying it in the wind tunnel, low drag not being vitally important for a hill-climb car. Its body was purely empirical and the car was actually raced before it went into the wind tunnel. Certainly the fact that despite the lower wheels and the slightly smaller frontal area the car's drag was no less than that of the Carrera 6 was nothing to be proud of. This is why experiments were made on the occasion of those wind tunnel tests, using tail extensions and undershields and cutting or blanking off air inlets. The 910 was never raced with such modified bodies, but these tests served as a basis for the design of the 907 body in which the frontal area was further reduced by using a narrower superstructure above the belt line.

In the design stage, every effort was made to reduce the weight further. The weight of the 910 was already down to the limit, both as a 2-litre and as a 2.2-litre, for which the minimum weight limit was set 25 kg higher, but it was kept in mind that the long-tail body planned for Le Mans and the additional lights and other equipment necessary in that race would otherwise make the car unnecessarily heavy. A further consideration was that most races were run clockwise and thus included more right-hand than left-hand turns which made it advantageous, both for the weight distribution and for the driver's line of sight, to have right-hand steering. This was first used on the 907 and has been a common feature of all subsequent Porsche racing cars.

The first event in which the 907 was to run was the Le Mans 24-Hour race of 1967 for which the use of a low-drag body is of primary importance in view of the 5-kilometre (3-mile) straight. Because of this, exacting tests were carried out in the wind tunnels of both the Stuttgart Technical High School and the Volkswagen factory. Of these we shall consider only the tests done in Stuttgart, as the two test series gave rather different results and the Stuttgart tests were confirmed much better by actual track tests. They are also more comparable with the tests carried out, also in Stuttgart, some months before on a 910.

The tunnel tests were carried out in accordance with the now established Porsche practice. The test car had its front wheels standing on a Teflon plate on which grease had been previously applied so that the wheels could move freely in and out to accommodate track variations. The car was then exposed to a 270 kph (approximately 170 mph) draught and was blocked at the resulting angle of incidence. The drag coefficient as well as the lift and downthrust were then obtained in this position. The car was a long-tail model with a removable scoop for the engine air intake above the rear deck and further air intakes to cool the gearbox in which the oil had reached a temperature of 120° C after only six laps of testing at Hocken-heim.

From the large amount of data obtained with the car in various states (with and without air intakes, bottom open and shielded, various spoiler settings and combina-tions and so forth) we can draw the general conclusion that the lift and downthrust conditions can change radically as the speed increases, mainly due to variations of the angle of incidence. An extrapolation of test results to speeds of a significantly different order is not acceptable and can lead to completely wrong conclusions. It is also interesting that wheel discs approximately flush with the tyre sidewalls reduce the drag by about 2.5 per cent.

For the car without wheel discs, as intended for driving at Le Mans, a drag coefficient Cw=0.273 was measured, a considerable improvement on the previously measured experimental 910 with an added long tail which had recorded 0.307, the same as obtained for the long-tail Carrera 6. Additionally, the 907 had a smaller frontal area (S=1.288 m²) than the 910 (S=1.319 m²).

The product Cw x S to which the total drag is proportional is as follows:
For the 907 long-tail CwS=0.273 x 1.288=0.352;
For the 910 long-tail CwS=0.307 x 1.319=0.405.
giving approximately 14.2 per cent lower drag for the 907.

Apart from the right-hand steering and the body shape, the main difference between the Type 910 and the Type 907 was in the front suspension. For some time, Porsche racing cars had had progressive rate front springs in which the variation was obtained by reducing the spacing between the coils at one end of the spring. As the spring was compressed, these end coils closed up solid and the effective length of the spring was reduced, increasing its rigidity. In the course of the develop-ment of the Type 910, test engineer Peter Falk had already suggested that the progressive rate should be obtained by suspension geometry (using a narrow angle between the spring unit and the lower wishbone) so as to reduce the number of coils and save weight. This proposal was put into practice on the 907. In addition, ventilated front brake discs were used from the start for this model, experience having shown that they reduced pad wear very considerably. An indication of this was given by the Nürburgring 1,000 km race in which an eight-cylinder 910 driven by Stommelen/Ahrens was fitted experimentally with ventilated discs at the front. On this car pad wear was approximately 2.5 mm (0.1-in) per 1,000 km, while the wear on the otherwise identical car driven by Mitter and Bianchi, which had non-ventilated discs, was as high as 11.2 mm (0.44-in) per 1,000 km and even the six-cylinder of Neerpasch/Elford wore its pads down at the rate of 6.1 mm (0.24-in) per 1,000 km. Another reason for using these discs on the 907 Le Mans cars was that, with ventilated discs fitted, additional air intakes and ducts could be deleted, an important contribution towards reducing air drag. Additionally—but this was certainly not decisive in the case of Le Mans—the ventilated discs weighed only 4.4 kg (9.7 lb) compared with 4.7 kg (10.3 lb) for the plain 910 discs.

The ventilated discs were first experimentally used on the original 910 001 Spyder of which the front wheels were driven by rollers at a speed corresponding to 100 mph. The test programme was to operate these brakes in the same way as on the Hockenheim Grand Prix course for a lap time of 2 m 10 s. The temperatures were measured with the aid of a brush fixed to the outside of the discs. Two test series were carried out: one with direct air cooling by means of a Porsche Carrera air blower, simulating the additional air cooling provided by air intakes in the body and flexible ducts, and one series without any additional ventilation. The front wheels constantly bore 160 kg extra weight, corresponding to the weight transfer on to the front wheels under severe braking. On the (warmer) right-hand side, the highest temperature reached with additional cooling was 480° C, without additional cooling 590° C, which is still tolerable. Twenty-one laps were simulated without loss of braking efficiency.

The first track tests of the 907 took place at Hockenheim with a long-tail car. After setting up the spoilers and taking off a shield around the exhaust tail pipes which apparently had the same effect as lengthening the pipes themselves, a speed of 272 kph (169 mph) was reached according to the rev counter reading, which in fact is nearer 285 kph (177 mph) if the increased dynamic rolling radius of the tyres is taken into account. It was found that the temperatures of the engine and gearbox oil were too high, and small intake scoops were added on the rear deck. The first two cars produced (907 001 and 002) were then sent to the Volkswagen proving ground for a destruction test in the course of which 001 broke its chassis tubes in several places above the gearbox supports which put an end to the tests after 725 km (450 miles) had been completed. Appropriate reinforcements were then made to the other car which went on until the test was stopped after 1,500 km (935 miles) had been covered. Other parts which proved inadequate to the battering were the experimental fuel and oil tanks made of 1.2 mm thick magnesium, lid and door locks and the half shafts of which one broke after 1,453 km (900 miles) even though it was of the latest reinforced type.

Following the tests at Hockenheim and on the destruction course, the following important modifications were carried out :

Frame reinforced at gearbox supports ;

Tail part of body reinforced ;

Opening at extreme rear of body closed (air extracted from engine compartment by means of ducts underneath the car) ;

Wheel arches widened towards centre line ;

Rear body part locked by Ski-type tensioners ;

Larger air scoops for gearbox ventilation ;

Door hinge screws locked ;

Magnesium tanks rejected because reinforced type as heavy as aluminium ;

The type 907's first race was at Le Mans. Both cars entered (907 003 and 004) were fitted with six-cylinder fuel injection engines, probably the only case in which the 907 was raced as a six-cylinder. In contrast to its sister car, 907 004 had space cam controlled fuel metering, the first time this was used in connection with the six-cylinder engine. In the race, it gave a notably improved fuel consumption of 13.3 mpg as against 10.8 mpg for the flat cam, which caused considerable concern to Mitter and Rindt when they discovered that they would have to stop twice more for refuelling in the course of the race than Siffert and Herrmann. But the flat cam car itself was more economical than the two less efficiently streamlined 910s, also fitted with flat cam injection pumps which did 10.2 and 10.4 mpg.

The wind tunnel tests had made it possible to calculate suitable gear ratios with such accuracy that no alteration was needed when the cars came to Le Mans. On the Mulsanne straight, the engines reached 8,000-8,100 rpm on the 28:23 fifth gear and they were officially timed at 185 and 187.5 mph for 003 and 004 respectively, these speeds reflecting an increase in dynamic tyre radius of approximately 8 per cent. The larger air scoops to cool the gearbox did their job efficiently as the temperature did not rise above 105° C while the engine oil temperature was 95° C After washers had been added under the springs to get a zero angle of incidence at high speed, the drivers were pleased with the straight line stability and general handling of the car. The running gear settings were as for the Type 910. As on their 27:25 fifth gear the Type 910 cars reached an indicated 8,500-8,600 rpm on the straight, it can be calculated that the long-tail 907s were 12 mph faster. This is also reflected in the lap times:

Best lap time (practice and race):
907   3 m 41.6 s   (Siffert in 907 004)
910   3 m 49.0 s   (Schütz in 910 017)
906   3 m 52.0 s   (Pon in 906 154 with carburettor engine)

In practice, comparative tests were done with and without wheel discs. With the discs fitted, the engine rpm were increased by about 50 (approximately 1.2 mph) but as no difference appeared in the lap times they were not used for the race.

Of the six works entries at Le Mans, four finished, the first three being placed fifth, sixth and seventh overall behind a 7-litre Ford Mk IV, two 4-litre Ferrari P4s and another 7-litre Ford. 910 017, the Schütz/Buzzetta car ran out of oil in the sixth hour and ruined its engine while 907 003 driven by Mitter/Rindt, dropped out in the seventh hour as a consequence of over-revving. At the finish, the Porsche contingent was headed by the Siffert/Herrmann 907, only one lap behind the fourth placed 7-litre Ford, having averaged over 125 mph for 24 hours—a fantastic performance for a 2-litre car. This also secured first place in the Index classification (in which the distance covered is related to the engine capacity) and second place on efficiency (relating the distance covered to the fuel consumption and weight). In 24 hours, the 907 had left 910 016, driven by Stommelen/Neerpasch, 59 miles behind, while the two Carrera 6s of Elford/Pon (906 154) and Koch/Poirot (906 156) averaged 114.4 and 112.5 mph respectively. Both 907s and also 910 017 were fitted with ventilated front brake discs, which were so efficient in reducing pad wear that the front linings actually wore less than the rear ones: they could have gone through two consecutive Le Mans races without being changed!

The only other race for which a Type 907 was used in 1967 was the Brands Hatch Six-Hour race for which one short-tail car, 907 007, was entered with an eight-cylinder engine for Neerpasch and Herrmann who finished fourth behind the Siffert/McLaren 910.

The same car was used later in the year in order to finalise the running gear data. Up to then, due to lack of time for proper testing, the 907 had been run on the same settings as the 910. The car was driven by Hans Herrmann on the southern loop of the Nürburgring and on the combined Monza course with chicanes (as used for the 1,000 km race) and the tests confirmed that the settings that had been used up to then (negative camber front —1° 30', rear —3°, toe-in front and rear 10' per wheel) were actually the best. Only the castor angle was slightly increased from 6.5° to 7° and shock absorbers with a slightly higher resistance to compression were adopted. It appeared, however, that on high speed courses on which speeds exceeding 155 mph were reached, a reduction of the negative camber to —1° front and —45' rear was beneficial both to straight line stability and to tyre temperatures. Subsequent tests on the Weissach circular track, however, indicated that even with 4.75/10.00-13 tyres on an 8-in rim at the front and 6.00/12.00-13 tyres on a wide 12-in rim at the rear, these settings slightly reduced the car's cornering power.

Unfortunately, it was not possible to compare 907 and 910 times on the Nürburgring and Monza tracks as at the time of the tests the southern loop of the Ring was still partly damp (despite which Herrmann did 2 m 16.7 s) and the only basis for comparison was a time of 2 m 16.8 s obtained by a six-cylinder 910 on a dry track. At Monza the 907 did 3 m 02.0 s, an improvement of 5 s compared with the best 910 time to date, but that had been obtained with a six-cylinder engine. In all cases

Dunlop 5.25 M-13 and 7.00 L-13 tyres were used front and rear respectively. As no wider and lower profile tyres were available at the time, comparisons could not be made, but the wider tyres showed a clear advantage on the circular track, producing the best ever time of 17.36 s obtained to date on the 190-metre diameter circle with a long-distance racing car. This is equivalent to a lateral acceleration of 1.287 g, but still lags a long way behind the time of 16.80 s obtained with the Bergspyder on the same Dunlop rubber mixture, or the time of 16.72 s reached on the 970 mixture. The effect of camber, rim width and tyres on cornering power clearly appears from the following table, recapitulating the results of the circular track tests carried out on November 20 1967 when the car was driven by test engineer Peter Falk on a cold and dry day.

Tyres	*Rims*	*Camber*	*Best times (secs)*	
			Right	*Left*
5.25 M-13	8-in	—1° 30'	17.98	17.88
7.00 L-13	9½-in	—3°		
Mixture 184 23/26 psi	8-in	—1° 30'	17.88	17.88
	12-in	—3°		
4.75/10.00-13	8-in	—1° 30'	17.92	17.64
6.00/12.00-13	9½-in	—3°		
Mixture 184 21.5/24.3 psi	8-in	—1° 30'	17.52	17.36
	12-in	—3°		
	8-in	—1° 30'	17.62	17.44
	12-in	—1°		

10

From 907 to 908

AT THE END OF 1967, the point had been reached where the 2.2-litre eight-cylinder engine had become usefully reliable following the modifications already mentioned to the crankshaft and oil and cooling systems. As a result of this, the 907 was used in 1968 only in eight-cylinder form. A further incentive was that the FIA had decided to limit the capacity of prototypes to 3 litres, though so-called homologated sports cars, of which at least 25 units had been built, were accepted up to a capacity of 5 litres, their power plant usually being tuned standard production American V8 pushrod engines. In the previous year, Porsche had lost the Championship of Makes to the 4-litre Ferrari P4 by only a very small margin despite the fact that most of Porsche's Championship points had been gained by the 2-litre six-cylinder car which had proved much more reliable than the more powerful eight-cylinders. With the eight-cylinder 2.2-litre engine now fully developed, the chances of beating the 3-litre prototypes and the 5-litre pushrod sports cars looked even better.

This was confirmed by the first two races of the season: the Daytona Inter-continental 24-Hour race in which the three factory-entered 907s took the first three places led by the Elford/Neerpasch car, and the Sebring 12-Hour race won by Siffert/Herrmann in 907 024, followed in second place by Elford and Neerpasch (907 026), after all their main opponents had retired. In Daytona the cars used a long tail, in Sebring they ran in short-tail form. Two of the Sebring short-tail cars retired: Scarfiotti over-revved the engine of 907 025 after only seven laps while 907 023 (Mitter/Stommelen) used unexpectedly large amounts of oil and ran a bearing after two hours as a consequence. The reason for the Elford/Neerpasch car finishing 11 laps behind Siffert/Herrmann is that a bearing outer race worked loose in a rear upright which had to be changed. This particular car had been used as a practice car and started the race with over 550 miles already to its credit.

At a preliminary practice session in Daytona, an idea which the Porsche racing people had been playing with for some time was put into practice: air inlets are known to increase the air drag and they wanted to reduce the entry of air into the cockpit to the volume necessary for the driver's breathing. No air was to be directed into the cockpit for cooling purposes which was taken care of by special overalls worn by the driver, incorporating a network of small tubes in which water contained in an ice bag was circulated by an electric pump. The weight of the installation was of no importance as the factory had enough experience of light weight construction to make the car's structure as light as necessary to get the total weight down to the regulation minimum. The set-up was not developed enough to be used in the race, however, as the cooling effect lasted for only half-an-hour and was insufficient at arm and leg levels.

In the course of this preliminary practice, for which the Daytona track was hired, Firestone tyres were tried in comparison with Dunlops but proved inferior in straight line stability, so Dunlops were used for the race; but the negative camber of the rear wheels had to be reduced from —3° to —45', because the inner shoulders of the tyres got too warm on the back banking, causing the rubber to come off in lumps.

The gearing of the victorious cars was as follows:

Daytona (907 005): 11:29, 17:30, 22:29, 25:27, 27:24 with crown wheel and pinion 7:31;

Sebring (907 024): 11:29, 17:29, 22:30, 25:27, 27:25 with crown wheel and pinion 7:31.

As the narrower tyres gave a slightly higher maximum speed, they were still used in Daytona, but as a result of the circular track tests carried out at the end of the preceding season, the new Dunlop lower profile tyres were used for all following races, starting with Sebring. The standard dimensions were 4.75/10.00-13 on 8-in wide rims at the front and 6.00/12.00-13 on 12-in wide rims at the rear. Under pressure from the tyre technicians, the negative camber was reduced to —1° at the front and —45' at the rear to keep tyre temperatures down and reduce wear, notwithstanding the fact that the skid pad tests had shown this to be slightly detrimental to the cornering power. The reduced negative camber was, however, believed to give better stability on the straights and under braking. As low profile tyres were too large for there to be room for the spare wheel in the car's 'nose', a Goodrich 'Space Saver' spare tyre and an air bottle were used.

Daytona was also the first long-distance race in which new light weight construction methods were tried out on 907 011 of which the chassis had aluminium tubes, and on which titanium suspension links and an aluminium steering rack were used. This car had done all the preliminary practice for the 24-hour race and was experimentally entered for the race itself. It would probably have won, driven by Schlesser and Buzzetta, if the experimental Motorola alternator had not had to be changed, but it still finished third. As it went over the finishing line, this car had done some 50 hours at racing speeds. For the first time the ventilated brake discs were additionally cooled by means of flexible ducts. Compared with the preliminary practice, where no additional cooling was used, the brake pad wear was reduced by 50 per cent.

Another novelty first used at Daytona was a pad-wear warning light. This lit up when an electric wire carried by the caliper made contact with the brake pad back plate, informing the driver that the lining was worn to the limit. The device cost Porsche the victory in the third race of the Manufacturers' Championship, the Brands Hatch Six-Hour race. In this race a change of brake pads was scheduled after the third hour, but after only 50 minutes the light went on in 907 027 driven by Mitter. During the ensuing pit stop, which lasted for $2\frac{1}{2}$ m, it was found that the electric contact had shorted. The unnecessary stop was decisive, however, as the Ickx/Redman Ford GT40 won by a margin of only 25 s over the Mitter car. Elford and Neerpasch drove 907 028 into third place while 907 022 driven by Siffert and Herrmann was securely in the lead when a defective front wheel bearing caused their retirement. This was only the beginning of a long run of bearing failures which was to cause the Porsche crew considerable headaches for the rest of the season, even though the rig tests undertaken the previous year had given the impression that the new grease used for bearing lubrication had solved the problem. In the particular case of the Brands Hatch race, it was discovered that the outer race of the taper bearing was not of the same make as the rollers and the case was dismissed as an assembly mistake. But it soon became obvious that the wrong outer race may have been partly responsible for the failure but it was not its real cause.

The first results of 1968 certainly showed that the 3-litre capacity limit gave

Porsche a better chance than ever. Although the limit was 'in the air' by summer 1967, the final decision by the CSI to introduce it only came in October, which was much too late to allow the manufacturers to really prepare for it. As a concession, homologated sports cars (of which at least 25 units had been made) up to a maximum capacity of 5-litres were also accepted. The practical (if not technical) justification for this derogation was that the cars eligible under this heading (mainly the Ford GT40 and the Lola T70, the latter being homologated under somewhat dubious circumstances) all used basically production American pushrod engines which, even if fully developed, could not be expected to produce a very high specific power.

As early as Summer 1967, the Porsche management was convinced that the 3-litre capacity limit would be enforced and it was decided to build an engine taking advantage of this capacity. This decision was well in line with the general Porsche policy, it being obvious that future Porsche production cars would need more powerful engines and it is the company's policy that production cars should benefit as much as possible from racing development.

In July 1967, the racing design office under Dipl-Ing Hans Mezger sat down to design an entirely new engine that was to replace the 2.2-litre eight-cylinder and was to be conceived as far as possible in such a way that it could eventually form the base for a production engine. Consequently it had to be comparatively simple and easy to assemble. That the latter requirement was achieved is evident from the fact that the new 3-litre engine could be assembled in approximately 25 working hours, nearly 10 times quicker than the Type 771 eight-cylinder which had been designed purely as a Grand Prix engine.

Despite all supply difficulties, the first engine was built only four months after the designers had got down to work and it took another four months to develop it far enough for it to be considered suitable for a 1,000 km race. The first time it went on the test bed, it delivered 320 hp, which had been increased to 335 hp at 8,500 rpm when it was first raced in the Monza 1,000 km. Further development and a 1 mm bore increase to 85 mm, as first used at Le Mans, resulted in a power figure of 350 hp by the end of 1968. The maximum bmep was 13.6 kg/sq cm (193 lb/in^2) at 6,600 rpm.

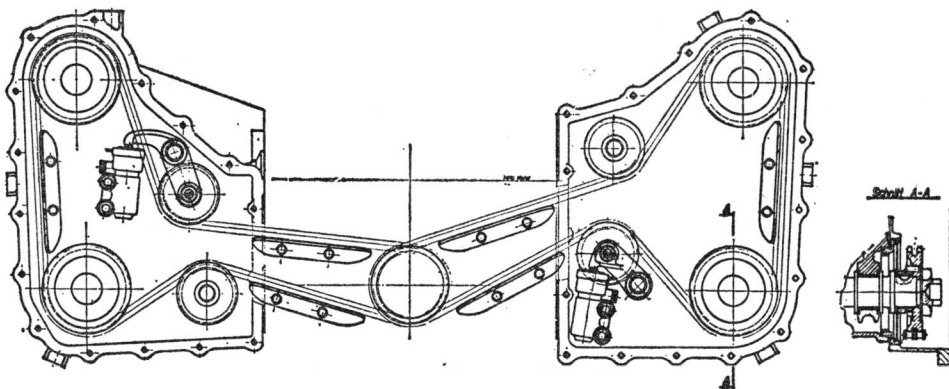

Camshaft drive of engine Type 908 and 916.

The design and development of the eight-cylinder was simplified by the fact that the engine was largely developed from the six-cylinder experimental 916 engine with twin overhead camshafts per bank that was seen in a 910 on the occasion of the Mugello race practice in 1967 and which had undergone endurance tests on the test bed. In contrast with the 771 engine in which all accessories (except for the injection pump which was added later) were gear-driven, the Type 908 had chain-driven camshafts (from the front of the crankshaft via an intermediate shaft) while the vertically mounted cooling blower which shared its shaft with the alternator was belt-driven. Originally this was a cog belt. As, however, several belt breakages were experienced on the occasion of the Le Mans preliminary practice, on April 6 1968 the first time the engine was seen publicly, a change was made on the spot to a V belt. The cog belt failures were due to the excessive load put on the belt by the inertia of the blower, as no slip was possible. But the V belt never proved fully reliable, even when twin belts were used. The power absorbed by the blower at peak revs was approximately 12 hp.

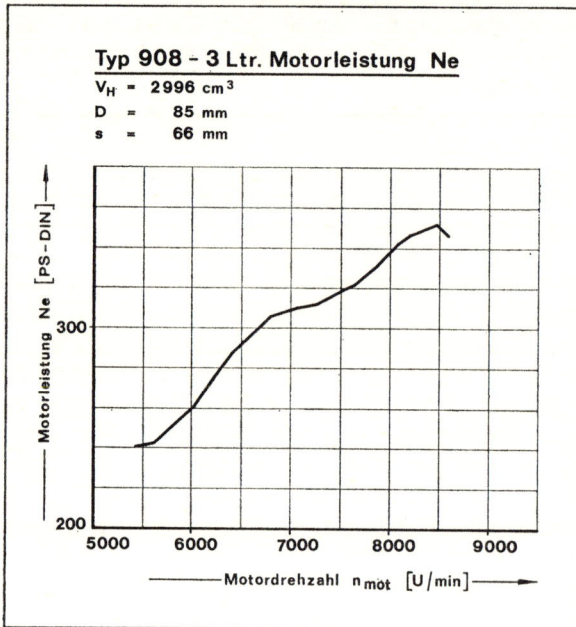

Power curve of 3-litre engine
Type 908.
Maximum bmep 195 psi.
Maximum torque 236 lb/ft at
6,600 rpm.

Though many manufacturers were already going over to four valves per cylinder, the Type 908 still had only two. This was because it was intended to remain as closely related as possible to a production engine and also because with four valves per cylinder, the cooling passages between the valves of an air-cooled engine do not allow a sufficient flow of cooling air. But, as in the Type 771 engine, all valves were hollow and sodium-filled for better heat dissipation. Because of their relatively large diameter (inlet 47.5 mm, exhaust 40.5 mm with a lift of 12.1 and 10.5 mm respectively) and also to obtain sufficiently large cooling air passages around the valve guides, the valves were set at the comparatively large included angle of 71°. In view of the resultant shape of the combustion chamber, the comparatively low compression ratio of 10.4 : 1 was chosen, so that the form should not be excessively shallow. The dry sump lubrication system was again designed in such a way that the crankshaft was fed axially from its front end, with drillings to lubricate the crankpins, while the main journals were lubricated directly from drillings in the block. As in all Porsche racing engines, the connecting rods and their bolts were made of titanium. As this metal has approximately only half the elasticity modulus of steel, any

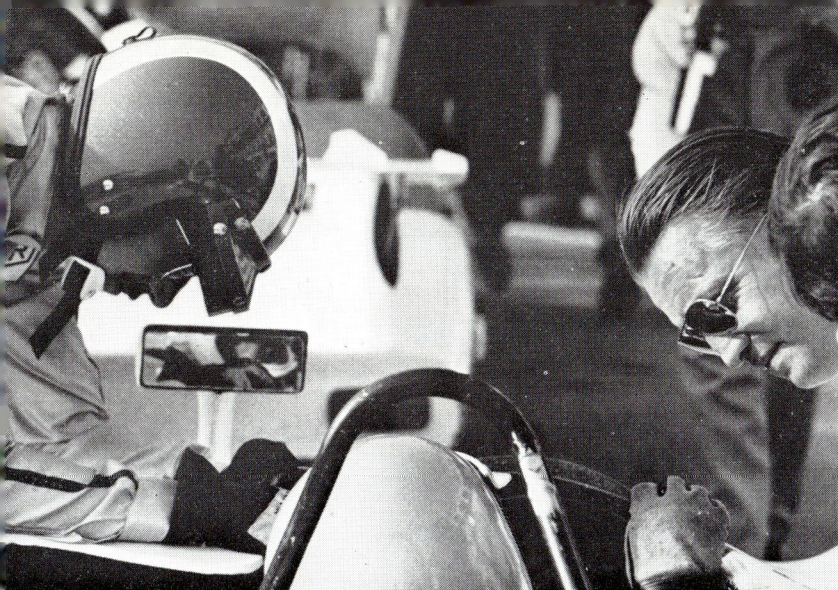

Jo Siffert with development engineer Helmut Bott, at the 1969 Le Mans race.

Jo Siffert (left) and Brian Redman. This was Porsche's star crew who played a decisive part in securing Porsche their first World Championship.

Le Mans 1969. The drivers Mitter, Herrmann and Kauhsen in a practice discussion with engineers Bott (back to the camera) and Piech.

908/02 Spyder. The cockpit is 100 per cent functional. The sliding driver's seat is an unusual refinement for a racing car.

Large front and rear spoilers literally spoiled the shape of the original 908/02 Spyder so that its drag coefficient rose to as much as 0.7. Here Mitter is seen winning the 1969 Targa Florio.

For the 1969 Le Mans race, a long-tail version of the 908/02 'Sole' was produced. Its total drag was nearly as low as for the long-tail coupes and its weight was 40 kg less.

Aluminium frame of the 908/03. Weight approximately 35 kg (78 lb). The diagonal tube over the engine bay is not fitted in this photograph.

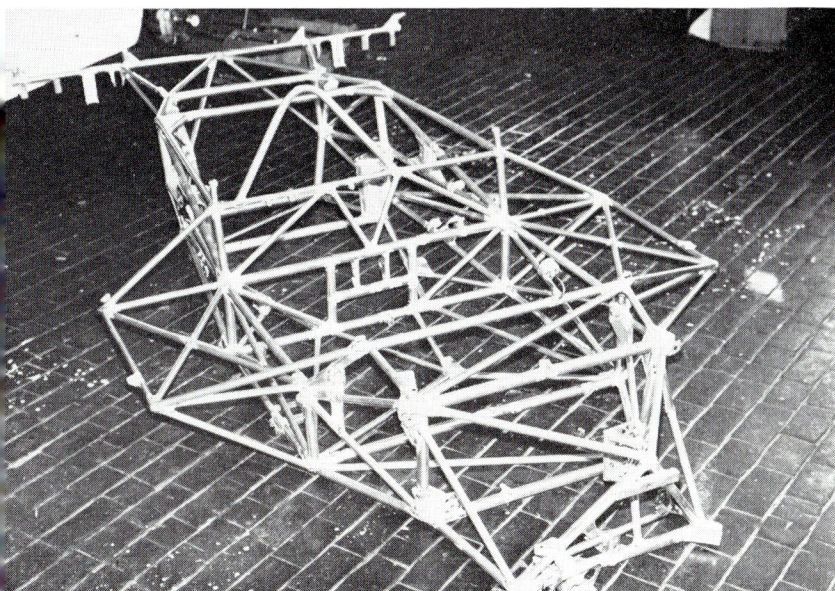

908/03 frame with front pyramid. The gauge on a front cross tube is used to check the welds by air pressure after assembly.

The author at the wheel of a development prototype of the 908/03 on the Nurburgring. The car has no headlights as Porsche 'discovered' that the CSI rules do not actually require them for daylight racing.

Right: The perforated rear brake discs of the 908/03 provide better cooling and a significant saving in weight.

Middle: The gearbox of the 908/03 is between the engine and the differential. All transmission housings are cast magnesium. The spare wheel seen in this picture was carried only in the Targa Florio.

Bottom: Type 908/03 in its final 1970 form, as used in the Targa Florio and the Nurburgring 1,000 km race which it won. The pedals are far in front of the front wheel centre. The very low and sharply cut front with a wrap-round 30 mm wide horizontal spoiler reduces the air flow under the car and makes any other form of spoiler unnecessary. Kurt Ahrens is seen at the wheel.

deformation of the bearing caused by stress or heat expansion will stress a titanium bolt less than a steel bolt. The nuts are made of steel, however, as experience has proved that titanium nuts tend to undo themselves on a titanium bolt. In the interests of quicker development, the Type 908 engine had the same bore and stroke dimensions (84 x 66 mm) as the well-proven 901 six-cylinder unit. But before the engine ran at Le Mans, the bore was increased to 85 mm which raised the capacity from 2,926 cc to 2,996 cc. Due to its larger bore, the 908 engine is slightly longer than the Type 771, but extensive use of light alloys—aluminium for the cylinders (the bores were chrome-plated) and for the cylinder heads, magnesium for the longitudinally split crankcase and for all covers—made it possible to keep the weight of the 3-litre engine down to 178 kg (394 lb), only 18 kg (40 lb) heavier than the 2.2-litre engine and the chassis needed only minor alterations to take the larger unit.

Having a 'flat' crankshaft, the Type 771 engine had the firing order 1, 7, 2, 8, 5, 3, 6, 4 which made the exhaust system rather complicated as each of the two tail pipes had to be fed from cylinders of each bank to prevent back pressure and to obtain an extractor effect. In order to simplify the exhaust system, the Type 908 engine had a two plane crankshaft, originally with the firing order 1, 8, 2, 6, 4, 5, 3, 7 which made it possible to treat each bank as a separate four-cylinder engine, as far as the exhaust piping was concerned. This, however, meant that, as in a four-cylinder engine, second order forces were not balanced: in fact, this type of flat eight being made up of two four-cylinder units, the unbalanced forces were additive.

The resultant vibrations are much more acceptable in a racing car than in a touring car and for comparatively short races (up to 1,000 km) for which the engine was first used, this did not cause any great difficulties. Despite a modification that had meanwhile been introduced, however, the situation was to prove very different at Le Mans, as we shall see later.

As already mentioned, the 3-litre engine fitted the 907 chassis without the need for any major modifications. On the passenger's side, the bulkhead had to be moved forward slightly to make room for the right-hand cylinder bank. Externally, the two long-tail cars 908 000 and 908 002 which took part in the preliminary Le Mans practice in April 1968, were nearly indistinguishable from the Type 907 car which had also been brought along. At this time, the 908 still used 13-in diameter wheels though the rim width and tyre sizes were different for the two 908 cars: 908 002 had the smaller 5.25 M-13 and 7.00 L-13 tyres on 8- and 9½-in wide rims, while 908 000 was fitted at the back with 12-in wide rims and used 4.75/11.50-13 tyres at the front and 6.00/13.50-13 tyres at the rear. This car had also been modified to take 15-in diameter wheels. The wheel openings had been enlarged and the wheel arches widened but there had been no time to put the car in the wind tunnel. As the currently used gearbox was unable to take the torque of the 3-litre engine, a new six-speed gearbox with dry sump lubrication was adapted to it. This transmission had been originally developed for the Bergspyder, but emphatically rejected when it finished up weighing no less than 25 kg (55 lb) more than the existing gearbox. The whole point of this dry sump gearbox was to reduce the power absorbed by oil splash in a wet sump gearbox, which is as much as 7 to 8 hp at speeds of the 185 mph order. To reduce clutch inertia and obtain quicker gear changes, the new transmission had a three-disc clutch located at the rear end of the gearbox and driven by a long shaft passing through the hollow gearbox lay shaft. From the clutch, the drive went through quickly interchangeable constant speed gears. Naturally all six gears had Porsche synchronisation while the half shafts not only had two universal joints and roller splines to take up length variations, but they were also divided by a

G

Giubo rubber universal the aim of which was to absorb shocks by giving the shafts a certain torsional flexibility.

This had also often been proved beneficial to lap times and in this form, used for the 907 since the beginning of 1968, the Giubo joints were not submitted to axial stresses reducing their durability. In order to compensate at least partially for the notably heavier power train (the engine and gearbox together weighed 43 kg or 95 lb more than in the 907) the side pannier fuel tanks were moved forward as far as possible. On the occasion of their first race at Monza, these early 908s turned the scales at 670 kg (1,475 lb) with oil but without fuel.

The six-speed gearbox was given a try-out even before the first 908 was completed, in March 1968, on the occasion of a preliminary practice for which the Brands Hatch track was hired in view of the forthcoming 500-mile race. This was also to serve as a try-out for the Sebring 12-Hour race. As fitted in 907 007, the six-speed gearbox used a twin disc clutch which was found to be slightly prone to slipping even in conjunction with the 2.2-litre engine. Two other standard 907s took part in this run in which a new, more wear-resistant Dunlop mixture 236 was also to be tried.

Compared with the previous year's models, the normal 907s had been modified by using wider 12-in rims at the back and low profile tyres front and rear while the camber settings had been altered to suit: they were reduced to —1° front and —45′ rear. Slightly higher gearing than the year before on the same circuit was also used in view of the smaller rolling radius of the new tyres. The ratios were 11 :29, 16 :29, 21 :30, 23 :28, 25 :26. The normal cars were actually lighter than permitted by the rules and carried a ballast of 15/20 kg (33/44 lb) at the front.

All the trials were done on the club circuit except for ten laps for which the long circuit was made available and which was lapped by Herrmann in 1 m 36.5 s, ie, 1.7 s faster than Graham Hill's best Porsche time the previous year on a 910 eight-cylinder. Altogether, the car fitted with the new gearbox and also using experimental brake discs incorporating a molybdenum additive covered nearly 1,000 km (625 miles) involving approximately 7,000 gear changes. The gearbox gave no trouble whatsoever and both this and the two other cars were absolutely trouble free. After the trial the brake discs, both normal and with molybdenum additive, were in excellent condition.

The Dunlop mixture 236 proved to be nearly twice as wear-resistant as the mixture 184, but the drivers said its grip was less which is confirmed by the lap times: on the club circuit (best time 50.6 s) they averaged between 0.6 and 0.8 s more to the lap. These tyres were not used in actual racing.

Though, to start with, the 907 chassis was to be used for the 908 with as few modifications as possible, an interesting experiment, in view of further developments, was made at that time in Weissach. Its aim was to reduce the understeering behaviour in small radius curves of racing cars set up for running on fast circuits. For the tests, a Carrera 6 (906 141) kept by the factory for experimental purposes was modified in such a way that the pivot axis of the front suspension transverse wishbones sharply converged towards the rear of the car, causing very important castor variations as the suspension worked up and down. It follows from the steering geometry that the castor angle induces camber variations as the road wheels are steered. The greater the castor angle and the greater the steering angle, the greater are the camber variations: both front wheels lean into the corner, a good way of reducing the slip angle and of combating understeer.

The modification of the experimental car was carried out in such a way that the steering and suspension geometries remained otherwise unaltered. The experiment was based on the fact that if the anti-roll bars were set to produce a neutral steer attitude on the largest (190-metre) diameter of the Weissach circular track, conventional cars would understeer when being tried on smaller diameter tracks. And what is really wanted in such cases is slight oversteer to help the car round a sharp corner. This could be achieved by increasing the negative camber of the outside front wheel when its lock is increased, which is precisely what this geometry achieved, the considerable castor angle being obtained by the compression of the outside suspension caused by body roll.

In practice, however, the scheme did not work out, mainly because the castor variations also produced a strong anti-dive effect: even moderate braking caused the nose of the car to lift so much that the suspension rebound stops came into action. The anti-dive effect was also noticeable during cornering, without any application of the brakes, when it was induced by the longitudinal component of the cornering force. This vertical reaction, which is obviously more pronounced on the more laden outer wheel, opposed body roll, so that the castor increase could not materialise. It was also observed that on the smallest circular track the force needed to hold the steering decreased as the speed increased and was finally inverted, so that the wheels would immediately go to full lock if the steering wheel was released. Measuring the suspension travel under fast circular track cornering, it was found that while the outside front suspension was only slightly compressed as a result of the conflicting actions of body roll and anti-dive, the inside front suspension, which anti-dive and body roll both tend to extend, was lifted up to the rebound stop, causing the castor angle to become negative and thus inverting the castor action. This was confirmed when the suspension of the experimental car was lowered so as to increase the static castor angle from 7° to 13°, when this castor reversal could not be produced. Lowering the suspension also decreases the anti-dive effect, but nevertheless the measures indicated that for a constant lateral acceleration of 1 g, the compression of the front outside suspension and the castor angle depending upon it become less as the diameter of the circle is decreased, which is the reverse of what is aimed at.

These experiments were thus momentarily abandoned, but the report concludes with the observation: 'Possibly the solution lies in an arrangement combining a much larger castor angle than usual with a normal trail' (so as to keep the steering force reasonable). This, in fact, was the arrangement later put into practice by BMW beginning with their six-cylinder touring models.

Le Mans preliminary practice: first appearance of the 908

It was not until the preliminary practice for the Le Mans race in April 1968 that the 908 was first driven at its absolute maximum speed. Both Linge and Stommelen, who drove the cars on this occasion, complained of instability under braking and (also on the 907) of bad transient behaviour when the car was driven from a straight into a bend. In the case of the 908, it could be assumed that the instability was caused by the greater rear weight bias, but this could not be so for the 907 (907 005) which was practically identical to the previous year's car. In the case of the 907 a likely reason could have been that the car was now running with less negative camber (—1° instead of —1° 30′ front, —45′ instead of —3° rear), but that the wider tyres for which these settings had been chosen were not being used at Le Mans. This was because there is no doubt that the narrower tyres gave a much higher maximum speed down the Mulsanne straight. According to the rev counter, 908 002, using the narrower tyres, reached 193 mph (2.5 mph more than the 907) while 908 000 on wide tyres and with a body sufficiently wide to cover them did only 189.5 mph. As changing spoiler settings until the car ran parallel to the road at high speed did not produce a complete cure, all cars were fitted at the back with two vertical fins. These notably improved straight line stability and reduced the sensitivity to side winds.

Various troubles with the gear change mechanism, broken cooling blower cog belts, Giubo rubber universals fouling the frame and finally a broken half shaft all prevented the new 3-litres from showing their true potential. The best 3-litre time was achieved by Stommelen in 3 m 47.3 s on the wide-tyred car, but he was 1.5 s quicker with the 907. But even his time of 3 m 45.8 s was a lot slower than the best 907 time of 3 m 41.6 s achieved by Siffert during official practice the previous year. No fast time was attempted at all with the narrower 908 which was driven by Herbert Linge.

Immediately after the preliminary practice at Le Mans, a private practice session was organised for April 9/11 on the Nürburgring in view of the forthcoming 1,000 km race. 907 024 (the Sebring winner) and 908 001 were used as test cars.

On that occasion the 908 was still virtually identical to the 907, except for the engine and transmission, and stood on 13-in diameter wheels, their width being 8-in front and 12-in rear. A large number of lightweight parts were used and 20 kg (44 lb) of lead had to be carried in the nose in order to get the weight up to the 650 kg (1,430 lb) required by the regulations. Titanium coil springs were used front and rear. The test, comprising 47 laps of the northern loop of the Ring (a total of 667 miles), indicated the need for additional small front spoilers and the drivers asked for the castor angle to be reduced from 7° to 6° and then down to 5° in order to make the steering lighter. And, as the tyres wore much more on the inside than on the outside, the negative camber was reduced by 15′ front and rear to —45′ and —30′ respectively.

The drivers rated the engine as very flexible, but very noisy and rough. Above 7,000 rpm, the entire car vibrated very noticeably, which was probably the cause of some damage experienced during the test run or discovered when the car was later dismantled. The throttle slide control bracket broke and so did a tail pipe hanger. Further trouble was experienced with split intake and exhaust manifolds, and after only six miles a fifth gear thrust washer broke as had already happened at Le Mans. As the crack initiated at the spline, the washer was replaced by one free to rotate on the shaft, a modification which made the part much less fragile.

As only two weeks later the 1,000 km race at Monza was to take place, the narrower of the two Le Mans cars, 908 002, was sent to Monza for some preliminary practice after being overhauled in the factory. This long-distance test took place in the period April 17/19 and was used for trying out further running gear settings.

Altogether 935 miles were covered in the course of which spoiler dimensions and settings were finalised, while two satisfactory combinations of shock absorbers, springs and auxiliary rubber springs evolved. In view of the two bankings included in the circuit which were to be taken clockwise, the car was set to ride slightly higher on the left hand side and a slightly higher rubber auxiliary spring was used at the rear on that side. The fastest lap was done by Scarfiotti in 2 m 56.2 s—more than 10 s quicker than the previous best by a 910/6 the year before; it should be remembered, however, that the long-tail body played a significant part in this improvement.

Much less satisfaction was derived from the long list of troubles which interrupted the test drive:

After 138 miles: self-starter defective;

After 169 miles: broken washer in gearbox (as had already happened at Le Mans and Nürburgring);

After 423 miles: clutch cable broken;

After 466 miles: brakes grab (front brake discs polished);

After 490 miles: bracket broken on right hand throttle slide;

After 565 miles: throttle slide bracket broken again;

After 580 miles: brakes pull strongly (all brake discs polished, new pads fitted at front);

After 688 miles: throttle slide bracket broken for third time;

Spare wheel broken through floor;

Right hand exhaust megaphone bracket broken;

After 869 miles: gear lever console tie-rod broken;

After 930 miles: gear mechanism jumps out of gear; selection of some gears has become impossible.

Thereupon the test run was stopped and the car was partially dismantled when the following additional faults came to light:

The diagonal tube across the engine bay was cracked;

a front wheel bearing was about to fail; it was already running roughly;

the gearbox housing was cracked at the starting motor flange;

two of the four exhaust manifolds were cracked;

a lockring was broken in the gearbox;

the flywheel internal splines driving the clutch shaft were damaged;

the left upper front wishbone spherical joint had worked loose in the wishbone arm.

In addition the drivers complained of heavy engine vibrations, of poor cockpit ventilation, that the front part of the body became heavily deformed by the air pressure, that the screen wiper lifted at speed and of other defects of lesser importance. Wear and consumption data for the tests were as follows and were later confirmed by the official race practice:

Fuel: 6.5 mpg;

Oil: 475 mpg;

Brake linings: front 0.92 in per 1,000 miles, rear 1.15 in per 1,000 miles.

In the course of official practice, the two 3-litres entered for the race did not run well either and various defects prevented them from getting down to satisfactory practice times. Together, the two cars 908 003 and 004 put in only 23 laps in the course of which there were two cases of breakage of the drive shaft going through the gearbox. There were also repeat performances of other well-known troubles: a clutch release cable broke (a specially made guide brought no satisfactory solution, as the race was to show), the front end of the body was still deforming (it was reinforced for the race) and the gearbox thrust washers were still a problem (a reinforced model was manufactured).

Despite these last-minute measures, the cars did not fare well in the race: in 908 003 (Siffert/Herrmann) the air duct to the rear brakes was destroyed, presumably by the Giubo elastic joint, and tore off the external pipes of the dry sump gearbox which was modified to wet sump at the pits. On the Mitter/Scarfiotti car (908 004), the clutch cable broke no less than three times, leading to the suspicion that these breakages might be caused by engine vibration. Vibrations were also no doubt responsible for the alternator failure on both cars, when the batteries were changed as required. After the race, the starter motor flange was found to be broken, as had already happened on the car used for preliminary practice: this was no doubt also caused by engine vibration. As a result of all this trouble, Mitter/Scarfiotti were only 11th and Siffert/Herrmann finished 19th. Their car had been standing at the pits for a total of 1 h 35 m! Porsche's reputation as well as precious Championship points were saved, however, by 907 005, driven by Stommelen/Neerpasch who finished second overall. The fuel consumption of the 907 was as low as 10 mpg, strongly contrasting with the 908's consumption of 7 mpg.

A week later the Targa Florio brought Porsche much more glory, but as only type 907 cars were entered for this race, it does not belong in the development story of the 908 and is of little interest to us, as the 907 had about reached the end of its development career. It is worth mentioning, however, that two of the four cars entered, 907 022 and 029, had to retire due to front wheel bearing failures. Hero of the day was Vic Elford (co-driving with Umberto Maglioli) who had lost a lot of time when his car (907 025) lost a wheel and he had to drive back to the pits on the Space Saver tyre. Only a terrific drive in which he established a new lap record in 36 m 01 s brought him ahead of the leading Alfa of Nanni Galli and Ignazio Giunti to clinch victory on the very last lap.

First 908 victory in the 1968 Nürburgring 1,000 km

After the dismal performance of the 908 at Monza, it came as a complete surprise when a similar car driven by Siffert/Elford won the Nürburgring 1,000 km race only three weeks later. In those three weeks, work had been going on at full pressure at the factory to remedy the defects that had plagued the cars at Monza—mostly by reinforcing the troublesome parts—while Bosch had dealt with the problem of making the alternators less sensitive to engine vibrations. In addition to this, the cars prepared for the race had been fitted with 15-in diameter wheels and correspondingly larger disc brakes. The rim widths adopted were 9-in front and 12-in rear. Following the April tests on the Nürburgring, the negative camber was only —45' front and —30' rear while the castor was down to 4° or 5°, according to the driver's preference, to make the steering reasonably light.

Three days before official practice started, the Nürburgring was hired for a preliminary test session with a practice car (908 007) identical to the race cars. The object of this practice session was to test the durability of the car and to find optimum settings for the Ring. On this occasion, too, trouble was experienced, but none that could be traced to hasty preparation. The main sources of worry were:

One front wheel bearing (which had already done the Monza race) failed: as a precautionary measure, both bearings were changed;

One fuel injection pipe was worn through by fouling the engine cover: the pipe was changed and the cover was filed down to give more clearance;

The clutch output shaft broke at the constant mesh pinion splines: the new shaft was polished before being fitted and care was taken to ensure that the boss of the constant mesh pinion completely covered the splines;

The constant mesh pinions broke and had to be changed.

Altogether 822 miles were covered in this brief practice session without any need for a tyre or a brake pad change. The fastest northern loop lap time was done by Mitter in 8 m 41.9 s, half a second slower than the best 907 eight-cylinder time by Jo Siffert the year before. On the southern loop, too, Mitter was fastest in 2 m 10.3 s, after the Bilstein dampers had been set harder on compression. The same car 908 007 was then used as a practice car during official race practice, so that a total of 1,185 miles were covered, which allowed two well-known weak points to show up again: the clutch cable broke (an improved version had meanwhile been prepared) and a throttle slide bracket broke. It is quite understandable that Porsche did not really trust the new car yet and spread their chances between the Types 908 and 907, especially as the fastest 907 with a 2.2-litre engine, driven by Stommelen, had been the fastest Porsche, lapping in 8 m 32.8 s as compared with 8 m 40.1 s which was the best Siffert could do with a 908. Another advantage of the smaller-engined car was that it could do 15 laps between fuel stops (which the race proved to be somewhat optimistic) while the 3-litre could do only 12 laps on a tankful, calling for 3 stops to cover 44 laps.

All cars entered for the race had a short-tail body. They were:

908 008 for Siffert/Elford

908 009 for Mitter/Scarfiotti

Tyres: Dunlop 4.75/11.30-15 front, 6.00/13.50-15 rear; pressure—26 psi front and rear.

Gear ratios: 17:34, 21:30, 24:27, 26:25, 28:23, 29:21, crown wheel and pinion 8:35, constant mesh pinions 22:28.

907 031 for Neerpasch/Buzzetta

907 032 for Herrmann/Stommelen

Tyres: Dunlop 4.75/10.00-13 front, 6.00/12.00-13 tear; pressure—26 psi front and rear.

Gear ratios: 12:29, 18:29, 22:30, 24:27, 27:25, crown wheel and pinion 7:31.

All cars were fitted with aluminium brake calipers and cast iron brake discs with flexible hose ventilation.

With a lap in 8 m 32.8 s, Stommelen driving a 907 was in pole position, with Ickx's Ford GT40 second fastest in 8 m 37.4 s and the Mitter/Scarfiotti 908 in third place, though it was actually Siffert who had driven the car around in 8 m 40.1 s. In the race, the Ford proved to be a real menace for the Porsches as long as Ickx drove, but Hawkins could not quite keep up the pace. A defective injection pump had prevented Siffert from getting a good starting position, but after only one lap, he was second behind Mitter, having started in 27th spot. He soon took the lead, but from the fifth lap on, Mitter was plagued by out-of-balance brakes. He made several pit stops but as they gave no result, the car was withdrawn. The other cars ran faultlessly and Siffert did the fastest race lap in 8 m 33 s, a new prototype record. His speed was kept up very well by co-driver Elford and the 908 finally proved to be more than a match for the Stommelen/Herrmann 907, even though they both drove very hard. This is reflected by a note in Porsche's internal race report: 'Twenty-eighth lap: Stommelen spins twice; the first time because a GT40 baulks him, the second time because he was furious about the delay'(!). In the end their ambitious driving paid off as the 5-litre Ford driven by Ickx and Hawkins was left 50 s behind to take third place, while Neerpasch and Buzzetta were fourth, having also covered the full distance.

Spa, Norisring, Watkins Glen

Those who enthused, however, and thought the 908 had already overcome its teething troubles were to be deeply disappointed. Porsche's aim was not only to win the Manufacturers' World Championship, but above all to win the Le Mans 24-Hour race and no occasion was missed to gain experience with the car. Two 908s and one 907 were entered for the Spa 1,000 km race, but a streamlined long-tail version (908 004) was also brought along and tried out in practice. The car was not actually raced as it did not handle as well as the short-tail version and this is much more of a handicap at Spa, where the circuit is essentially made up of very fast curves, than at Le Mans where the long straight is the overruling factor.

In an effort to reduce the vibrations which had destroyed the alternators and many other components at Monza, the firing order of the 3-litre engines had been altered. Instead of 1, 8, 2, 6, 4, 5, 3, 7, it was now 1, 5, 2, 7, 4, 8, 3, 6. One of the two engines tried had a crankshaft with additional counter weights and of which the crankpins were drilled hollow, which made it much smoother, but as the engine did not seem to produce the required power (which of course had nothing to do with the new crankshaft), it was not used for the race.

All cars were fitted with 13-in brake discs (Spa is not hard on brakes) so that both 13-in and 15-in diameter wheels could be tried. According to the drivers, handling was much better on the latter. Of the long-tail car with 13-in wheels, the drivers said it was very dangerous and even though it was better on 15-in wheels, Elford still called it a tricky car. Even apart from this, practice problems were quite numerous : a clutch cable broke again (though it was said to be an improved version) and on a short-tail car, the main pin of the clutch withdrawal fork fell out. Some of the rivets securing the cooling air blower wheel to its hub were found to have broken and two alternators were shaken to pieces, one of them by the engine with the new crankshaft. In addition, two rear wheel bearings had to be changed.

For the first time, the 3-litre proved to be faster than the 2.2-litre : both the 908s got round the circuit in 3 m 46 s, driven by Elford and Herrmann while Elford did the best long-tail time, getting round in 3 m 47 s, which compares with Schlesser's best 907 time of 3 m 49 s. There were three cars on the track faster than the Porsche, however : Frank Gardner went round in a 3-litre Ford prototype using the DFV Cosworth engine in 3 m 36.3 s and two Ford GT40s did 3 m 40.3 s and 3 m 45.7 s driven by Ickx and Mairesse respectively.

As the race itself was run in pouring rain, the Porsches, helped by the fact that the fast 3-litre Ford fell out on the first lap, finally did better than expected, taking second and third places. No one could hold a candle to Ickx, however, who won with ease while rain tyres and Schlesser's determined driving put the 907 into second place, just in front of the surviving 908, the other car having been crashed by Neerpasch who was hurt in the accident.

New gearbox for the 908

The six-speed gearbox of the 908 had the one defect Porsche engineers are unlikely to forgive : it was heavy. If throughout the 1968 season, the 908 was some 20 kg (44 lb) overweight compared with the minimum of 650 kg required by the regulations, it was mainly the fault of its gearbox. Neither was the fact that this over-weight was overhanging the rear axle particularly desirable. Consequently the design for a new gearbox Type 916, based on the transmission Type 822 usually used with the 2- and 2.2-litre engines, was rushed through. It had five forward gears with Porsche synchronisation and one reverse gear, and the Fichtel & Sachs clutch was in a conventional position, between the engine and the transmission. The oil was carried in the bottom of the casing, but additional lubrication of vital parts was provided by small jets fed via external pipes from a gear type pump. The new gearbox was first tried in 908 007 which was entered for the Norisring race in Nuremberg on June 30 1967 and driven by Mitter. The car had 13-in diameter wheels and several experimental features. Among these were articulated flaps operated by the rear suspension as on the Bergspyders and, in view of the wide tread pattern of the rear 6.00/12.00-13 tyres, the anchorage points of the rear suspension had been moved to reduce camber variations induced by suspension movements. This was not a happy move, as Mitter complained of sudden breakaway. For the race, first gear was blanked off altogether, as the first gear stop of the selector mechanism was not satisfactory. In spite of these defects however, Mitter managed to lead the race, heading David Piper's Ferrari, until the experimental aluminium clutch housing broke.

Whereas the Norisring race had been entered mainly for experimental purposes, the Watkins Glen Six-Hour race was much more important as it carried precious World Championship points. No risks were taken here, as indicated by the fact that all cars used the well-proven six-speed gearbox, but all cars were now fitted with the articulated rear flaps and 15-in diameter wheels fitted with Dunlop 184 mixture tyres 4.75/11.30-15 front and 6.00/13.50-15 rear. Apparently the camber settings had not yet been finalised: at Monza the 908s ran with —1° front and —45' rear. Following the April Nürburgring tests, these settings were reduced by 15' front and rear, while for Watkins Glen all cars had —45' camber front and rear.

The Watkins Glen practice once more showed how unreliable or impressionable test drivers can be in their judgement: after having put in some practice laps, Elford came slowly into the pits and asked the crew to change a wheel of which he said the tyre had burst with a loud bang and he had been lucky to be able to hold the car! Everybody looked around and saw no flat tyre. What actually had burst was the compressed air bottle for the Space Saver spare tyre, but this could hardly have in any way affected the handling of the car!

In the case of Mitter, a favourite complaint was about the Giubo rubber coupling incorporated in the steering column to reduce kick-back and make the action more progressive. Once, after early development testing, the resilience of this joint had been finalised, none of the drivers ever gave it a second thought, but not so Mitter: whichever was used for his car, it was always the wrong one for the particular track and before almost every race the mechanics had to change it. But back to the Watkins Glen practice:

In an effort to cure the front wheel bearing troubles experienced on previous occasions, the Watkins Glen cars had been fitted with twin track ball bearings designed to take both radial and axial loads and lubricated by a very heat-resistant grease. In view of the forthcoming Le Mans race in which the reduction of the drag factor was all important, making it desirable to blank off any unnecessary air intakes, overalls cooled by tubes in which ice-cold water was circulated were again tried, but the pump circulating the water in the ice box was still unreliable and a full year went by before this set-up, which was rather unpopular with the drivers, was tried again.

Two of the Watkins Glen cars, 908 005 and 908 012, were new. 908 009 and 908 011 had taken part in the Nürburgring and Spa races respectively, though 908 009 had not gone very far. Thanks to its aluminium frame, 908 012 weighed only 660 kg (1,460 lb), approximately 20 kg (44 lb) less than the steel-framed cars. 908 011 was also used for some preliminary practice and it was soon clear that the new front wheel bearings did not provide the answer to the problems: after 87 laps (200 miles) the left-hand bearing seized up and its replacement lasted for only 67 laps. The same failure happened yet again in the course of official practice. Another already-known trouble repeated itself on 908 009 when the clutch release fork pivot fell out of its boss. In this car too and in 908 012, the reverse gear pinion would not slide into engagement.

The drivers complained of bad handling on the aluminium-framed car but any fears that the frame might be at fault were dispelled when an increase in the mobile tail flap surface and in rear wheel toe-in from 10' to 30' brought the car up to par.

As a precautionary measure, the engine of the practice car was changed for the race and so was the entire left front suspension, as three consecutive bearing failures on that side seemed suspicious, though no obvious cause for them was found. All cars were also fitted with air scoops to provide some oil tank cooling, as despite the oil cooler, the temperature had gone up to 110° C.

The best Porsche practice time was, as usual in those days, done by Jo Siffert in 1 m 10.2 s and was also the fastest overall. The other Porsches were third, fourth and fifth fastest. Only the John Wyer Gulf GT40 driven by Jacky Ickx and Lucien Bianchi could challenge the Porsches with 1 m 10.8 s. This proved that for performance, the 908 was quite competitive, but reliability was another question. Only one of them finished and only in the case of 908 001, driven by the American George Follmer who over-revved the engine on the 15th lap, was the car not to blame. 908 009, the only surviving Porsche, driven by Herrmann, the Japanese driver Ikusawa and finally Jo Siffert, finished 29 laps behind the victorious Ickx/Bianchi Ford.

Wheel bearings did not fail on this car but other troubles more than made up for it:

53rd lap: oil pressure gauge tube burst. Replaced at pits.

77th lap: battery overcharged. Replaced at pits.

126th lap: battery overcharged. Replaced at pits.

127th lap: accelerator linkage broken. Repaired at pits.

200th lap: accelerator linkage broken. Repaired at pits.

234th lap: battery overcharged. Replaced at pits.

As part of the 908 development programme, a car was sent to the Solitude race on the Hockenheimring (20 laps-94 miles), Hans Herrmann driving the Norisring car 908 007. The rear suspension, with reduced camber change, was again used but meanwhile the front suspension had been modified on the same lines. This time 15-in diameter wheels were used. The car was fitted with the new (Type 916) five-speed gearbox, but the housing of the Fichtel & Sachs single plate clutch had been changed from aluminium, which had caused the car's retirement at the Norisring, to steel.

Despite the fact that the front suspension now matched the rear suspension better and that in view of the smaller camber variations, the static negative camber of the rear wheels had been increased from —45' to —1° 15', Herrmann was not satisfied with the car's handling, particularly objecting to its rapid rear end breakaway. Apart from this, however, the car ran like clockwork, but though Herrmann had done the best practice time, he was narrowly beaten in the race by David Piper's private 3-litre Ferrari (a modified and lightened P3) which was faster in a straight line.

Seven weeks later on the same track, the result was reversed in the Preis der Nationen after Piper had been faster in practice than Herrmann. In this case, however, Herrmann drove 908 005 with standard suspension (but —1° 15' rear negative camber) and a six-speed gearbox. Herrmann had fitted better biting but less reliable Energit 395 brake pads to his car in an endeavour to outbrake Piper into the last corner, but this was not to prove necessary as Piper had to make a quick pit stop after having lost a rear spoiler on his Ferrari.

Porsche were lucky that the Le Mans race that normally takes place in June was postponed until September as a result of the tense French political situation of May 1968: in June, the 908s were still so unreliable that a withdrawal would probably have been inevitable.

At Watkins Glen the team had been fortunate in its misfortune. Two cars retired following front wheel bearing failures. The only car that finished was only saved from the same fate by the fact that it lost 29 laps in the pits due to various difficulties. As it was dismantled in the factory after the race, it was found that the grease used for the bearings had become a sort of rubbery paste and that the bearing itself was already running roughly. The fact that by chance the bearing had been dismantled just at this stage, gave a hint as to the cause of the failures and, following this, skid-pad tests were performed in which the outer front bearing was destroyed regularly after 12 to 15 laps. The test being perfectly reproductive, lubrication experts were consulted. They recommended a new grease on which the car could be driven around the circular track 100 times without any trouble, as a consequence of which it was also used for the rear wheel bearings. To make quite sure, however, the small twin track ball bearings used at Watkins Glen were replaced by large taper roller bearings, the same as used in the 2.5-ton Mercedes 600, and new rear uprights incorporating a Simmerring seal were fitted.

The specific preparation for the Le Mans race began immediately after these development tests, when the Zeltweg circuit was hired for a private practice session shortly before the Austrian Grand Prix. Three cars were tried out: a short-tail, 908 007, the Norisring and Solitude car with reduced camber variation front and rear and two long-tail cars prepared for the Le Mans race—908 015 and 908 013, the latter with the same front suspension geometry as 908 007.

As from 908 012, all cars had an aluminium tube frame, including the long-tail cars prepared for the Le Mans race. This decision was taken following the experience with the 907 that had run for 50 hours as a preliminary practice car for Daytona and in the race itself and with the 908 that had given no trouble as far as the chassis was concerned on the bumpy Watkins Glen circuit. Argon welding was no problem for the factory's specialised welders and theory showed that the aluminium frames should be more fracture-resistant than the steel frames. This is because the elasticity modulus of aluminium alloy is much lower in relation to its tensile strength than steel, so that an aluminium frame designed to have the same overall bending and torsional stiffness as a similar steel frame, automatically offers more resistance to those forces which tend to break it up.

In practice a slightly lower torsional stiffness than that of the 908 steel frame was accepted for the aluminium frame, in the interest of light weight. In fact, tests comparing the torsional stiffness of the two types of frames were only done later, when the aluminium frame for the open-bodied car used in 1969 was compared with a similarly modified steel frame:

	Torsional stiffness
908/02 Spyder aluminium frame	1,700 lb ft/deg
908/02 Spyder steel frame	2,190 lb ft/deg
For comparison:	
910 steel frame	1,750 lb ft/deg
906 (Carrera 6) frame	1,420 lb ft/deg

Car 908 007 used for the preliminary practice at Zeltweg was fitted with the new front wheel bearings and the new rear uprights incorporating better seals: it also had the previously-used mobile rear flaps and the new five-speed gearbox in which the crown wheel and pinion broke after 51 laps (95 miles) when the usual six-speed gearbox was fitted and the car driven on until, after about 500 miles, the engine started missing. The breakage of a front suspension attachment bracket was an unusual failure, but nobody found it unusual that a cooling blower belt broke or that, after some 320 miles, the starter motor would not start the engine any more: it was now a well-known fact that the electrical equipment could not withstand the vibrations set up by the 'double four-cylinder' engine. Additional crankshaft counterweights had reduced the vibrations but there was simply no means of suppressing them with the existing crankshaft layout.

The car with reduced camber change was again unsatisfactory, the drivers reporting unpredictable changes from understeer to oversteer and vice versa, which could not be corrected by altering the anti-roll bar settings. The same comments applied to the long-tail car 908 013, using similar front suspension, for which bad straight line stability was also reported. Increasing the front negative camber from —45' to —1° 45' brought no improvements.The other long-tail car, with the normal suspension geometry, proved much more satisfactory: it was better both in a straight line and in curves, being much easier to drive than even the short-tail car with the modified suspension. This is reflected by the lap times obtained by Stommelen: 1 m 05.9 s with the long-tail car 908 015 using the standard suspension and 1 m 06.7 s with 908 013 with reduced camber change. Neither of the two cars gave any trouble in the course of some 125 miles of driving each.

Four cars were entered for the 500-km long Austrian Grand Prix, of which only Elford's 908 006 was new. The others, 908 005 for Siffert, 908 009 for Herrmann/Ahrens and 908 011 for Neerpasch/Lins, had all been raced before, but with a different engine. The new front wheel bearings gave no trouble, but most of the other well-known weaknesses related to engine vibrations were still with them. In the course of official practice and the race, an alternator shaft (also driving the cooling blower) broke, there were four cases of throttle linkage breakage, one fuel tank cracked and on Siffert's winning car the long shaft transmitting the drive from the engine to the clutch broke on the slowing down lap, after the car had crossed the finishing line. On this car, the diagonal stiffening tube above the engine bay was also found to be broken. Fuel consumption was 6.7 mpg and it is interesting that when, in practice, washers were removed to lower the front and rear suspensions by some $\frac{3}{4}$-in (which was done on all cars), the lowered centre of gravity brought a mean lap time improvement of some 1.3 per cent.

Le Mans 1968

Meanwhile every effort had been made to improve the drag and lift conditions. the influence of various modifications being tested in the wind tunnel of Stuttgart University. Both the short- and the long-tail cars were investigated. They had an identical frontal area of 1.375 m², ie 0.09 m² more than the Type 907, the difference lying in the greater width of the body and the slightly higher wings required to accommodate the taller and wider tyres: the 907 was 68 in and the 908 72.5 in wide.

To start with the short-tail car 908 006 was tried as driven by Elford at Zeltweg. It had front spoilers (angle of incidence —18.5°) and fixed (but adjustable) tail flaps (angle of incidence —25°). In this state, the following results were obtained for a wind speed of 93 mph:

Cw=0.422; lift, front —5 kg (negative); rear —16 kg (negative).

Increasing the rake of the rear flaps to —35° raised the drag to:

Cw=0.448, with a rear lift of —24 kg, the front lift being as before.

A flatter position of the rear flaps (—18°) decreased the drag to:

Cw=0.402, with the rear downthrust reduced to —10 kg and no change in the front downthrust, the rear flap being only slightly overhung.

Removing the rear flaps brought a further decrease in drag to Cw=0.382, but the rear lift became 2 kg positive.

The influence of the front spoilers on drag was practically nil, but removing them caused the front lift to become 7 kg positive with the rear flaps in their original (—25°) position, Cw being then 0.421.

The car was also tested with the front suspension raised 45 mm (1.8-in) above its normal position, as occurs when the car is driven over a hump. This increased Cw from 0.422 to 0.452, but much more important was the fact that the front lift changed from 5 kg negative to 16 kg positive. This means that the front wheel adhesion was reduced by 21 kg while the downthrust on the rear axle was increased by 4 kg. A lift of 16 kg (35 lb) may not sound very disturbing, but the picture changes when one considers that it was measured for a wind speed of 93 mph : at 180 mph, the lift would be increased to 60 kg (132 lb) !

If we consider that the original state gave the best compromise between drag and lift conditions, we can assume that the short-tail 908 had a drag factor Cw=0.422, which doesn't compare too well with Cw=0.354 obtained for the 910.

As the Le Mans race was close at hand, the wind tunnel tests of the long-tail 908 were more important. The car was investigated with front spoilers (angle of incidence —18°) and both with and without the aerodynamic devices specially developed for the Le Mans race. These consisted of two vertical tail fins connected by a horizontal aerofoil incorporating an articulated flap at each end. These were connected to the rear suspension, as in the Bergspyder and in the experimental short-tail 908.

Many data were obtained, of which the following are of particular interest :

The drag coefficient was the same with and without the rear aerodynamic devices : Cw=0.345. This was confirmed during practice for the Le Mans race, when the cars were tried with and without the rear aerofoil assembly : with this removed, they were much less stable at speed down the straight but, according to the rev counter, they were no faster. The drag factor Cw=0.345 was obtained in the wind tunnel with the rear flaps at a positive angle of incidence of 6°, which gave a front downthrust of —5 kg and still maintained a rear downthrust of —10 kg. Without the fins and wing, front downthrust could not be obtained.

As it seemed illogical that the additional rear aerofoil assembly should not increase the drag, the matter was further investigated with the help of cotton threads. This showed that without the assembly, the air stream running along the tail of the car was rather turbulent and tended to become detached, while the flow was much smoother with the aerofoils in place. For the Le Mans race, two large air scoops were added to the tail in order to improve the gearbox ventilation. These slightly increased the drag to Cw=0.360 (for comparison the long-tail 907 as used at Daytona in 1968 had Cw =0.299) with a downthrust of —5 kg front and —7 kg rear (corresponding to approximately —22 and —28 kg respectively, —49 and —62 lb, at 195 mph.)

In the meantime every effort was made in the racing division to improve the reliability of the 908 with the 24-Hour race in view. 908 005, which had won at Zeltweg, was used for the development tests. It had already covered some 840 racing miles at Watkins Glen and Zeltweg and had meanwhile been brought up to the latest specification and fitted with the additional gearbox-driven alternator to be used at Le Mans. The main blower-driven alternator was of the latest type developed by Bosch specially for this kind of car.

In the period September 6-27 1968, the car covered some 3,800 miles in 47 h 10 m driving time on the Hockenheimring, Nürburgring and on the Weissach proving ground, including the practice and the race at Hockenheim which Herrmann won, as mentioned earlier. For these 3,800 miles, four engines were used : the first was an 84 mm bore engine which was still in good order when exchanged for the latest type of 85 mm bore engine to be used at Le Mans; this engine was ruined when it was over-revved and a valve broke as a result of a broken input shaft in the gearbox. Its replacement broke a sprocket support in the camshaft drive after some 2,240 miles and the last engine was still in good order when a split gearbox casing put an end to the long-distance tests only one day before the Le Mans race was due to start.

As expected, many other difficulties cropped up in the course of the long-distance tests, but as far as possible all the defective parts were replaced, where available, by parts that had already been used and of which the previous history was known. This was the case with the three gearbox housings which were used up in the course of the tests, and every time an engine was changed the entire fuel injection system, including the throttle slides and all the linkages as well as all the electrical accessories, was taken over from the previous engine.

Some satisfaction was derived from the fact that the hitherto so troublesome front wheel bearings went through the tests with flying colours. Neither was there any trouble with the rear wheel bearings and the new, better sealed rear uprights proved satisfactory. No defects were found in the frame, the clutch, the Bilstein suspension dampers or the suspension springs (titanium front, steel rear). The only reason why titanium springs were not used for the rear was that only a very small number of them were available and in view of the price and long delivery times for titanium, the engineers preferred to use steel springs for development tests and then to order titanium springs of the rates that would be required.

Unfortunately, some of the well-known old troubles cropped up again: a starter motor failed, the input shaft broke in the gearbox, one half shaft broke and on another the flange bolts failed. And again there were difficulties with the ball joints of the throttle slide linkage. To everyone's satisfaction, however, there were no more throttle linkage failures and the alternators satisfactorily withstood the long-distance tests. But the Weissach tests indicated that the gearbox-driven alternator alone could not provide enough current to keep the batteries charged for a whole night, and this was to prove catastrophic at Le Mans. Taking an optimistic view, the fact that a starter motor securing screw broke and ruined the starter ring on the engine flywheel can be put down to chance, but this was certainly not the case with two other weaknesses which the long distance tests brought to light: the brake caliper supporting bracket broke on both the front wheel uprights, and the differential housing or cover split three times.

For the input shaft breakage, a solution had already been found: a polished and shot peened shaft was fitted and gave no trouble for the further 2,420 miles covered until the test was interrupted. As far as the other weaknesses were concerned, little could be done before the Le Mans race which was due to start only a few hours after the end of the endurance test. They were merely brought to the notice of the staff at Le Mans and recommendations were made that the screws and bolts securing the weak parts should be locked as well as possible.

Following the endurance tests, the following recommendations were made to be incorporated after the Le Mans race:

Reinforce front wheel uprights at brake caliper supporting brackets;
Use larger half shaft flange bolts;
Use larger diameter half shafts or stronger half shaft material;
Reinforce differential housing and cover by enlarging the ribs;
Improve oil-tightness of differential cover by using an O-ring gasket;
Use slightly longer or stronger input shafts;

Bond wire mesh covering intake trumpets instead of using screws which might become loose and fall into the intake.

As all these modifications could be carried out only after the Le Mans race, the much fancied Porsches, three of which had been faster in practice than their fastest opponents—the Ford GT40 driven by Pedro Rodriguez and Luciano Bianchi—faced the starter with very little hope of success as no 908 had ever run for over 3,000 miles without meeting serious trouble. But only those with a deep inside knowledge knew this and they certainly also knew why they had prepared three privately entered 907 long-tail cars, driven by first-class crews, as carefully as if they had been works cars.

The works entires were four long-tail 908s:

908 013 for Stommelen/Neerpasch
908 014 for Patrick/Buzzetta
908 015 for Siffert/Herrmann
908 016 for Mitter/Elford

After the Zeltweg trials, 908 013 had been modified back to standard suspension geometry and all cars were fitted with the rear fins and horizontal wing incorporating two flaps connected to the rear suspension. This arrangement not only resulted in better straight line stability but also made the car more stable under severe braking, presumably because of better rear wheel adhesion. All cars had the 85 mm bore engine and their maximum speed on the straight was approximately 200 mph.

The suspension settings included the now usual —45' camber front and rear, but in the interests of straight line stability, which at Le Mans is all-important, the castor angle had been increased to 7°. In spite of the aluminium frame, all cars weighed between 702 and 708 kg. ie, more than 50 kg over the minimum weight, this being caused by the long-tail body, the rear fins and wing, the six Marchal headlights, the supplementary battery and the supplementary alternator. The gear ratios were as follows: 15:35, 18:32, 22:28, 25:26, 27:23, 29:21 with crown wheel and pinion 8:35 and constant mesh pinions 24:26.

Apart from some minor trouble, some difficulties experienced during practice indicated that the cars were still far from mature. An example of this occurred when the bush centring the constant mesh shaft of 908 014 in the end cover came loose and was trapped between the flywheel and the gearbox housing which it split. Following this a locking screw was added on all cars to keep the bush in place. No such easy remedy could be found for the two alternator failures which occurred during practice, making the outlook for the race rather gloomy—quite literally. The gearbox cooling scoops proved quite efficient, however: they lowered the oil temperature from 135° C to 118° C.

The three 907s were 005 for Lins/Soler-Roig, 006 for Linge/Buchet and 008 for Spoerry/Steinemann. Except for their 2.2-litre eight-cylinder engines and the very slightly lower first and second speed gearing, they were identical to the cars used the previous year. They were back on narrow tyres, as in 1967, in the interests of lower drag and also weighed some 50 kg over their 600 kg minimum weight limit.

As expected, the Porsches took the lead from the start, but after only $2\frac{1}{2}$ hours of racing, the Siffert/Herrmann car stopped with a broken gearbox casing, probably following a ball bearing failure. On all cars which ran for more than three hours, the free movement of the clutch pedal had to be adjusted several times as the fulcrum pivot of the release lever worked its way further and further into the magnesium housing, a problem that they had not met before, and on car 908 013, the only one which finished the race, the cooling blower belt broke three times in quick succession, probably due to insufficient tension. In this and the two other cars still in the race, the main alternators failed after three to four hours. On 908 014, the alternator suffered a mechanical failure which led to the car's retirement.

Meanwhile the bracket taking the auxiliary alternator had broken on all three cars still in the race and, in the case of 908 016 (Mitter/Elford), a new alternator was fitted which led to the car's disqualification as, according to the rules, only parts but no complete units may be changed. In 908 013 the auxiliary alternator worked to the end of the race, though due to its low output, the battery had to be changed once in the course of the night. Altogether this car spent 1 h 27 m 45 s in the pits but Neerpasch and Stommelen still finished in third place behind the Rodriguez/ Bianchi GT40 and the 907 driven by Spoerry and Steinemann who spent almost exactly one hour less in the pits: their only unscheduled stop was made to replace the windscreen wiper. The two other 907s also retired, 006 after six hours' racing due to a defective starter motor and 005 when a big end failed, probably due to a low oil level in the tank of the dry sump system.

For the first time the Constructors' World Championship went to Ford, and only the Porsche (and probably also the Bosch) engineers knew that a miracle alone could have brought victory into the Porsche camp: pre-race investigation had indicated that the main alternator on the blower shaft was submitted to accelerations up to 120 g originating in engine vibrations.

Developing the 908 for 1969

Although, since July, work had been proceeding on the design of the $4\frac{1}{2}$-litre 12-cylinder Type 917 which was to be homologated as a sports car, it was not to be expected that this more powerful model could be sufficiently developed in time to become Porsche's principal asset in the 1969 season. For another year, Porsche would have to rely on the Type 908, and every effort was made to make it really competitive. Obviously, they were going to take advantage of the fact that the CSI regulations for 1969 did not require a minimum weight any more for prototype cars, that both the so-called luggage room and the spare wheel could be deleted and that minimum dimensions were no more required for the windscreen.

These modified regulations made light weight the order of the day once more and led to the adoption of an open body, the higher drag coefficient of which could more or less be offset by lesser frontal area. Consequently, only open-bodied cars (which Porsche call Spyders) and long-tail coupés were built for 1969 and used as required. The first Spyder, fitted with front spoilers and articulated rear flaps, was tried in the wind tunnel in December 1968 and, after a few modifications had been made to its main shape, an air drag coefficient with driver on board of Cw=0.506 was arrived at with a downthrust of —15 kg front and —37 kg rear (respectively —33 and —82 lb) at an air speed of 93 mph.

Related to the frontal area S=1.266 m², the total drag S x Cw was 0.6406, comparing with S x Cw=0.05803 for the short-tail coupé, showing the Spyder to have a 10 per cent higher drag than the previous year's car. To compensate for this, however, the Spyder weighed only some 590 kg (1,300 lb), about 60 kg (130 lb) less than the 1969 long-tail cars without special night equipment and this represents a saving of some 45 kg (100 lb) compared with a hypothetical short-tail coupé which was never built. The weight distribution in the Spyder was 37 per cent on the front axle and 63 per cent on the rear axle. Another advantage of an open-bodied car is that it is always driven slightly faster (at least in good weather) thanks to the better visibility. Unfortunately, however, the Spyder's drag factor was notably increased by the additional large front spoilers which, in practice, were found to be

Twenty-five Type 917 coupes lined up in the factory forecourt in April 1969 for homologation by the CSI in the 'sports car' Group 5.

917 aluminium frame (1969). Weight 47 kg (103 lb).

The 917 was placed eighth in its first race, the 1,000 km of Nurburgring in 1969.

Type 917 engine with two-row fuel injection pump. The cooling blower is driven from the central power take-off gear on the crankshaft. Thanks to the space cam control of the injection pump, the injectors could be located at the top of the intake pipes as in the 90° engine, improving the homogeneity of the mixture.

Below: Porsche 917 long-tail coupe with mobile rear flaps (Le Mans 1969)

Flat twelve-cylinder flat 12 engine in Type 917. Note the diagonal tubes stiffening the engine bay and the pivot of the rear upper radius rod.

Type 917 transmission unit of cast magnesium suitable for four- or five-speed gear sets.

Jo Siffert trying out the 917 PA at Weissach. This car had larger tanks but was otherwise generally similar to the 917 coupe. Its main purpose was to gain experience for developing the 917 for the 1970 season.

917 PA. The rear pyramid and diagonal reinforcement of the engine bay are clearly visible.

The 908/03 in its last race as a works car, the 1971 Nurburgring 1,000 km race. The new finned tail reduced the drag compared with the 1970 version.

necessary, especially when in May 1969 the CSI declared the mobile rear flaps to be illegal. Later wind tunnel tests indicated that the drag coefficient had been raised to a horrifying Cw=0.7.

The first wind tunnel tests of the Spyder brought some interesting points to light. One of them was that lower tyres reducing the ground clearance from 11 to 10 cm (ie by 0.4-in) reduced the drag coefficient by 2 per cent from the original Cw=0.523 to Cw=0.514, without notably altering the (negative) lift conditions. Another interesting finding was that compared with a normal windscreen protecting the two seats, a screen of which the upper edge is turned up, so as to form a rain gutter, reduces the drag by another 2 per cent, giving a 0.01 lower Cw factor. This was explained by the fact that in the case of the turned up edge, the air stream was deflected by the windscreen so that it rejoined the upper rear deck of the body tangentially, whereas with the smooth screen, it came down into the cockpit and was sharply deflected again by the rear bulkhead. Tests were also made with the air stream directed at an angle to the car's longitudinal axis (to simulate side wind driving conditions) : they indicated that in this case, the downthrust was reduced and that the aerodynamic centre of pressure was some 0.92 m (36-in) ahead of the centre of gravity, a fact hinting at a certain side wind sensitivity.

Further developments in the course of the winter 1968/69 were aimed mainly at the following points :

Improving the brakes ;

Developing titanium rear wheel spindles and hubs ;

Increasing body stiffness and reducing body weight ;

Developing the five-speed gearbox Type 916 that had already been used in less important races and which was to replace the much too heavy six-speed gearbox;

Increasing the life of the alternator and starter motor by better insulation from engine vibrations and heat transmission.

In many cases the brake pads had been worn into a wedge shape. Rig tests showed that this was the result of the pad being pressed so hard on to the caliper by tangential force from the rotating brake disc that it was prevented from moving out at the trailing edge. It was even found that with aluminium brake calipers the aluminium deformed plastically under the high pressure, forming an indentation retaining the brake pad supporting plate and taking up part of the pressure applied by the piston. The remedy was to move the piston towards the abutment on the caliper to apply the pressure assymetrically to the brake back plate, to chrome-plate the abutment and to modify the brake pads in such a way that the back plate projected approximately 0.3 mm (1/10-in) beyond the side of the lining material This experimental solution apparently never found its way into an actual car however, as drilled brake discs soon brought a simpler solution with other attendant advantages.

For the new cars, the width of the front brake calipers was increased to accommodate nearly 18 mm (0.7-in) thick linings. Provided the ventilation was sufficient it was reckoned that this would allow them to get through the Daytona and Le Mans 24-Hour races without a change of brake pads, which proved to be correct.

The development of titanium rear wheel hubs which were some 0.75 kg (1.65 lb) lighter than steel hubs, mainly consisted of investigating the operating conditions of the wheel bearings at the higher temperatures resulting from the lesser heat conductivity of titanium. The tests, which were done in an oven, showed that the play in the bearings did not change to any great extent if the hub material was titanium instead of steel. Neither did it make a significant difference whether the central hub locking bolt was tight or loose.

H

In the body department, the main object pursued was to lighten those parts which, in the previous season, had been stiffened up by adding balsa wood, without reducing their stiffness. This object was achieved by Porsche's plastics department by incorporating Lonza-Tubus mats into the panels. The front body lid which was reinforced by this means weighed only 1 kg, ie 600 gr (1.3 lb) less than the old balsa-reinforced lid.

Such small savings in weight may seem unimportant, but when every part is closely investigated to save weight, as is the case with Porsche, many small savings finally add up to several hundredweights and only this can explain that, for instance, at Le Mans, where all cars are carefully weighed, the Porsche 908s of 1969 were from 100 to 140 kg (220/310 lb) lighter than any other 3-litre prototype.

The previous racing season had indicated that the alternator troubles were caused primarily by engine vibrations. It was thought that the trouble could be cured by removing the alternator from the blower shaft and relocating it on a rubber-mounted bracket where it was driven by a cog belt from one of the camshafts. This was still only a makeshift solution, but for the time being no measures were taken to suppress the vibrations at their origin by using a different crankshaft design.

As part of the development programme for 1969, two long-tail cars were sent to Monza for a long-distance test in view of the forthcoming Daytona 24-Hour race. The full 10 km circuit including the two bankings was used, and the opportunity was taken to compare three different types of Dunlop tyres.

The two cars sent to Monza were 908 014 and 015 to which the following major experimental components and parts were fitted:
The engine crankcase was cast in RZ 5 magnesium alloy;
The injection pump had a new space cam;
The cooling blower was driven by twin V belts;
The alternator was relocated as explained above;
A modified five-speed Type 916 gearbox was used;
A new tooth design was adopted for the crown wheel and pinion;
The clutch discs were reinforced and a new type of release bearing was used;
Reinforced front uprights were used with titanium stub axles and hubs;
Titanium rear hubs were fitted;
The starter motor, alternator, silver zinc battery and the Marchal and Cibie headlights were all experimental;
An electric rev counter was used.

The new RZ 5 magnesium alloy used for the crankcase had a better high temperature strength than the AZ 91 alloy used for previous prototypes and also for production cars. The RZ 5 alloy contains 5 per cent zinc and 0.7 per cent zircon. It is in use for all cast parts operating at comparatively high temperatures in current Porsche racing cars, such as engine crankcase, transmission casing, etc.

The main difficulties experienced with the experimental parts were a broken V belt which had insufficient clearance from the blower cowling, vibration in the injection pump drive causing the engine to run irregularly, unreliable electric rev counters, and too weak batteries which, after some time, did not deliver enough current to operate the self-starter. Following this, the 45 amp-hour silver zinc battery was removed from one car and replaced with two lead batteries of 27 amp-hours each, of which only one was connected at a time, the other being kept in reserve for emergencies.

Slight directional changes were noted when accelerating and braking; they were traced to insufficiently stiff steering box mountings which had already been reinforced in later cars. The Cibié headlights were found to be the better ones and in view of the 1969 regulations which did not require a spare wheel, both cars were run without one for part of the tests.

Unfortunately, neither of the two cars completed the long-distance tests: after some 625 miles, Willy Kauhsen crashed 908 014 which was completely gutted. According to the driver's report, the accident could have been caused by a defect in the steering. The other car, driven by Karl von Wendt, ran off the road after some 18 hours of driving (in which it had covered some 2,140 miles) probably due to the formation of ice in the Lesmo bends. In this case too, the car was destroyed by fire. Both drivers were unhurt but the fire damage made it difficult to draw full conclusions from the endurance run and this curtailment was to have catastrophic consequences. After one of the cars had run for 18 hours at Monza without any great difficulties, the Porsche engineers were looking forward with some confidence to the Daytona 24-Hour race for which five brand new cars (908 022 to 026) sporting long tails with mobile flaps had been entered. All were up to the latest specifications which included a light alloy gear driving the intermediate shaft of the camshaft drive. This broke in all five cars. The first of them stopped after 9 h 23 m of racing, the last after 17 h 6 m when the car was leading the race, 45 laps (approximately $1\frac{1}{2}$ hours) ahead of the Lola which ultimately won! As the Monza engines were also fitted with this new type of gear, it can be assumed that if the endurance tests had proceeded for a full 30 hours, as scheduled, this weakness would certainly have been discovered. And at Le Mans, another weakness which would probably have been discovered put several cars out of the race. Just as unexpected was the fact that all cars broke their exhaust system, a trouble that had not been experienced at Monza. This can easily be explained by the fact that with the Daytona gearing, the engines ran much more frequently in a range setting up critical vibrations in the exhaust system. At Daytona there was another case of V belt breakage, a trouble that plagued the cars throughout the season, even though twin belts were now used. These breakages could never be reproduced on a test rig and were probably caused by brutal gear changing in racing. Needless to say, the light alloy timing gear was quickly discarded!

The Sebring 12-Hour race had nearly as catastrophic results as the Daytona 24-Hour race. In this case too, the problems encountered can be traced to the fact that the preliminary test run could not be completed as scheduled.

The new Type 908/02 Spyders were entered for the first time in the Sebring race. Their aluminium frames were very similar to those previously used for the coupés, except that because of their light and short tail, the rear pyramid type girder had been discarded.

Before the cars were sent to America, one of them was to be tested on the Weissach destruction course, as was now normal practice for any new type of car. Unfortunately, snow made the track unusable until very shortly before the cars were due to depart. There remained only enough time for roughly setting up the suspension on the circular pad. As a replacement for the endurance test, two cars were sent in haste to Sebring where the track was hired for private testing. They ran for 16 hours, but as rain fell for nine of these, the cars were not submitted to the same stresses as they would have been on a dry track. Nevertheless, hopes were running high in the Porsche camp, as both cars had gone through the test with very little trouble. Only after five hours further official practice, a chassis tube holding a rear suspension bracket broke on one of the cars used for the preliminary test. As the car had run for 21 hours when this happened, however, the breakage didn't seem to be a cause for great alarm. But in the race, for which five cars had been entered, a real chassis breakage epidemic broke out.

Ironically, the first car to stop was the one driven by the smoothest driving crew of Herrmann and Ahrens. Then Siffert came in with a broken frame and, as he had already spent some time in the pits following an off-road excursion, his car was also retired. But when Mitter came in with the same disease, the mechanics set down to repair the frame and he eventually finished the race, and when, finally, Stommelen brought in his car with a broken frame, the mechanics had become so efficient at effecting the necessary repair that, co-driving with Buzzetta, he still drove his car into third place. Only Elford, who went off the road twice tearing a front wing away and crushing the oil tank, was unable to break his car in the weak place. The race was eventually won by the John Wyer GT40 driven by Ickx and Oliver who overtook the ailing Ferrari 312P of Amon/Andretti in the last hour.

Though it failed to show up the weakness in the frame, the private practice session organised on the Sebring track before the race had not been without interest and drew attention to some weak points:

Weight reduction had been taken a little too far as far as one gear in the gearbox was concerned; a heavier gear was fitted for the race.

The throttle cable stuck. Another type was fitted following rig tests at the factory.

The tail flaps had levers which were too short causing excessive stresses in the linkage. They also seemed to have little effectiveness. This had already come to light in the wind tunnel when, as an experiment, the right- and left-hand flaps had been tested at different angles. Apparently the tail was too short for the flaps to act with a sufficient leverage on the body.

A very important innovation tried out in the course of the Sebring preliminary practice was an engine with a flat crankshaft in which second order reciprocating forces cancelled each other out instead of adding up. This very noticeably reduced the engine vibrations, though a much more complicated exhaust system was required. In this engine the firing order was as in the Type 771 engine: 1, 7, 2, 8, 5, 3, 6, 4. The drivers definitely rejected this type of engine as having less punch than the old one. This was not reflected in the lap times, however, and for the race all the cars were fitted with an engine incorporating this new crankshaft.

As the long-distance tests at Sebring had confirmed previous experience with titanium front stub axles and hubs, these were used for all Type 908 Spyders made.

Of the Sebring cars, two had slightly more angled steering levers, producing a steering geometry which more closely approached the Ackermann principle. As they were certainly not found to give any advantage, they were not used for other races and up to now all Porsche racing cars have an approximately 50 per cent Ackermann steering geometry.

In the meantime, investigations on self-starter failures had shown that these were not always caused by vibrations; neither in many cases could the battery be held responsible when the motor would not crank the engine. In the course of the private practice session at Monza, it had been noticed that the engine would restart without any difficulty immediately after it had been stopped, but would not restart after it had stood still for a few minutes. The explanation for this was that, with no draught to cool the starter motor, the heat transfers from the engine caused the motor to overheat excessively. Following this discovery, a cooling duct was added before the Daytona race to cool the self-starter, but despite this a temperature of between 60° and 70° C was measured after five minutes' standing in the course of the Sebring preliminary practice. As a remedy a titanium plate was inserted between the starter motor flange and the engine crankcase, titanium having a much lesser heat conductivity than steel. Supplementary ducts to cool the gearbox were also found to be

Zünd folgen   908   *Zünd Abst 90°*

908   1. Zündfolge   18 26 45 37

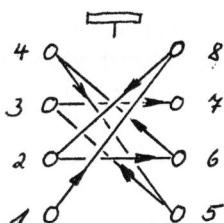

4			8
3			7
2			6
1			5

Kw Hub3. versetzt
Massenausgleich
Sehr schlecht

908   2. Zündfolge   15 27 48 36

4			8
3			7
2			6
1			5

gleiche KW u. NoK. W
Massenausgl.
Sehr schlecht

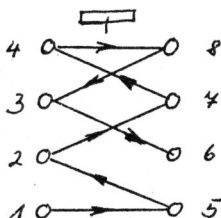

908   geänd. Kw   1 4 28 53 64

4			8
3			7
2			6
1			5

2x4 Hub3.in 1.Ebene

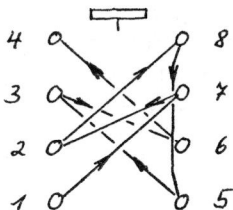

The three firing orders of the 908 engine. In the first two arrangements (upper two drawings) the crank pins are in two planes at an angle of 90° to each other. In the third and final arrangement, all the crank pins are in the same plane. In this case, the inertia forces of the second order are fully balanced.

necessary to lower the gearbox oil temperature from 130/140° C to about 110/120° C.

Originally it had been intended to use Dunlop tyres of the new dimension 4.75/10.00-15 on the front wheels and 5.50/13.60-15 on the rear wheels. Following comparative tests at Sebring, however, lower profile tyres of the dimension 4.50/11.60-15 were used at the front, these improving lap times by anything between two and three seconds (best lap time by Siffert in 2 m 43.0 s).

On the occasion of the preliminary practice at Sebring, another interesting idea was tried out and finally adopted: the aluminium tube frame was fitted with a valve that made it possible to pressurize it. Where necessary, the frame tubes were drilled so that the air circulated through the whole frame. After assembly, the frame was put under pressure and the pressure drop, due to inevitable small leaks in welds, was recorded against time. This made a quick subsequent check for any cracks very easy, the frame becoming suspect as soon as the pressure dropped appreciably faster than originally.

For the record, the gear ratios used at Sebring were 13:29, 18:29, 22:29, 25:26, 27:23 with crown wheel and pinion 7:31.

The race also showed that the Ferrari 312P would certainly become Porsche's main opponent in the course of the season: it was heavier than the 908 but made up for it by a more powerful 12-cylinder engine and it did the fastest practice lap.

Brands Hatch 1969: first victory for the 908/02

While the racing department was under full pressure to get 25 units of the 917 ready for homologation by mid-April 1969, two problems had to be solved in connection with the 908 before the next Championship race at Brands Hatch. One was the frame problem. After some hesitation it was decided to revert to the rear pyramid girder which added 2 kg (some 4.2 lb) to the frame rather than to reinforce the existing simplified frame. The modified frame could not be tried out on the destruction course at Weissach before the Brands Hatch race, but proved fully satisfactory when it was eventually put to the test before the Targa Florio. Just before the cars departed for Brands Hatch, news came from Sicily, where a 908/02 Spyder was involved in some preliminary practice for the Targa Florio, that a lower rear suspension wishbone had failed. The lower rear wishbones were reinforced in a last minute effort on all the Brands Hatch cars which were also fitted with larger diameter radius rods.

The second task that had to be done quickly was to evolve a system to accelerate refuelling with funnel and can, as prescribed at Brands Hatch, without risk of overfilling and spilling the fuel. This problem was solved by the use of a funnel with a quick screw connection and a spill tube.

At Brands Hatch, the Ferrari driven by Amon and Rodriguez again proved to be the strongest opponent for the Porsches: only Siffert could keep in contact with it. For the first time in the history of Porsche, except for trials at Weissach, a works entry was fitted with Firestone tyres (all weather profile R125, rain mix B11). With appropriate anti-roll bar settings, Siffert was 1.5 s quicker with these tyres than with the new Dunlop mix 212 and 1.7 s quicker than with the usual Dunlop dry mix 184. He finally secured the pole position with a time of 1 m 28.8 s, 0.2 s quicker than Amon on the Ferrari and 5.8 s quicker than the previous best time he had achieved the year before on an eight-cylinder 907.

In view of the high rate of wear of the Firestone tyres, which would not last for more than three hours, and the cramped pit situation at Brands Hatch, which did not allow more than two cars to be serviced at a time, it was decided to run only Siffert's car on Firestone tyres and to change his front tyres after $1\frac{1}{2}$ hours, his rear tyres after 3 hours and his front tyres again after $4\frac{1}{2}$ hours of racing, so that only one jack would have to be used at a time.

Of the cars entered for the Brands Hatch Six-Hours, 908/02 007 and 908/02 008 (Herrmann/Stommelen and Mitter/Schütz) had an engine fitted with the new crankshaft, while 908/02 010 and 908/02 011 (Elford/Attwood and Siffert/Redman) drove the old 'rockers'.

When Siffert's engine was warmed up, 20 m before the start, there was a great panic: only one ignition circuit was working. In great haste, the electronic control box was changed but there was no improvement. Then the mechanics changed the distributor : no improvement either. There was no time to try a change of coil and only 30 s before the start did the mechanics close the bonnet.

But Siffert was in great form and, with only one ignition circuit functioning, he left the Ferrari behind, even if on the straight the revs were 300/400 rpm below normal. Only when the car was back in the factory was it found that only the first electronic control box was actually defective and that, in the haste before the start, the replacement box had been wrongly connected.

As the Ferrari had a puncture and slowed down at the end of the race because the throttle cable had stretched, Siffert and Redman won comfortably while Mitter/ Schütz and Elford/Attwood took second and third places. Tyre changes and refuelling stops went exactly according to plan and only the Stommelen/Herrmann car fell back when one of its tanks was damaged by debris left on the track by Bonnier's crashed Lola.

Incidentally, just for a check on the modified chassis' reliability, this car was the one that had already done some 625 miles' destruction testing at Weissach. All the Brands Hatch cars used slightly different gearing, the set chosen by Siffert being 13 :29, 17 :31, 19 :27, 23 :28 and 25 :26.

Only after the Brands Hatch race could a Spyder be taken to the Nürburgring for final setting up. It was found that the handling could still be improved by different shock absorbers.

In the meantime, five long-tail cars, of which one was to be used for practice, were being prepared for the Monza 1,000 km race : 908 026 for Siffert/Redman, 908 027 for Mitter/Schütz, 908 028 for Elford/Attwood, 908 025 for Herrmann/ Ahrens and 908 024 as a practice car. Gear ratios were 13 :29, 18 :30, 20 :25, 26 :25 and 28 :23 with crown wheel and pinion 7 :31. All but the Herrmann/Ahrens car used an engine with the new type of crankshaft. 908 025 and 026 had already run at Daytona ; the others were brand new. All were without front spoilers and were fitted with tail fins and a horizontal mobile flap wing. Again comparative tests were made with Firestone and Dunlop tyres, mainly on the practice car, whereupon all drivers decided to use Firestones 4.25/10.20-15 front and 5.50/12.20-15 rear, profile R125, mix B14. These tyres were certainly faster, but as it turned out they were less reliable than the Dunlops. Nevertheless, both the Ferraris were clearly faster than the Porsches and only Siffert could keep up with them : his best practice lap of 2 m 48.7 s was the second best overall, just half a second slower than Chris Amon's best in a Ferrari, while the second Ferrari driven by Rodriguez and Schetty was faster than the other Porsches.

Both practice and race proved that contrary to drivers' impressions, the new engine, easily recognisable by the cross-over layout of the injection tubes, was by no means slower than the old 'rocker'. In the race itself, again only Siffert could keep up with the Ferraris, but to everyone's surprise the long-tail Porsches were hardly any faster on the straights than the open-bodied Ferraris which were at an advantage in the fast bends. Then the treads began to fly off the Italian car's tyres. The Porsche camp, which used similar tyres, was plagued by the same trouble when Udo Schütz lost a tread and a tyre burst on Elford's car shortly before the end of the race, which led to the complete destruction of the car while the driver was fortunate to escape injury. The final decision came when the Amon/Andretti Ferrari stopped with a blown engine while Rodriguez went off the road as a consequence of another tyre failure.

Mitter had trouble with the gearchange linkage in which a small plastic bush in the flange connecting the linkage with the gearbox selection shaft broke and had to be changed. After a short time, the part again broke and the engine was over-revved as the driver missed the gearchange. Investigation at the factory showed that there were blowholes in the moulding, notably reducing the effective wall thickness: from then on, those bushes were turned from a solid piece of plastic. On Elford's car, the V belt driving the cooling blower broke twice, an old trouble which was never quite eradicated, even by the use of twin belts, as it proved impossible to reproduce racing gearchange conditions on a test rig. Elford's driving seemed to be particularly hard on those belts.

Targa Florio and Spa 1969

Five 908/02 Spyders were entered for the Targa Florio where the competition was rather weak, Ferrari not having entered and Alfa Romeo being present only with rather slow 2- and 2.5-litre cars. In this case, there was no alternative to Dunlop tyres as a special type with reinforced sidewalls had been developed at Porsche's request for this particular race in which tyres are very easily damaged.

For the development engineers, the race was not without interest, however. A cooling blower V belt broke again in Elford's car (908/02 013) which probably cost him and Maglioli the victory. On 908/02 015 (Herrmann/Stommelen) a rubber bush came out of the steering box bracket and had to be replaced while on the Larrousse/Lins car (908/02 010) one of the taper bolts of the gearchange linkage flange broke and could not be replaced, as the broken part could not be removed. This apparently was caused by the taper of the bolt not exactly matching the taper of its seat. But except for 908/02 012 which Attwood crashed, all cars finished, Mitter/Schütz on 908/02 014 winning ahead of two other Porsches while Elford again broke the lap record, this time in 35 m 08.2 s, nearly 1 m faster than his previous record with an eight-cylinder 910, but it must be borne in mind that the circuit improves from year to year. The gear ratios of the winning car were 13:29, 18:30, 19:26, 23:27, 27:25 with crown wheel and pinion 7:31. The other cars were very similarly geared.

For the Spa 1,000 km race, long-tail cars were used again and a 917 (917 002) was also brought along for its maiden race, mainly with the aim of roughly sorting it out during the practice period. Though the new car ran with a short tail, it was very unstable and continuous rain during practice hardly afforded any opportunity for trying out various settings. Without much hesitation Siffert decided to drive a 908 and Mitter took the 917 round for only one lap before retiring with a broken valve, possibly as a consequence of over-revving the engine at the start. As race day was dry, the three 908s used Firestone tyres which practice had shown to give better straight line stability, though the inconsistent weather had not allowed any time comparisons to be made. The gearing chosen for the long-tail 908s was 13:29, 18:29, 23:28, 26:25, 28:23 with crown wheel and pinion 7:31 for Siffert/Redman and Elford/Ahrens. Herrmann/Stommelen used an even higher fifth gear: 27:23.

With Pedro Rodriguez at the wheel of the lone works Ferrari, only Siffert could keep up with the Italian car, but then the Ferrari was delayed by an incident with another car and the ensuing pit stop made it lose contact. But again it was observed that the open-bodied Ferrari was just as fast down the straight as long-tail Porsches and a similar fact had been observed with regard to the open Matras on the occasion of the Le Mans preliminary practice.

11

Revised Spyder aerodynamics

FOLLOWING THESE OBSERVATIONS and in view of the fact that the long-tail Porsches had a notably higher maximum speed than the Spyders, it was thought that the latter which had the very high drag coefficient $Cw=0.7$ could be improved aerodynamically. With this in mind, the development team set about producing a new Spyder body differing from the existing one mainly in its higher scuttle and a straighter wing line between the wheels. These modifications quite drastically improved the drag coefficient to $Cw=0.486$, which later tests showed to have deteriorated to $Cw=0.576$ after the inevitable spoilers had been added to improve its stability. Even in this form, however, the improvement compared with the original Spyder was nearly 20 per cent which showed up in a maximum speed increase on the Nürburgring straight of nearly 10 mph. Due to its flat shape, the new Spyder was soon to become known as the 'Sole' among the works personnel. It was developed from the original Spyder by reshaping it with plasticine.

Thanks to its better shape, the 'Sole' required a higher fifth gear so that the gearing adopted for the Nürburgring 1,000 km race was as follows:

908/02 006 (Siffert/Redman), 908/02 010 (Elford/Ahrens), 908/02 011 (Kauhsen/von Wendt), 908/02 015 (Mitter/Schütz), all old type cars: 13:29, 20:31, 22:29, 25:27, 26:25.

908/02 018 (the 'Sole' driven by Herrmann/Stommelen) had a 27:25 fifth gear, the other ratios being similar to the above.

Several of these cars had already been raced before, showing that the policy of entering only brand new cars had now been abandoned, cost being the main reason.

As usual, the track was hired for a private practice session before official practice began. Two cars with the old type body were submitted to a 1,000 km run in the course of which tyre and brake pad wear as well as fuel and oil consumption were checked.

For the race itself, three cars with the new shape of body had been prepared but two of them were destroyed even before the race: Siffert came off the road on the southern loop in the course of a setting-up session and Elford crashed his in official practice. The only remaining car was allotted by ballot and fell to Herrmann and Stommelen. That these incidents happened to the new cars, may not have been just a matter of chance, as later wind tunnel tests showed that they had less down-thrust than the old cars until they were modified accordingly.

In addition to the five 908 Spyders, the factory had also entered a 917 coupé (917 002), which was sorted out as well as it could be during practice but was not considered competitive enough to be entrusted to one of the works crews. In practice, it was driven by the BMW factory drivers Quester and Hahne, when it did a lap in 8 m 37.8 s, but as BMW would not release them for the race, it was finally driven consistently by Frank Gardner and David Piper who had strict instructions to take no risk whatsoever and bring the car over the 1,000 km distance. This was important as a try-out before Le Mans and the car eventually finished eighth overall.

Again the only serious opposition to the 908s came from the lone Ferrari driven by Amon and Pedro Rodriguez. Siffert had done the best practice lap in 8 m 00.5 s on Firestone tyres, while Mitter/Schütz and Herrmann/Stommelen had brought their car round on Dunlop tyres in 8 m 01.3 s and 8 m 04.2 s respectively. Amon had lapped only 0.1 s slower than Siffert and also achieved a new official prototype record in 8 m 03.3 s during the race. But Rodriguez apparently had an off day and could not hold Redman, the Italian car being finally put out of the race by gearbox trouble. In the end, the five works Porsches took the first five places, headed by the Siffert/Redman car, which clinched the World Manufacturers' Championship for the Zuffenhausen factory with Le Mans still to be run.

Le Mans 1969: a great chance jeopardised

As recorded in the chapter dealing with the development of the Type 917, four 908s were entered for the 1969 Le Mans 24-Hour race in addition to the two long-tail 917s from which the reliability necessary for a 24-hour race could not be expected. Three of the 908s were long-tail cars on which, following a last-minute decision by the CSI, the mobile tail flaps had to be fixed. The fourth car was a new long-tail version of the 'Sole' (908 028) to be driven by Siffert and Redman. This new car was based on the existing 'Sole' and had been developed in the wind tunnel which had shown that the good drag originally measured for the 'Sole' ($Cw=$ 0.486) had been spoiled considerably to $Cw=0.576$ by the additional front and rear spoilers that had to be added when the car was track-tested. Replacing the short tail by the cut-off long-tail considerably improved the drag coefficient of the original spoilerless 'Sole' from 0.486 to $Cw=0.363$, though in this condition the downthrust was very small front and rear. As the frontal area of the open car was notably smaller than for the coupé, the product S x $Cw=0.46$ was even better than for the long-tail coupé in which it was 0.474. This explains why the 'long-tail Sole' was as fast on the straight as were the long-tail cars even after the inevitable small front spoilers were added. As it was faster round corners and on acceleration, this was definitely the fastest of the 908 brigade. Accordingly, higher fourth and fifth speed gearing was fitted during practice, the same as for the long-tail cars, except the one driven by Lins and Kauhsen which had an even higher fifth gear. When comparative tests were later made on the Hockenheim track, the maximum speeds reached on the straight, at the braking point for the East Curve, were as follows (according to uncorrected rev counter readings):

908/02 original form	162 mph
908/02 'Sole'	168 mph
908/02 'Le Mans Sole'	174 mph

As a side wind can make a car very unstable down the Le Mans straight, the long-tail Spyder was fitted with twin rear fins which wind tunnel tests had shown to move the centre of pressure back to a position some 1.2 ft ahead of the centre of gravity instead of nearly 3 ft as for the normal 'Sole'. But having very small down-thrust, the car was still unstable at speed: as soon as it was driven over a hump and the front suspension was slightly extended, the downthrust was inverted into strong aerodynamic lift which raised the suspension by as much as 2 in. This was measured in the usual way by attaching a vertical rod to a front wishbone and leading it through a hole in the body: the rod was painted in various colours, and the lift was indicated by the colour which showed up above the wing. Some improvement was obtained by using stiffer springs front and rear, so as to reduce the attitude changes, and in addition stiffer shock absorbers were used at the rear. Despite these, however, it proved essential to add small front spoilers which were fitted high on the front wings, where they presumably had the least effect on drag. With the car in this state, and running on Firestone B14 tyres, Siffert did a lap in 3 m 29 s, 3 s quicker than with the long-tail coupé 908 029 on the same tyres and eventually decided to drive the open car in the race.

Following this decision, the teams were formed as follows:

Long-tail cars—908/01 029 for Lins/Kauhsen; 030 for Mitter/Schütz; 031 for Herrmann/Larrousse.

Open car—908 028 for Siffert/Redman.

All cars were fitted with Cibié quartz iodine headlights and had the following gear ratios: 13:29, 18:28, 23:27, 27:25, 28:22 with crown wheel and pinion 7:31 except 908 029 which had a 29:22 fifth gear.

Siffert/Redman and Lins/Kauhsen were on Firestone B14s, profile R125, the other cars on the usual Dunlop 184 tyres.

In order to obviate a recurrence of the previous year's difficulties, all the 908s used the new smoother engine with a flat crankshaft and everyone expected a 908 to win the race and to beat the faster 917s on sheer reliability.

In contrast to these expectations, however, the first two Porsches which struck serious trouble were 908s. After six hours of racing, a front wheel bearing failed on the Herrmann/Larrousse long-tail car. This had not happened since the large taper roller bearings had been introduced in conjunction with a new type of lubricant in August the previous year. The interference between the outer bearing race and the stub axle was known to be very critical, and apparently insufficient attention to this point had allowed the race to turn on the shaft, causing overheating and destroying the bearing. The whole upright had to be changed which cost the car 20 m in the pits and, as it turned out, victory: in the closest finish ever seen at Le Mans, Herrmann crossed the finishing line only 2 s behind the winning Ford GT40 driven by Jacky Ickx and Jackie Oliver.

But even before the long-tail car stopped for repairs, the long-tail Spyder had shot its bolt. In this car there were no air ducts to cool the gearbox as in the coupés, and the longer tail caused the transmission to overheat so much that the external plastic pipes which fed the gearbox from the oil pump melted, causing the box to run dry. Then, quite unnecessarily, Udo Schütz crashed during the night when lying second behind the 917 driven by Elford and Ahrens. But two Porsches were still comfortably leading the race after some 20 hours of racing when they almost simultaneously came into the pits and gave up: on Elford's 917, the clutch had failed (as described later) and in the Lins/Kauhsen 908, the bearing of the differential driving pinion had failed. This was certainly another weak point as, when the Herrmann/Larrousse car was later dismantled in the factory it was found that this bearing would obviously not have lasted for very much longer. Again this failure can be traced down to the uncompleted endurance test at Monza, the previous winter, for had this gone on for 30 hours as scheduled, such weaknesses would most probably have been discovered.

It remains to be explained why, in the last two hours of the race, as Ickx's Ford and Herrmann's 908 were fighting wheel to wheel for victory, Herrmann, who had the faster and more manoeuvrable car, could not leave the Ford behind. The reasons for this are twofold and have little to do with the fact that at the time

Ickx was about half the age of Herrmann, who, on important occasions, was still almost as fast as anyone.

One reason is that the Ford had been driven very cautiously until the last stages of the race while after its prolonged pit stop to change a front upright, Herrmann and Larrousse had understandably tried to make up time and at the end of the race, with a rather tired engine, the 908 was no faster than the Ford along the straight. It is doubtful, however, if the Porsche's advantage on the straight could have been as great as was thought anyway, as when the engine was put on a test bed after the race it had lost only 10 hp compared with its original power which should not have made the car more than about 2 mph slower.

The second reason is that when Herrmann took over the last spell, he drove the car for only two laps before the brake pad wear warning light lit up. It had been calculated that with the new wider front brake calipers, introduced on the occasion of the Daytona race to accommodate 0.7-in thick brake linings, no brake pad change would be necessary, but nobody had anticipated such a hard-fought finale. To stop and change the pads would have entailed giving the victory away to Ford, so Herrmann, who knew that when the warning light lit up there were still some 2 mm of pad on the back plate, decided to continue but he had to use the brakes with discretion and could not take advantage of the shorter braking distance made possible by the Porsche's lighter weight.

This was the end of the 908 long-tail cars' career with the factory. The 908/02 Spyders were entered for the last World Championship race of the year at Watkins Glen where they took the first three places, whereupon all those still in running order were completely overhauled and sold to private teams or drivers. For 1970, the factory's main weapon would be the 917. But not for every circuit was a 5-litre car with a compulsory minimum weight of 800 kg considered to be the best proposition. In view of the experience gained with the Bergspyders, the development engineers knew how to make a 3-litre car even lighter than the 908/02 which would probably be a better bet than the more powerful 917 on circuits where manoeuvrability was at a premium. The decision was thus taken to develop the 908 further, along with the 917.

The 908/03 Spyder

The new 908 Spyder had practically only the engine in common with the previous version. It took form as early as 1968 as a plasticine 1 : 5 scale model which was tried in the wind tunnel in October that year. Contemporary documents indicate that the intention was to race it in 1969, being then officially called 908/69, but in view of the 917 crash programme and following the great promise shown by the 908/02, its development was shelved for some time.

Being a specialised design intended mainly for comparatively slow circuits, the 908/03, as it was later called, was to be kept as compact and light as possible. As originally designed, the 1 : 5 scale model had a drag coefficient of 0.413. A large number of trials led to a modification of the original shape lowering this to 0.342, with a slightly increased frontal area. However, as the decreased drag required a longer and slightly wider body, it was decided to stick mainly to the original dimensions in the interests of light weight and optimum manoeuvrability.

The first as yet non-running full scale car was tried in the wind tunnel in July 1969. As expected, it had a higher drag coefficient than the scale model, but several modifications improved this from $C_w = 0.495$ to $C_w = 0.375$. In addition to drag and lift data, pressure checks were made at various places on and in the car. An interesting indication was that louvres cut into the top of the front wings increased the depression in the wheel arch (indicating a faster air flow) but had practically no influence on lift conditions. Several shapes were investigated in an effort to prevent positive lift when the front suspension was extended by 80 mm (just over 3 in) producing a positive angle of incidence of 2°. Unfortunately no means was found of achieving this. For the car as originally built and with an air velocity of 155 mph, the following data were obtained:

	Normal position	Front suspension extended 3.15 in
Cw	0.495	0.524
Front lift	—34,5 kg (downthrust)	+21.6 kg
Rear lift	—106.0 kg (downthrust)	—97.0 kg (downthrust)

After several trials, the shape considered to give the best compromise between drag, lift, dimensions and weight produced a drag figure Cw=0.460 with a downthrust of 38.5 kg front and 90 kg rear. But when, early in 1971, a car was again tried in the wind tunnel as actually raced in the Nürburgring 1,000 km race of 1970, the drag was found to have deteriorated to Cw=0.557, as reported later.

An important feature of the 908/03 body is its very low and clear-cut bow. Its aim is to prevent the air from being rammed under the car, which would increase the lift. This feature was also incorporated in the 908/02 Spyders sold by the factory to private owners for 1970.

In general shape and design, the 908/03 closely follows the trend set by the 2-litre eight-cylinder Bergspyder Type 909 which appeared in the last two Championship hill-climbs of 1968. In view of its very light weight, the driver's seat and the engine were moved forward in the aluminium tube frame by moving the five-speed gearbox from its overhung position to a position between the engine and the differential. This was necessary to keep enough weight on the front wheels and the reduced polar inertia gave improved manoeuvrability.

When the car was designed it was borne in mind that the whole exercise was justified only if the vehicle could be kept as light and as small as possible. Not even the smallest detail aimed at achieving this requirement could be neglected; all known means of keeping the car light were to be used and new ones were to be explored. An example of what was achieved in this quest is given by the body shell, made of PVC foam sandwiched between two layers of epoxy plastic material, which weighs only 26.5 lb (excluding the seats), but is nevertheless so rigid that no reinforcement is needed to keep the nose in shape at maximum speed.

Originally this car was due to be fitted with beryllium brake discs which, as already mentioned in an earlier chapter, saved more than 30 lb.—all unsprung weight—compared with cast iron discs. Several surface treatments were tried to increase their life, but no really successful solution could be found within the short time available and the car was finally built with cast iron discs. Several holes were drilled through the discs, however, which not only reduced the weight, but notably reduced the discs' working temperature as some of the holes communicated with the internal cooling vanes, establishing a centrifugal circulation. These perforated discs, known in the factory jargon as Gruyère discs, were successfully tried for the first time on a 917 on the occasion of the private practice preceding the 1970 Daytona 24-Hour race. As part of the weight saving programme, the usual aluminium brake cylinder units with steel pistons were replaced with magnesium cylinder units with aluminium pistons. With these, however, five consecutive applications of the brakes from high speeds made the brake fluid boil. Later investigations on the brake test rig confirmed this boiling problem—it was thought at the time that it could have been cured by using titanium pad back plates or titanium pistons, this metal having only one third of the heat conductivity of steel, but for the time being they were not tried. Unfortunately, for the same braking pressure, the magnesium cylinder units also opened up 1.72 times more than the aluminium units, which made the brakes feel spongy and they were never used.

Titanium was widely used for the new car, not only for those parts that had already been made of this material but also for several others. One of the applications was the differential cage, another the gear selector shaft. At the end of September 1969, a complete car which now had titanium stub axles at the rear too, was ready to face a deadly rig test for which an additional load of 90 kg (200 lb) was carried over the rear axle. The test consisted of accelerating at full throttle right through all the gears and then braking as soon as maximum speed was reached, while simultaneously changing down through all the gears again for a full 24 hours. One complete cycle lasted from 50 to 55 seconds, corresponding to some 12,700 gear changes in 24 hours. Bearing in mind that a completely new gearbox had to be designed for the new car, very satisfactory results were obtained. Only the location of the selector forks on their shaft gave any serious trouble and made it necessary to take the gearbox apart in the course of the test. The titanium differential cage and stub axles went through the test with flying colours and when it was dismantled, the clutch was found to be in such a good state that it was decided to fit it to another car for further testing.

The engine of the 908/03 was practically the same as the previous model. In an effort to remedy the V belt breakages a fluid coupling was incorporated in the blower drive to limit the torque set up by blower inertia. The coupling was driven at 0.83 engine speed and had a slip of approximately 1.5 per cent at peak revs. This solution at last proved entirely satisfactory.

The decision to continue the development of a 3-litre car along with the development of the 917 was taken primarily for the Targa Florio, but even on the Nürburgring the smaller car which only weighed 545 kg (1,200 lb) in its original form was so quick around the German track, even though its engine did not develop more than 350/360 hp, that it was given preference to the 917 for the 1,000 km race. This performance on a mixed course was almost expected after comparative tests had been done, with Hans Herrmann at the wheel, on the new so-called Can-Am course at Weissach just before the Targa Florio, when the following times were obtained:

908/02, 56.2 s
908/03, 52.0 s
917,   52.2 s

The 908/03 was running on 13-in diameter wheels of 9.5 in width front and 14-in width rear as intended for the Targa Florio, though a change to 15-in diameter rear wheels was already contemplated at the time. The 13-in wheels were those used on the Bergspyder Type 909 from which the 908/03 chassis was developed and there had not been time for a change to 15-in wheels. The reason why these were now preferred was the same which had dictated the change from 15- to 13-in wheels three years before when the 910 superseded the Carrera 6: as the 3-litre Formula 1 cars now all used 15-in rear wheels, more modern tyres of lower profile were available for this size.

The change from 13- to 15-in rear wheels took place at a time between the Targa Florio and the Nürburgring 1,000 km race and called for new rear uprights and wider rear rims to fit the new lower profile tyres. The rear rim width was increased to 15-in while the front rim width went up to 11-in, still with 13-in diameter. Driving a car with this equipment and on Firestone tyres, Jo Siffert did a lap in 7 m 41.0 s in the course of a private preliminary practice session before the 1,000 km race, one second faster than the absolute record (official or unofficial) set up only a few months before, in August 1969, by Jacky Ickx on a Formula 1 Brabham using a Ford engine developing some 60/70 hp more. Siffert's time was also 19 s faster than his previous best on a 908/02, which illustrates the enormous advance achieved by the new car using an identical engine.

Despite its very light weight, the 908/03 withstood perfectly the tremendous bashing it took on the Targa Florio course on which it had done some preliminary practice six weeks before the race. Of the four cars entered (two by the Gulf-Wyer team and two by Porsche Salzburg) only one failed to finish, and that was because Umberto Maglioli crashed it on the first lap when the track was still wet. None of the others had the slightest trouble and they finished first, second and fifth with Siffert/Redman ahead of Rodriguez/Kinnunen. The latter also set up a fantastic new lap record in 33 m 36.0 s to overtake the 5-litre Ferrari 512S of Vaccarella/Giunti just before the finish. Fourth place was taken by the privately entered 908/02 of van Lennep and Laine.

While there had never been any question of running a 917 in the Targa Florio, one such car was brought along for the Nürburgring 1,000 km practice to be driven by Jo Siffert for comparison with the 3-litre. Though the big car lapped in 7 m 47.7 s, nearly 50 s quicker than an early car had done the previous year, it was still nearly 7 s slower than the more agile 3-litre. As it was also more tiring to drive and would have required three refuelling stops during the race, where the 3-litre only required two, it was not difficult for Porsche to decide which type of car to use.

In the race two Ferrari 512S, one of them a works car driven by Surtees/Vaccarella, were no match for the more agile 908/03s, of which the two Gulf-Wyer team cars running on Firestone tyres were faster than the two Porsche Salzburg cars on Goodyear tyres. But the latter took the finishing flag in first and second places, driven by Elford/Ahrens and Herrmann/Attwood respectively, after Kinnunen had gone off the road and the engine of the Siffert/Redman car had seized after running with a too low oil level.

As for the rest of the season, the 917 was the more suitable car, the 908/03s of which nine had been made—two development prototypes in 1969 and seven race cars in 1970—were temporarily stored, while development proceeded on the 3-litre engine in view of the proposed ban on any engine above 3 litres for the Manufacturers' Championship, commencing in 1972. The development went along the lines of four valves per cylinder, which made it necessary to provide the cylinder heads with water cooling, as with 16 valves per head the air passages between the valves became too small for efficient cooling. A 32-valve 3-litre engine with air cooled cylinders but water cooled head was eventually fully developed before the factory management decided to pull out from the Manufacturers' World Championship, starting from 1972, when the 12-cylinder cars could not be used any more. One reason for this decision was that the new rules required a minimum weight of 650 kg, which made all the data obtained on lightweight construction useless.

As the new 3-litre engine project was shelved, the 908/03s were taken out of their retirement very much as they had been left the previous year to defend the Porsche name once more in the Targa Florio and the Nürburgring 1,000 km race. But before that, they were taken to the wind tunnel for a check on drag and lift after the minor modifications carried out in the course of the racing season, the most important of which were the adoption of wider wheels and of a 30-mm wide wrap-round horizontal front spoiler.

It was found that from Cw=0.46 the drag coefficient had deteriorated to 0.557 with front and rear lift coefficients of —0.172 and —0.407 respectively. Various modifications including rear wheel spats and reduced front wheel arch openings were tried with little success, the best results being obtained by the addition of vertical tail fins which improved the drag coefficient to Cw=0.532 with little change in lift and these were consequently adopted for 1971 when the 908/03s were again used for the Targa Florio and the Nürburgring 1,000 km race only.

Meanwhile the 3-litre Alfa Romeo 33 had become quite competitive and, though the Targa Florio indicated that the Porsche was slightly faster, the fact that three of the drivers crashed suggests a certain nervousness on their part. But Larrousse was leading at two-thirds distance when he had to proceed for several miles to the auxiliary depot on a flat tyre, leaving the victory to the Italian make and the local schoolmaster Vaccarella co-driving with Nanni Galli.

Before the Nürburgring 1,000 km race a change was made from 15- to 17-in wide rear wheels which private trials on the track had indicated improved the lap times by some 7 s, and the rear part of the body was widened accordingly. With the now compulsory central fire extinguishing system and reinforced roll bar, plus larger wheels and tyres, the weight had gone up to 565 kg, a 20 kg (44 lb) increase on the original version, but this being the model's last race as a 'works' entry, no attempt was made to make up for it elsewhere.

Since the seven cars built in 1970 had now done two Targa Florios and one Nürburgring 1,000 km race between them, two new cars were made and entrusted to the top drivers Siffert and Rodriguez, bringing the grand total of 908/03s made up to 11.

Much to the satisfaction of the pundits who 'were sure these ultra-light cars were dangerous', and to the no lesser consternation of the Porsche engineers who had proved by winning both the Targa and the Nürburgring race the year before that their chassis was up to the worst conditions encountered in racing, the chassis of both the new cars broke (though Rodriguez just reached the finish). As was discovered later, the reason was that the new chassis had not been built up according to the original designs: at the point of breakage where several tubes converge to a welded spider, there should have been one straight-through main tube to which the others were welded, but in the two new chassis what was intended to be the main tube had erroneously been made up of two tubes assembled at the welded nodal point at which the stresses were too high for such an assembly.

At Nürburgring the lone Ferrari was clearly faster than the Porsches which developed nearly 100 hp less, but the 908/03 had their own back on the Alfas, being both faster (except for the Alfa driven by Stommelen) and more reliable, and they had an easy one-two-three victory after engine trouble had stopped the Ferrari.

As trials had proved the 17-in rear wheels to be a definite advantage, it may be surprising that this was not reflected in the lap times achieved either in practice or in the race itself. The reason is that up to 1970 only the best of the 3-litre engines, giving up to (but never more than) 370 hp, were used for important races, but by 1971 the stock of really good engines had been exhausted and the cars were using whatever engines were available, some of which probably had no more than 350 hp, the minimum required to be passed as 'OK'.

After the Nürburgring victory and just to round up the 908 development pro-

Porsche models at the end of 1969: front to rear, 917, 917 PA, 908/02 Spyder, 908 long-tail, 914, 911 S (Monte Carlo), 911 S and 911 R.
The lateral air outlets and the absence of side exhaust pipes indicate that the 917 PA had been brought up to the latest stage when this picture was taken.

Below: This view of the 917 PA cockpit reflects an important aspect of the Porsche racing policy: function is all important; finish is irrelevant.

The general shape of the 917 for the 1970 season was arrived at in October 1969, when experiments were carried out on one of the original 917 short-tail coupes at Zeltweg. The widened wheel arches (to take 15-in wide wheels) and the raised tail can be seen in this picture.

917 drive shaft with Giubo rubber doughnut and ball race sliding joint.

917 rear wheel brake with (at this stage) unperforated aluminium cone. Titanium hub and brake saddle, aluminium brake cylinder units (ATE) with automatic adjustment for pad wear.

Variable rate coil spring made of conical titanium wire for Type 917.

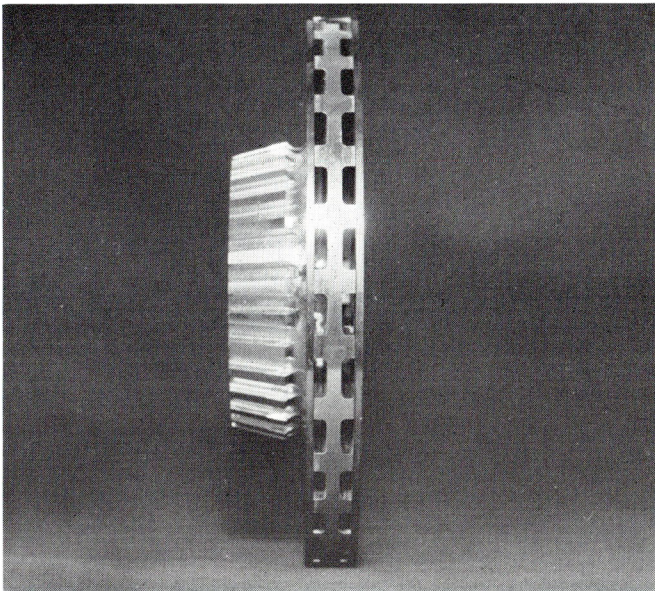

Aluminium copper chrome brake disc for 917. The integral aluminium cone and disc cooling vane carry the riveted copper chrome alloy rings forming the disc.

Front suspension of 1972 Type 917/10 with progressive anti-dive geometry and aluminium alloy wishbone tubes. This also shows the holed alloy 'cone' and the perforated brake disc.

Porsche 908/03. Note the flat front with a small wrap-round sill to deflect air from underneath the car. Also note the near central position of the steering.

Weight is being saved everywhere: the wires of this resistor, part of the electronic ignition system, are wound on a balsa wood frame.

gramme, a car was again tried in the wind tunnel and, as raced at Nürburgring, a drag coefficient of Cw=0.504 was obtained with front and rear lift coefficients of Clf= —0.181 and Clr= —0.233 respectively. Possibly the drag figure, which is lower than before, was improved by smoother shaped tail fins than the roughly made up ones experimented with in the earlier wind tunnel test, but the figure for frontal area given as 1.400 m² in the earlier wind tunnel report is up to 1.570 m² in the final report, mainly due to the wider rear wheels, the widened tail to accommodate them and also to the compulsory full cockpit width, large diameter roll bar, so that in the end the total drag was slightly higher than before. A great merit of the shape, however, was that any change of the angle of incidence or ground clearance obtained by compressing or extending the front and rear suspension up to 30 mm, creating positive or negative angles of incidence of $\frac{3}{4}$°, always *increased* the downthrust effect, except for a slight but insignificant reduction in front downthrust when the front suspension alone was extended.

After 1971 most of the existing 908/03s were sold to private owners, but their main asset of a very light weight had to be sacrificed to the minimum 650 kg rule enforced for 3-litre cars and, even though many of the lightweight parts were exchanged for cheaper and less costly to maintain steel ones, the cars still have to carry some ballast under the present rules.

12

917: the big jump

IN APRIL 1968 I visited the Porsche factory to interview Dipl-Ing Ferry Piëch, Dr Porsche's nephew, who led the company's research and development division from 1965 to the end of 1971. 'Had we known earlier', he said, 'that cars with an engine capacity of 5 litres would have been admitted to take part in the races for the World Championship of Makes, under the proviso that 25 identical units had been made, we would have designed a car to this specification instead of developing a 3-litre.'

This would have been quite compatible with the Porsche racing policy of the period when new cars were built for any important long-distance race, after which they were overhauled and sold to private owners at the end of the season. In the case of the 910, of which more than 20 were sold in accordance with this scheme, this policy had proved to be not much more expensive than running the same cars throughout the season, overhauling them as required and still risking a fatigue failure which would not happen in a new car.

Even the 908 could not have been ready to race in 1968 if Porsche had not started work on it on the assumption that a 3-litre capacity limit would be imposed on Prototypes for 1968, since the CSI's official decision was not taken before October 1967 to come into force on the January 1 1968! But the admission of existing 5-litre cars, like the Ford GT40 and the Lola T70, powered by tuned American V8 pushrod production engines to fill the gaps left by the scarcity of up-to-date 3-litre machinery, took Porsche completely by surprise. They soon recovered from it however and, if someone was to jump at the chance of getting absolute mastery of the situation by making 25 units of a 5-litre model to full racing specification, why should it not be them?

This is how, in July 1968, design was started on a flat-12-engined car of the 5-litre class called the 917, while its engine was cunningly given the 912 project number which was already borne by a production model. In fact however, the production models 911 and 912 were originally known as 901 and 902 (they still are for spare parts numbering) and were renamed only after Peugeot objected to the similarity to their own type numbers. The engine type number 912 no doubt helped to keep the project secret, specially as Porsche had never shown any interest in large engined cars. Certainly Enzo Ferrari, a most interested party, was far from suspecting anything and when, back in 1968, I once told him that Porsche regretted having developed a 3-litre rather than a 5-litre, he would not believe it and said it would be impossible to build an air-cooled engine of that size anyway. He was later to know better.

Not only were the sceptics proved wrong, but Porsche could also muster other weapons than sheer power: they had become experts in light weight construction and aerodynamics. At Le Mans, where all cars are carefully weighed before the race, the 3-litre Porsche longtail coupés of 1969 were 220 lb lighter than the rival 3-litre prototypes of Ferrari, Matra and Alpine-Renault, of which the Matras were open, while the open Porsche was over 300 lb lighter than any of the direct opposition. And if the drag was also 10 per cent lower (which was certainly true of the long-tail cars), they should have been competitive with 10 per cent lower engine power, which they in fact proved to be.

In practice, the 917 engine never had any problem in matching the power of the only opposition which materialized—the Ferrari 512. The Ferrari was not to appear until 1970 however, and, being convinced they could produce their car at the minimum weight required by the rules for Group 5 sports cars over 3 litres, ie, 800 kg (1,750 lb), Porsche did not even bother to bring their flat-12 up to the full 5-litre capacity. In order to speed up its development, the same connecting rod length, the same valve and port sizes and the same bore and stroke of 85 ×66 mm were used as for the 3-litre 908 engine. This gave a total capacity of 4,494 cc. The same valve timing and settings for the fuel injection plant could also be used, the only modification made at the 'top end' being a slight reduction of the included valve angle from 71° to 65° to obtain a more compact combustion chamber. The inlet valve was inclined 30° and the exhaust valve 35° from the cylinder axis, these being the narrowest angles compatible with adequate cooling air passages around the valve guides. As in the 908 engine, all valves were hollow and filled with sodium for cooling, sizes and timing being as follows:
Inlet: diameter 47.5 mm, lift 12.1 mm, opens 104° btdc, closes 104° abdc
Exhaust: diameter 40.5 mm, lift 10.5 mm, opens 105° btdc, closes 75° abdc.

The crankcase arrangements bear no resemblance to the 908 engine however. Just adding four cylinders to the flat-eight would have led to an unacceptably long crankshaft and insurmountable problems of torsional vibrations, specially in view of the fact that, in an air-cooled engine, a slightly larger distance is required to accomodate the cylinder head fins than in a water-cooled unit. In order to keep critical periods above the normal revolution range of the flat-12 engine, the power take-off is located in the middle of the crankshaft rather than at one of its ends. The long crankshaft is thus basically turned into two half-crankshafts of which the common central flywheel is a gear in mesh with another gear driving a layshaft located under the crankshaft and parallel to it. All the timing gears and accessory drive gears are also driven from this main crankshaft output gear and so are not subject to any vibration of torsional origin. This is because the location of

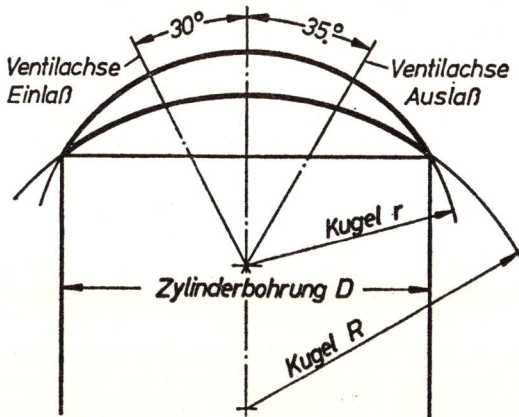

Basic shape of combustion chamber, engine Type 912 (for car Type 917). Ventilachse=valve axis; Einlass=inlet; Auslass=exhaust; Kugel=sphere; Zylinderbohrung=cylinder bore.

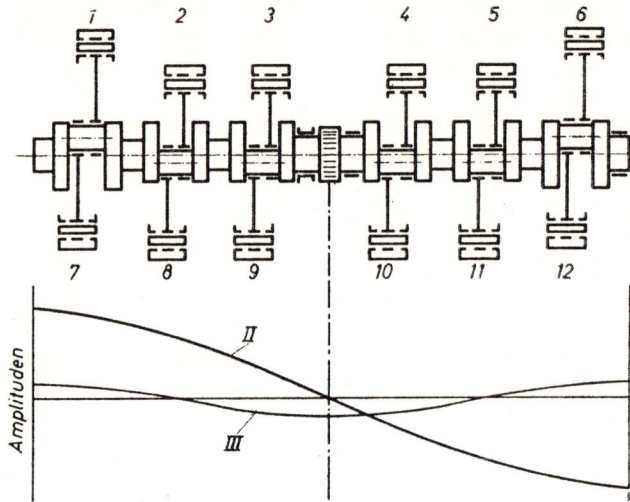

Crankshaft of engine Type 912 with diagram of fundamental (Curve 2) and first harmonic (Curve 3) vibrations.

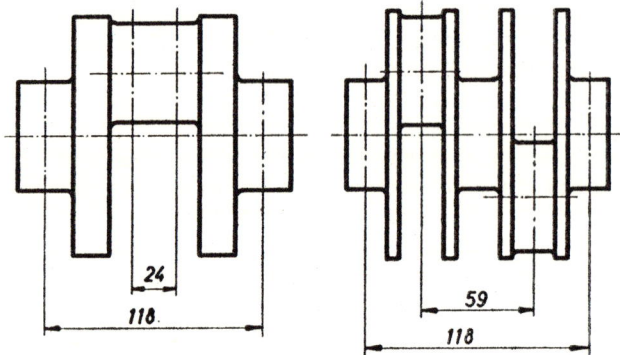

Comparison between a crankshaft with two connecting rods side by side on one crank pin and a crankshaft with one connecting rod per crank pin.

the output gear in the middle of the crankshaft coincides with the node of the fundamental torsional vibration, where the amplitude of the vibration is nil.

Advantage has been taken of the fact that in a flat-12 the same full balance can be obtained as in an in-line-six using the same crankshaft configuration but with the connecting rods of two opposite pistons working side-by-side on a common crankpin. This allows the number of main bearings to be reduced, thus making room for more robust crankshaft webs.

As the central driving gear is supported on both sides, the crankshaft has a total of eight main bearings. This is a comparatively small number for a 12-cylinder engine and reduces friction losses. Compared with the eight-cylinder engine, another gain in this direction was made by reducing the big end diameter from 57 to 52 mm, experience indicating that this would be possible without loss of reliability.

A further contribution towards keeping the crankshaft compact while maintaining an adequate bearing surface is made by feeding the oil for the lubrication of the big ends to both ends of the axially drilled crankshaft. This avoids the necessity for the usual peripheral oil groove in the main bearing shells that would be necessary if the big ends were to be lubricated by oil branched off the main bearings, and these can be made narrower by the width of the groove. The

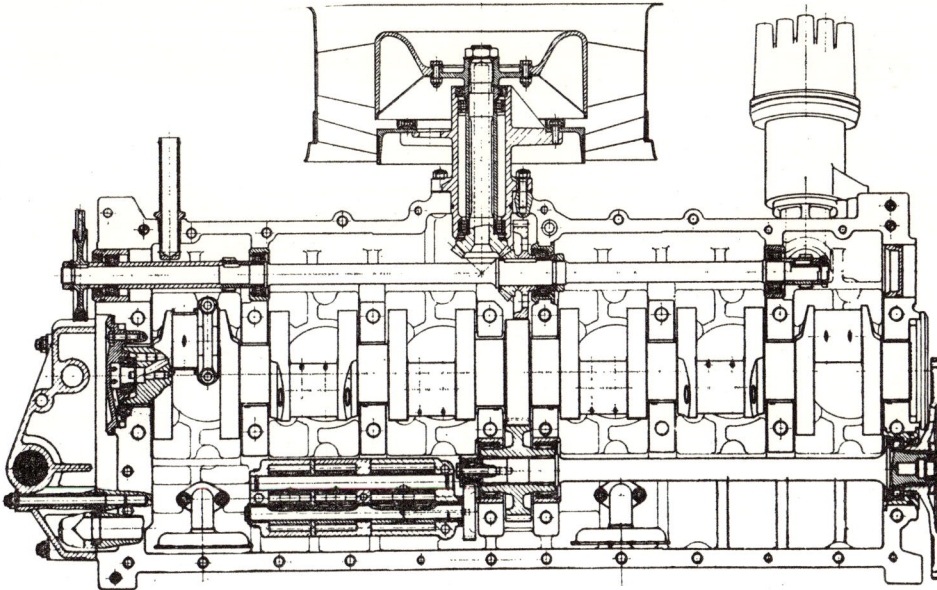

Longitudinal section of engine Type 912.

arrangement also allows the oil to be fed into the crankshaft at a notably lower pressure and the blow-off valve in the pressure pump is set to open at only 70 lb/sq in, which reduces the power absorbed by the lubricating system. The main and big end bearings are the only plain bearings in the engine and another interesting detail is that 1-mm diameter jets, fed from the main gallery, direct oil into the piston to lower the crown temperature by some 30-35° C.

The main bearing shells are held in the two halves of the magnesium crankcase split vertically along its centre line. The magnesium alloy used is the heat-resistant RZ5, as for later Type 908 engines. The two crankcase halves are held by long bolts going through the entire width of the crankcase. In order to avoid excessive stresses or distortion caused by the high coefficient of expansion of magnesium, these bolts are made of a special alloy called Dilavar which has a coefficient of expansion nearly as high as magnesium and aluminium. The same material is used for the long bolts securing the cylinders and cylinder heads to the crankcase, but in this case they are coated with an insulating layer because they are directly exposed to the cooling air and would otherwise run too cold.

In early engines, two alternative crankshaft constructions were used. In one of them, the central power take-off gear is in one piece with the crankshaft, both the gear and the crankshaft being case-hardened. In the other, introduced after the factory had acquired an electronic beam welding machine, the case-hardened gear is welded to the two crankshaft halves of which the pins and journals are induction hardened. This type of welded-up crankshaft was used for most of the unblown 4.5-litre engines. As gears are more durable if the teeth in mesh are not always the same, the 32-tooth power take-off gear drives a 31-tooth gear on the power output shaft which is itself calculated to act as a torsion bar to cushion the drive to the clutch. On its opposite end, the 31-tooth gear drives the triple gear-type oil pump of which two chambers scavenge the crankcase through two individual pick-ups and one feeds the main engine components under pressure. Also there are two pairs of additional scavenge pumps, driven from each end of the exhaust

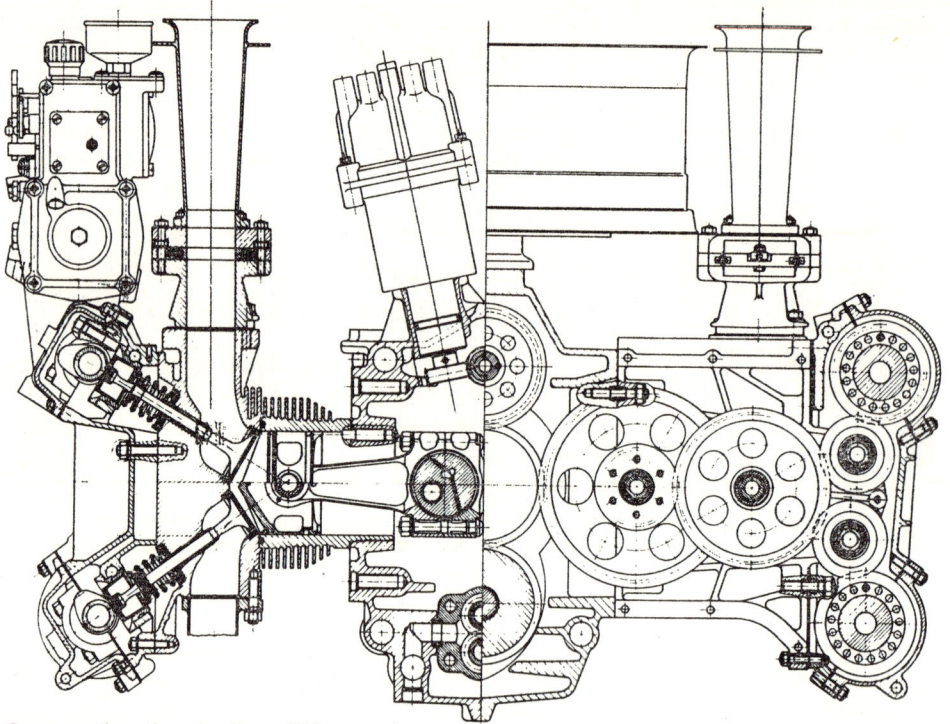

Cross section of engine Type 912.

camshafts, to return excess oil from the cam boxes to the oil tank. The two distributors of the electronic ignition system feeding the 24 plugs, the cooling blower running at 0.895 engine speed and the belt-driven alternator are all driven from a lay-shaft running above the crankshaft. The timing gears to the twin overhead camshafts per bank of cylinders are also driven from the 32-tooth power take-off gear and run in a self-contained magnesium housing. A cog belt drives the Bosch 12-plunger injection pump operating at 260 psi from the left intake camshaft.

The controlled oil feed to the inverted cup tappets is another feature adopted from the 908 engine. The drilling feeding the tappet bore is uncovered only when the tappet is pushed down by the cam, thus reducing the volume of oil going through the cam boxes by some 60 per cent. The cylinder head gasket arrangement is new, however, the gasket taking the form of an 'O' ring inserted into a groove on the upper cylinder face. When the head is tightened down, the gasket is completely compressed and the head and cylinders make direct metal-to-metal contact giving improved heat transfer.

The development of the Type 912 engine was accelerated by the fact that data could be obtained from the Type 916 six-cylinder engine with four camshafts used in practice for the Mugello race in 1967 and later used in a 911 entered for the Tour of Corsica. Most of the inlet and exhaust tuning data were obtained on that engine, while pending the delivery of the flat 12 crankcase, the cooling air flow was studied on an engine having a wooden crankcase. This advanced development was certainly worthwhile as the first flat 12 tried on the test bed immediately produced 542 DIN hp and gave very little trouble, except for a weak point in the crankcase which had to be modified before the model was raced.

In the course of further development for the 1969 Le Mans race, this output was raised to 580 hp at 8,400 rpm with a maximum torque of 52 mkg (376 lb/ft) at 6,600 rpm. The total weight of the engine, without clutch, was 240 kg (528 lb). With gear drive and a horizontal blower wheel, the cooling system was much more efficient than in the 908 engine, absorbing only 17 hp at peak revs. This is only 3 per cent of the total net horsepower and was eventually to become only 2.7 per cent when the engine was further developed and its capacity increased to 5 litres.

Right from the beginning, every effort was made to keep the type 912 engine as light as possible, substituting lighter materials for steel and iron. The interchangeable cylinder heads were, of course, made of aluminium and so were the individual cylinders which had chrome plated bores (the so-called Chromal cylinders); the crankcase, timing gear casing and cam boxes were all cast in magnesium. Titanium was used for the connecting rods and their bolts as well as for several spindles, brackets, linkages etc, while the air ducts and the cooling blower wheel were plastic. In the course of further development, new applications of light alloy or titanium were tried and some permanently adopted. Both these alloys were used for timing and other gears and even a main output shaft made of titanium was tried successfully in the Sebring 12-Hour race of 1970, though the experiment was not repeated as post-race examination showed that the permanent deformation was greater than would be the case with a steel shaft. Even sodium-cooled titanium inlet valves have been developed, with such success that they were used for all the turbo-charged engines which won both the 1972 Can-Am and Interseries Championships. Of the total weight of the original engine, 160 lb or 29.5 per cent was magnesium.

No existing Porsche gearbox was strong enough to take the torque even of the

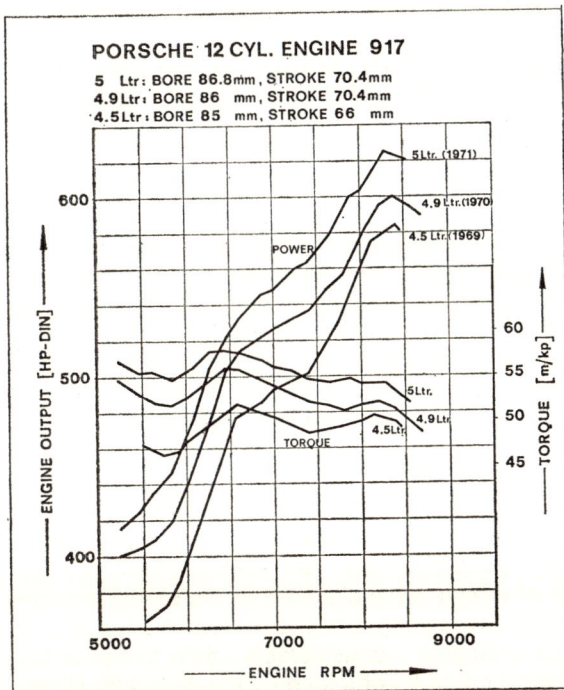

Power and bmep curves of Type 912 engines of 4.5-, 4.9- and 5-litre capacity. Maximum torque 4.5-litre 376 lb/ft at 6,600 rpm. 4.9-litre, 415 lb/ft at 6,400 rpm; 5-litre, 425 lb/ft at 6,400 rpm.

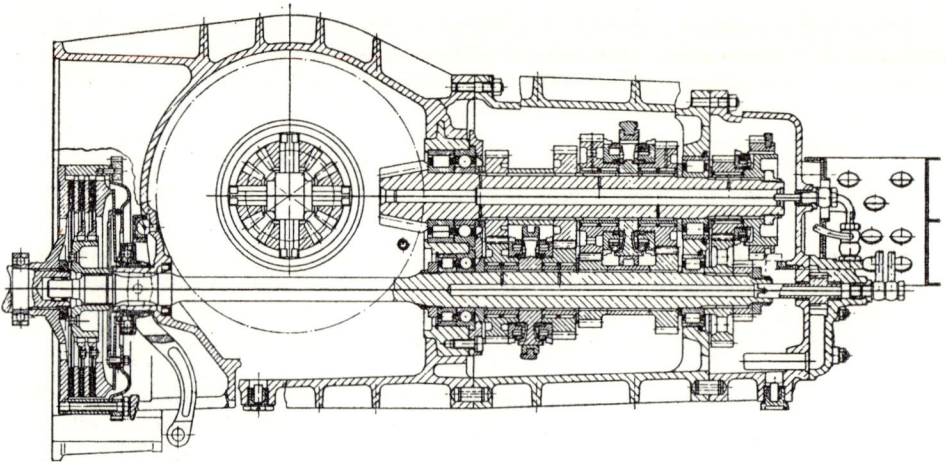

Five-speed gearbox for Type 917.

original 4.5 litre engine. With a magnesium casing and five speeds and reverse, of which all forward gears had full Porsche-type synchromesh, a new heavy duty box was developed, of similar general design to the 908 transmission. Its two shafts ran in two roller bearings each with additional ball thrust bearings at the front end, fifth gear being out-rigged at the rear. Wet sump lubrication was used and, as in the 908, oil was additionally circulated by an external gear-type pump feeding both to the hollow gearbox shafts and to jets spraying the crown wheel and pinion. Following the unfortunate experience at Le Mans when heat melted the external plastic pipes on Jo Siffert's 908 Spyder, the plastic pipes used in the original design were replaced by cast-in passages. A wet sump was prescribed in preference to a dry sump on the grounds of lightness, better reliability through less piping and the fact that a pump of lesser capacity can be used, partly making up for the higher churning losses. The clutch was a Fichtel & Sachs three-disc unit with bonded organic linings and the ZF limited slip differential had a 75 per cent locking factor with pre-loading.

The welded aluminium tube chassis, in which the tubes were as far as possible stressed only in tension and compression, was largely an adoption from the existing 3-litre Type 908, with the characteristic rear pyramid and the detachable diagonal tube across the engine bay. Chassis tubes were used to circulate oil from the front mounted radiator to the engine, the other tubes being interconnected for quick air pressure crack detection as on the 908. Both wheelbase and track dimensions were the same as for the 908 but the cockpit had to be moved forward considerably to make room for the big engine, so that the pedals were actually ahead of the front wheel axis while the spare wheel was moved back over the gearbox. As with all other Porsche racing cars, the frame had to withstand over 600 miles of hard driving over the rough destruction course of the factory's proving ground. Even then, the complete frame with all its brackets weighed only 47 kg (104 lb).

Despite the enormous power, light weight was as much the order of the day as ever. For many years Porsche had used progressive rate springs. Such springs usually have unequally spaced coils of which some close up as the spring is compressed. This entails many coils and a heavy spring. For this reason, the Types 907 and 908 had the front spring units working at a considerable angle to the wishbones, so that the required rate variation could be obtained by the geometrical layout, using non-progressive springs. The same principle was also applied to the 917. At the rear, however, space considerations preclude such a layout and progressive rate springs have to be used. In order to achieve this without weight penalty, the springs are made of tapering titanium wire, the taper accounting for the rate variations. In addition, titanium housings are used, as in the Type 908, for all ball- and Unibal-joints. Only continuous efforts to save weight can prevent addition of weight to a given model as its development calls for reinforcements, and new rules have to be observed. Typical examples of weight-adding rules are those introduced for 1970 requiring an automatic fire-extinguishing plant and safety bag-tanks containing a non-flammable sponge material.

The glass fibre coupé body was certainly not the least interesting part of the car. The final design was a result of extensive wind tunnel test and two alternative interchangeable bolt-on tails were offered: a short one for normal circuits and a long one for very fast circuits. The glass fibre reinforced plastic material used for the construction of the body was Porsche's own development and the original short-tail coupé, complete with seats, very spartan interior trim and mobile flaps weighed only 83 kg (183 lb) to which 12 kg (27 lb) was added by the long tail which reduced the drag coefficient from Cw=0.4 to Cw=0.33. Compared with Cw=0.273 obtained with the long-tail 907, as run at Le Mans in 1967, this is not particularly good but it must be remembered that the 917 was 72 in wide whereas the 907 was only 68 in wide which made the new car more stubby, while the wheel arches were higher. As the frontal area was increased from 1.288 m² to 1.40 m² for the 917, the total drag of the latter was 31 per cent higher than for the 907, but nevertheless with twice the horsepower available, it reached no less than 236 mph on the Le Mans straight in 1969, according to rev counter readings. This is some 20 mph faster than any car had reached there before.

At such speeds, stability is largely a matter of aerodynamics. It is essential, especially with a very light car, that the aerodynamic centre of pressure should be close to the neutral steer centre to avoid instability in side winds and, above

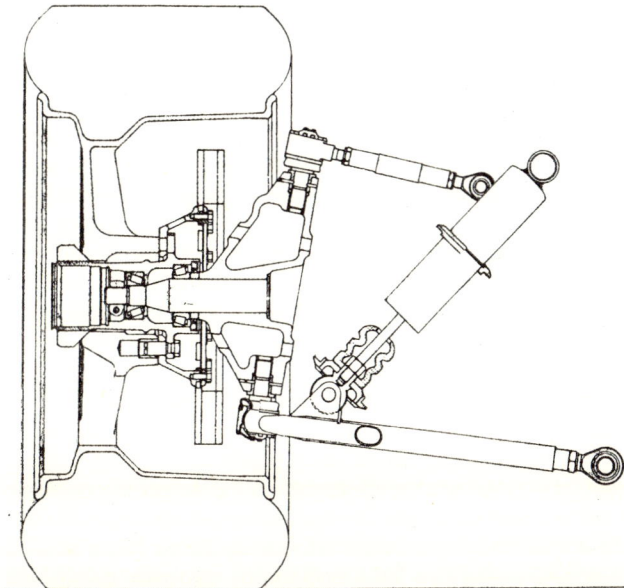

Late 1969 917 front suspension. The hub rotates on the stub axle

all, it must be ensured that no aerodynamic lift can occur. Whereas the side wind problem can be solved satisfactorily by the use of vertical tail fins, the lift is very dependent on the angle of incidence of the vehicle, as indicated by wind tunnel tests reported in earlier chapters. If a hump on the road surface or even only the driving torque reaction raises the front of the car, designed downthrust can easily change to lift and this being cumulative, it can cause the vehicle to take off at very high speeds—a sort of accident that has happened before. This could be avoided by designing the car so that it had very strong downthrust at its normal, static angle of incidence, but at high speed this would cause the suspension to be

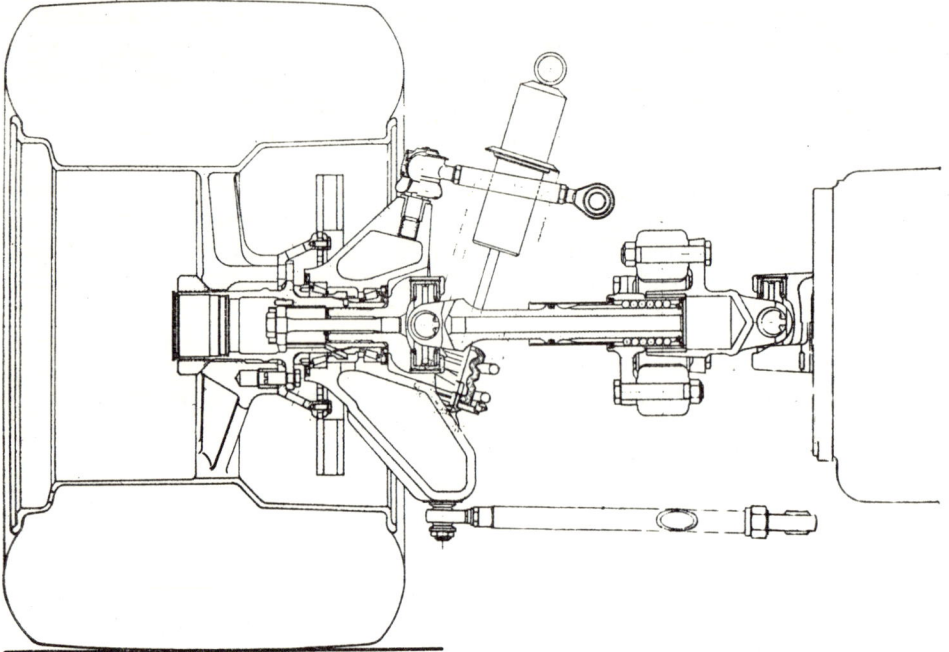

917 rear suspension and half shaft.

compressed down to its stops, again making handling unacceptable. At the design stage, this problem was solved by the use of pivoted spoilers at the front and mobile flaps at the rear, both connected with their respective suspensions, and successfully tried at the back on Bergspyders and 908s. Even before the Le Mans pre-practice, the mobile front spoilers were deleted, as experiments carried out showed that the rear mobile flaps were sufficient, while it was felt that if the front flaps were damaged accidentally during the race, as so often happens, the car's handling might be completely upset. The flaps were individually connected to the right and left suspension by a bell crank linkage in such a way that if the rear suspension was extended, the flaps would angle up to push the tail down again and restore full contact between the tyres and road surface; if the rear suspension was compressed, giving the car a positive angle of incidence generating lift over the front axle, the flaps would angle down to create an aerodynamic force raising the tail. On corners, body roll would make the flaps operate in opposite directions

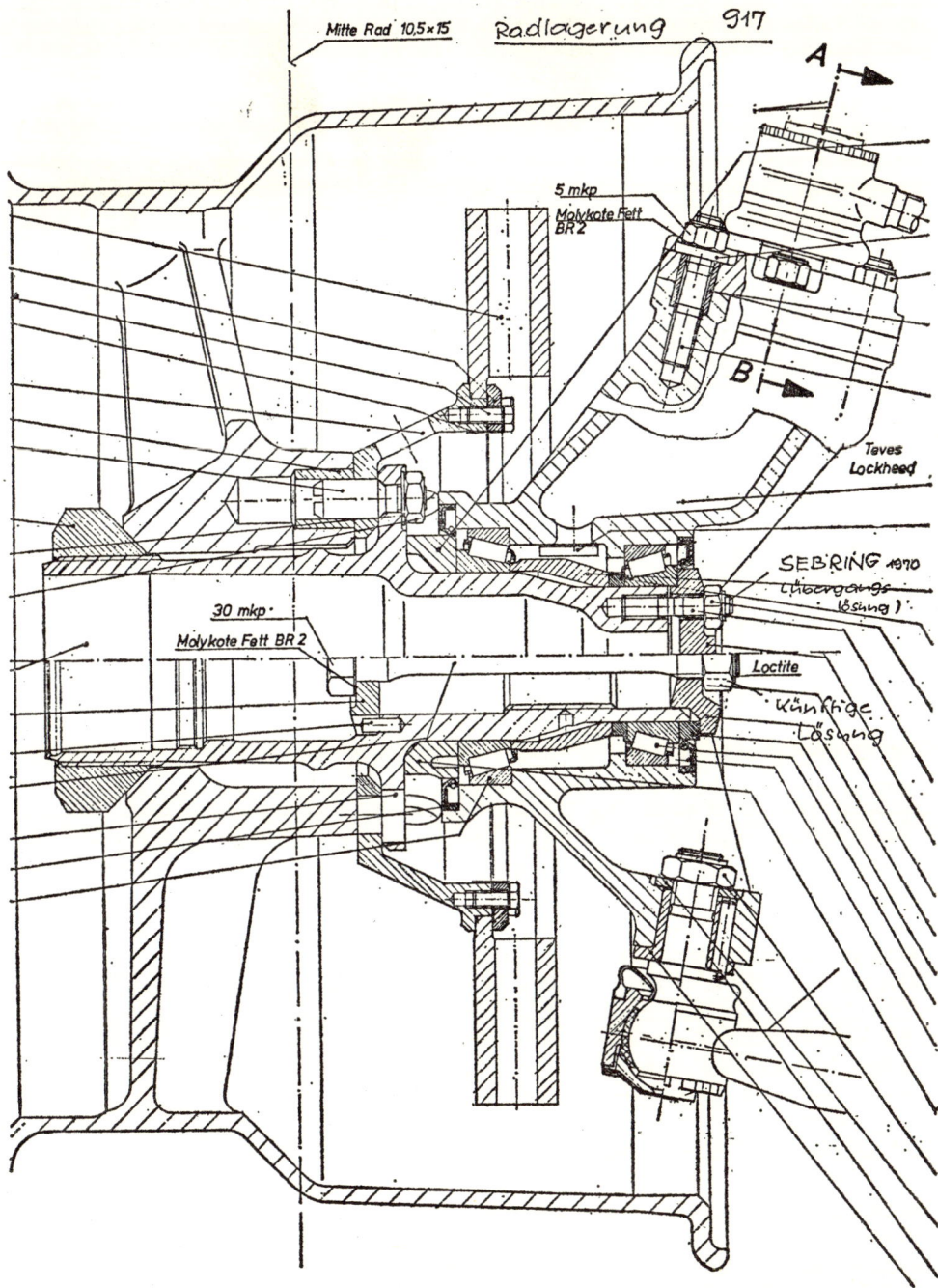

917 front upright and hub, 1970 model. The hub rotates in the upright. The bearings are much bigger than in 1969. The upper half of the drawing shows the intermediate solution which failed at Sebring.

to counteract roll and weight transfer, which in principle should improve cornering power. Earlier tests had shown, however, that this advantage was more academic than practical.

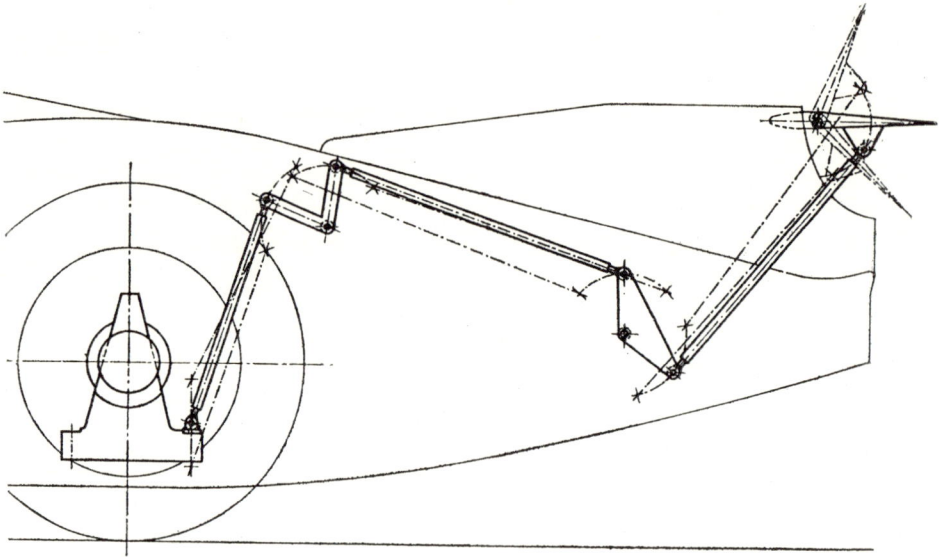

Linkage for operating mobile tail flap on 1969 long-tail 917.

Even though the chassis was largely adapted from the 908, it was a fantastic achievement that the first sample of the new car could be shown to a startled world on March 13 1969, the opening day of the Geneva Motor Show, barely $8\frac{1}{2}$ months after Dr Porsche had given his approval to go ahead with the project. A catalogue had been printed and the car was officially listed at 140,000 DM. And by the end of April, the 25 units required by the CSI for recognition as a Group 5 sports car had been built and homologated. A few days later Gerhard Mitter drove one in its first official outing, the Spa 1,000 km race, though a broken valve stopped him after only one lap. Two weeks later the car did much better to finish eighth in the Nürburgring 1,000 km race in the hands of guest drivers Frank Gardner and David Piper, and in mid-June long-tail versions led at Le Mans for the first 20 hours out of the 24!

This was much more than anyone had expected, but it was fairly obvious that the car still needed a lot of development before it could be really competitive on any course other than Le Mans where sheer speed is the overruling factor. No development testing had been possible at Spa due to pouring rain during all the practice sessions, so the only race the 917 had done at all before Le Mans (except for one lap in the actual race at Spa) was the Nürburgring 1,000 km. Its best practice lap was done in 8 m 37.8 s by Quester (who did not drive the car in the race) ie over 37 s slower than Siffert's best 908 practice time for the same race and the car running in short-tail form was said to be very difficult to drive and very unstable at speed. The only significant modification that could be made before the Le Mans race, however, was to the front suspension geometry: the anti-dive effect was reduced from 50 to 5 per cent.

At Le Mans, the two long-tail cars entered were eliminated by clutch failure. After some time, the clutch started to slip because the pressure exerted by the diaphragm spring was insufficient with part-worn linings. The heat generated broke the linings loose, eventually causing total failure after nine hours in the case of Stommelen/Ahrens, whereas by careful driving Elford and Attwood kept their car running for 20 hours. When it was later dismantled, it was found that the bell housing was cracked, so it is doubtful if it would have lasted through the 24 hours anyway. One point of interest is that the fuel consumption of the 917 was not significantly higher than that of the Type 908 cars; they did 6.6 and 7.5 mpg respectively. As in 1969 the larger car was still allowed to carry 140 litres of fuel whereas the 3-litre was limited to 120 litres, this meant that the 917 would go just about as far on a tankful as the 908.

13

Development of the Type 917

AS THE RACING CAREER of the 917 as a works car considerably exceeds that of any other Porsche racing model, it would not be possible to recall its development almost race by race as we have done for previous types. From 1970 onwards it has also proved to be so successful, being progressively developed to keep ahead of the opposition, that a detailed description of the various races for which it was entered and of the preparation of the individual cars would soon become uninteresting. Neither are there accurate reports on preparation and practice available from the factory as they were for the period before 1970, because beginning with that year, the factory's racing policy underwent an important change: it was felt that too many engineers, technicians and highly qualified workers, who were badly needed elsewhere, were involved in the preparation of the cars and the actual race organisation. Consequently it was decided that while the factory would get on with all the development work and would continue to build and recondition cars, engines and other mechanical units, the actual preparation work and race organisation would be entrusted to private teams officially representing the factory under a contract agreement. The most important of these teams was the Gulf-sponsored team of J.W. (John Wyer and John Willment) Automotive Engineering based in Slough which in 1970 and 1971 ran the cars in the well-known pale blue and orange Gulf colours. In 1970, the second team was that of Porsche Salzburg, a firm owned and run by Frau Luise Piëch, Dr Ferry Porsche's sister, which imports Volkswagens into Austria and looks after Porsche interests in that country. For 1971, Porsche Salzburg's racing organisation was taken over by the Martini Racing Team, but whereas the Wyer team got its engines straight from the racing department, the other two teams had to rely on the factory's service department for re-conditioning their mechanical units.

If the 917 had done surprisingly well at Le Mans where it had been entered more as a development exercise than anything else, everyone concerned was perfectly aware of the fact that on most other circuits its handling deficiencies would overrule its superior power. And in addition to this, another problem had to be solved: only two weeks before the Le Mans race any sort of mobile aerodynamic device was banned by the CSI on the grounds of serious accidents caused by such devices in Formula 1 racing. So by the time the Le Mans practice began, the flaps on the 917 Le Mans cars had become illegal, which gave rise to some intense discussions. But the flaps were part of the model homologated by the CSI itself only a few weeks earlier and as the cars were proved to be undrivable without them, the matter was finally settled by an agreement between all entrants that the 917s would be allowed to race as they were, though the flaps had to be disconnected on the 908 long-tail cars, which Porsche accepted in recognition of their rivals' courtesy.

The first development exercise after Le Mans was to enter two cars for the Austrian 1,000 km race on the Zeltweg circuit. This is a fairly fast circuit, with lap speeds in the 130 mph bracket at the time and it gave the 917, driven by Siffert and Ahrens, an occasion to gain its first victory, admittedly without much opposition. More importance must be attributed to the test runs for which the track was hired after the race. Here, partly on the initiative of John Wyer and his team who were to race Porsches the following year, the coupé body was modified with the aid of aluminium sheet, self-tapping screws, tape and plasticine to take a shape that in profile was very much more wedge-shaped than before. Wider 15 x 15 in wheels had already been successfully tried at the rear in the race itself and stiffer springs were used to reduce angle of incidence variations. These modifications improved the lap times by some 4 s or 3.5 per cent. When the first car modified along these lines was completed, it was found that the drag coefficient had increased by some 15 per cent to Cw=0.46, compared with the original short-tail coupé, but the rear of the body now being open, the total weight was reduced by 33 lb to some 150 lb.

Other worthwhile tests were performed on the steering pad, comparing different types of tyres, alternative rim widths and various running gear settings. A first series of test runs was carried out with the usual pre-stressed limited slip differential with a 75 per cent locking factor. The front wheels had the 9 x 15 in rims used throughout 1969 while at the rear 15 x 15 in rims were used as found to be beneficial at Zeltweg. Camber settings were —45' front and —30' rear, the castor angle was 3°. Dunlop, Firestone, Goodyear and Bridgestone tyres were tried, the anti-roll bar settings being altered as required to get the best results. These were as follows:

		Time	Lateral g
Dunlop, Profile CR 82, Mixture 184			
Front: 4.50/11.60—15	Rear: 5.50/15.00—15	17.72 s	1.233 g
Front: 4.50/11.60—15	Rear: 5.50/13.60—15	17.92 s	1.210 g
Firestone, Profile R125, Mixture ZB14			
Front: 4.25/10.20—15	Rear: 5.50/12.20—15	17.82 s	1.221 g
Goodyear Blue Strike			
Front: 4.80/10.50—15	Rear: 6.00/15.50—15	18.14 s	1.179 g
Bridgestone, Profile RA13, Dry-weather Mixture			
Front: 4.90/12.00—15	Rear: 6.00/14.00—15	19.10 s	1.080 g

In the course of these tests 12-in rear rims were also tried but gave inferior results. It is, however, interesting to note that the wider Dunlop tyres 5.50/15.00—15 which gave the best results of all on the 15-in wide rear wheels produced slower times than the narrower 5.50/13.60—15 tyres when mounted on the narrower rims which indicates that very wide tyres are beneficial only if mounted on appropriately wide rims.

As an experiment, the castor was first reduced to 1°, then increased to 5°. The small castor angle which made the steering noticeably lighter also fed back little information to the driver when the limit of adhesion was reached, which resulted in slower times, while a 5° castor made the steering certainly too heavy for racing but provided exceptional sensitivity giving very good times, as indicated below (Dunlop tyres 4.50/11.60—15 front, 5.50/15.00—15 rear):

Castor	1°	3°	5°
Time	17.82 s	17.72 s	17.58 s

Still with 5° castor, the negative camber angles were then increased by 1° to —1° 45' front and —1° 30' rear. This further improved the lap times on the circular pad from 17.58 to 17.48 s, but with the wide tyres used, such high negative camber angles are not practicable for racing except over very short distances because of too high temperatures and tread wear.

Though the best results were obtained on Dunlop tyres, these unfortunately could not be used after 1969 because of the teams officially representing Porsche in racing: at that time John Wyer and Martini were under contract to Firestone and Porsche Salzburg were with Goodyear.

In a second test series, the effect of various settings of the limited slip differential was investigated, using the fastest Dunlop tyre combination. Three different types of differentials were used:
a) pre-loaded with 75 per cent locking factor, as currently used;
b) no pre-loading and 25 per cent locking factor;
c) no pre-loading and 75 per cent locking factor.

On these occasions, the car was driven not only on the 190-metre (622 ft) diameter pad but also on the two smaller ones of 60- and 40-metre diameter (197 and 131 ft respectively) as the tendency to understeer on small radius corners was expected to be less with a low locking factor than with a high one. This was confirmed by test engineer Falk who drove the car, though he could detect no difference on the large diameter circuit. From the times recorded, it emerges that the lower locking factors consistently produced slightly faster times, the best recorded on the large diameter circuit being 17.34 s (1.31 g) with 25 per cent locking factor. The biggest difference, however, lies in the way the vehicle reacts on suddenly shutting the throttle: with 75 per cent locking factor (with or without pre-loading) there is practically no reaction on the large (190-metre) diameter circle but some tuck-in takes place with a 25 per cent locking factor. On the smaller diameter circles, there is some noticeable tuck-in with 75 per cent locking factor but the car with 25 per cent spins as soon as the accelerator is released. The logical conclusion of these tests was to stick to the currently used type of differential with 75 per cent locking factor and pre-loading.

In order to get more experience of the 917 in actual racing conditions, a single car was made to take an open body on a standard 917 frame modified accordingly. It was entrusted to the late Jo Siffert and sent to America in August 1969 to participate in all the races of the Can-Am Championship still to be run. This car 917 027 was called 917 PA Spyder (PA standing for Porsche-Audi, the company importing cars of these makes in the USA and by which the car was sponsored and entered). There had been hardly any time for a weight saving exercise and despite the open body and the fact that no spare wheel was required, the 917 PA still weighed some 775 kg (1,700 lb) and was not expected to be competitive against the 7- and 8-litre McLarens and other specialised cars taking part in the series. Its total tank capacity was increased to 190 litres (41.5 gal) and its general lines were largely inspired by the 908 'Sole' but its wedge shape was more pronounced.

At 125 mph, the original body produced a front downthrust of 36.6 kg (80 lb), increasing to 55 kg (120 lb) when a full width spoiler was added across the front edge of the body. Though, in view of the 17 in wide rear wheels to be used, the body was wider at the rear than at the front, the by no means bad drag coefficient of Cw=0.456 was obtained but, as the car was 84 in wide, its frontal area of 1.583 m² was certainly not small and the Cw x S product was rather large at 0.723. This was raised further when experience dictated the use of larger front spoilers to increase the front downthrust. Before its departure to America, the car was briefly set up on the Weissach steering pad and there were further trials on

917 long-tail car as it appeared at the Le Mans pre-practice in 1970. The air outlets in the front wings increased the circulation of air over the front brakes. There is no horizontal tail fin and the nose is not concave.

Below: Leo Kinnunen (left) and Pedro Rodriguez brought Porsche their first three victories of 1970.

In 1970 John Wyer added an adjustable aerofoil to the cars entered by his team. This made it possible to reduce the height of the rear spoilers, though wind tunnel tests did not indicate any serious benefit.

After the mobile rear flaps had been ruled out, the long-tail model was reshaped as shown here (Le Mans pre-practice 1970).

Hans Herrmann and Dickie Attwood drove this 917 short-tail car with 4.5-litre engine to victory at Le Mans in 1970.

The fastest car in the 1970 Le Mans race was the 917 L with 4.9-litre engine which Vic Elford drove to a new absolute unofficial practice lap record in 3m 19.8s, an average of 151 mph. Note the concave shaped nose and the rear aerofoil. Drag coefficient Cw=0.361.

The 917 short-tail in its 1971 version with a new shallower and finned tail part which reduced the drag by about 15%.

The one-off 917/20 with 'Sera'-designed short-tail low-drag body. Note the large side overhang and shaped wheel arches. The car was known as 'Big Bertha' but the Porsche styling people thought it looked more like a pig and decorated it accordingly. The raised centre section of the front is to make room for the regulation 'box' with which the ground clearance is checked by the scrutineers.

Rear of the 917/20 showing the transmission oil cooler and the regulation 'luggage boxes'.

Type 917 long-tail coupe as it appeared for the 1971 Le Mans pre-practice. Note the blunt 'nose' and the tail part covering the rear wheels with side air inlets for brake and tyre cooling. The front wing louvres are seen here partly blanked off as part of practice experiments.

917 L in 1971 Le Mans race.

The first open-bodied 917 was produced in 1969 for Siffert to race in the Can-Am series of that year. It was called the 917 PA and is seen here in its original form.

The evolution of the 917/10 Spyder 1971-72. This is the original car 917/10/001 driven by Siffert in the 1971 Can-Am series. In 1971 another car was built for the Can-Am series as the first stage of the development of the 1972 Group 7 917/10. It was also driven by Siffert.

First evolution of the front and rear parts of the 917/10. The rear aerofoil reduces the total drag, compared with the earlier tail, as it is more efficient in producing downthrust. Mark Donohue drives the car, still without a supercharger.

Second evolution with a larger overhung aerofoil. Kinnunen drives an unsupercharged 5.4-litre version of the car.

The 917/10 in its final 1972 form with a sharply concave front. George Follmer is driving the Porsche-entered turbo-charged 5-litre car with which he won the Championship. An identical car with 4.5-litre engine won the European Interseries Championship, driven by Leo Kinnunen.

the Zeltweg circuit mainly with the object of getting data on brake development. The original 917 had fairly heavy brakes, the performance and the weight of the car dictating the use of four-piston calipers of ATE manufacture with 18 mm thick pads acting on a ventilated cast iron disc. For the sake of lightness, this was reduced to a ring of a width corresponding to the area swept by the pads and mounted on a steel flange carried by the titanium hub. When wider wheels were used, it became necessary to off-set the hub farther from the disc, which was achieved by giving the flange a conical shape. Further weight was saved by making it of titanium, after rig tests had shown this to be reliable. Except for the wider wheels and tyres, the brakes modified to fit them and a clutch with a stronger diaphragm spring, the 917 PA was sent to America in a state of development generally corresponding to that reached by the car that had won the Austrian Grand Prix.

As expected, it was not fast enough to compete directly with the specialised Can-Am cars, but it finished second in one of the races and took fourth place in the Championship, even though it had taken part in only six of the 11 races in the series. Only once did it fail to finish when the driver missed a gear and over-revved the engine and in one race it finished with the cooling blower out of use after its driving gears had failed. Following this, the blower was fitted with a rubber spring hub to cushion the drive and reduce the inertia loads on the driving gears.

Chassis developments 1970/71

To the casual observer, there is very little difference between the 917 which won the Daytona Intercontinental 24-Hour race in 1970 and the cars which ran in the last race of the 1971 World Championship, the Watkins Glen Six-Hours. In fact, however, track and wind tunnel tests carried out during 1970 and 1971 led to subtle modifications to the body shape and there were of course some modifications dictated by new rules introduced by the CSI such as reinforced roll bars and the addition of an automatic fire extinguishing plant with a 5 kg bottle as developed by the Deugra Company.

The main differences between the 1969 models and the cars which took part in the Daytona Intercontinental 24-Hour race of 1970 were as follows:

According to the latest CSI requirements, the tank capacity had been reduced from 140 to 120 litres, all the fuel being contained in a single flexible safety bag tank on the left of the chassis;

An almost completely new wedge-shaped body based on the experience gained at Zeltweg in August 1969;

A three-plate Borg & Beck clutch with sintered metal linings instead of a similar Fichtel & Sachs clutch with bonded organic linings;

A reinforced transmission casing;

A four-speed and reverse gearbox (four or five speeds could be used alternatively);

Ultra-light Sarma rear radius rods (these were found to be dangerously brittle and were later discarded in favour of ordinary aluminium alloy rods, though the Sarma were still used on the lighter 908/03 cars);

A spring hub-driven cooling blower;

Modified brakes which will later be discussed in more detail.

Throughout the two racing seasons 1970/1971 wheels of 10.5 and 12 in were used alternatively at the front and wheels of 15 and 17 in width at the rear, the choice being in most cases dictated by the circuit and the weather conditions.

J

The narrower wheels were always used when rain tyres were fitted. With the ultra-wide flat-treaded tyres now used at the rear, it became impossible to use any negative camber; in fact, whereas at the front zero camber was usually specified, the static settings provided for some slight positive camber at the rear so that when the rear suspension was compressed by both the aerodynamic downthrust and the weight transfer due to acceleration, the camber variation designed into the suspension reduced the camber to a value around zero. Usually, the suspension settings were adjusted on every individual car in accordance with the tyre temperatures reached in practice and measured on the occasion of every pit stop. With those ultra-wide tyres, individual temperature checks are always made at the inside of the tread, in the centre of the tread and at the outside. Camber corrections are then made to equalise the temperatures reached. According to the circuit, the speeds reached and the rear spoiler adjustment, a static camber of between 15' positive and 45' positive was generally adopted for the 917 coupés' rear suspension.

After winning the 1970 Daytona Intercontinental in which they were first opposed by the Ferrari 512S (one of these cars finishing third), Porsche lost the next race, the Sebring 12-Hours, to its Italian rival, mainly due to the introduction of an insufficiently developed modification. In 1969, some difficulties had been experienced with the braking system of which the fluid tended to boil due to heat transfer from the brake pad. A very simple remedy was found (and is still being used) by inverting the pistons in the caliper so that they pushed the back plate with their hollow end. By this means, the brake fluid was kept further away from the pad and the contact surface between the back plate and the piston was considerably reduced. With this make-shift solution, however, the automatic adjustment mechanism was put out of use and there was nothing to prevent the pistons from being pushed back accidentally, apart from their seal. This did happen when, submitted to a high cornering force, the stub axle flexed very slightly or slight play developed in the bearings and in some cases the pistons were pushed back sufficiently to increase the pedal travel to the point of making pumping necessary. To obviate this, a completely new stub axle and upright unit was designed in which the stub axle rotated in large taper roller bearings. These units were fitted to the cars entered for Sebring before they had been properly endurance tested. Unfortunately, the four bolts retaining the stub axle in the bearings failed and the time lost cost Porsche the race. The design was then modified to replace the four small bolts by a single large axial bolt and no more trouble was experienced. The new uprights (cast in magnesium alloy) increased the front track by about 2.2 inches.

Another modification to the front running gear was introduced on the occasion of the 1970 Le Mans race. In this case, the dish of the front wheels was increased to reduce the steering off-set, while the wishbones were lengthened so as to keep the track unaltered. The aim of this modification was to improve stability both at speed and under braking and also to reduce steering kick-back.

The most important chassis development of the 1970/71 period was that of a frame made up of welded magnesium tubes. Magnesium is about 30 per cent lighter than aluminium, but it is more brittle and extremely difficult to weld: welding must take place at a strictly controlled temperature and under complete exclusion of oxygen. The first experiments early in 1971 on the Weissach destruction course were extremely discouraging: the first frame, using tubes of the same diameter as the current aluminium frame, required a lot of development and reinforcement to stop it breaking up. But finally a completely new, suitably reinforced frame was made (917 052) which successfully passed the 620-mile test on the destruction course which included the hill-climb circuit and a hump where the car takes off. This test, which was by no means uneventful, but not as far as the frame itself is concerned, started on April 21 1971 and was concluded on May 31.

Just before it started on its endurance run, the car (917 052) had taken part in the Le Mans preliminary practice for which it had been completed just in time. After the experience gained with the first magnesium chassis, the development engineers felt the magnesium frame could now be tried on the high-speed Le Mans course without endangering the drivers, even before it had passed the destruction test, which proved them to be right. But as a precaution, the car was run for 15 laps only, driven by Derek Bell and Jo Siffert. To get an unbiased judgement on the behaviour of the car using the new frame, the drivers were not told of its existence and, as it had a rather old and shabby body, they were far from suspecting anything as non-standard as a completely new frame. So when Siffert lapped faster with the magnesium frame car than with the standard model using a similar 4.9-litre engine, and passed a better overall judgement on it, everyone was very pleased.

As soon as it came back from Le Mans, the practically brand-new engine of the magnesium frame car was changed for one that had seen hard service during Le Mans practice and was taken to Weissach for the destruction tests. The engine was a 4.9-litre unit, and the five-speed gearbox used at Le Mans was changed for a four-speed box with ratios appropriate to the so-called Weissach hill-climb course (as opposed to the faster Can-Am course). It had ventilated and perforated brake discs and was fitted with the following experimental lightweight parts:

Aluminium front wishbones;
Magnesium steering box supports;
Light weight instruments.

In the course of this destruction test, there were three major incidents, none of which had anything to do with the frame itself:

the right hand half shaft broke after some 150 miles;
the replacement half shaft broke after it had done about 200 miles;
a lower rear suspension wishbone (steel) broke after 320 miles due to faulty material.

When the car was subsequently dismantled, the front and rear suspension Unibal joints were found to be rather worn, some wear had taken place in the front wheel bearings, one shock absorber was leaking and some wear was noted in the aluminium steering rack. For investigation of the magnesium frame, the body was completely detached and no cracks or breakages could be detected. Except for one reinforced tube in the structure between the cockpit and engine, this frame was identical to the original magnesium frame 917 051 as finally modified in the light of previous testing. In this form, and including the brackets for the fire extinguishing installation, the complete magnesium frame weighed 42 kg (93 lb) and it is interesting to note that as brought to Le Mans for the preliminary tests, the complete car weighed 766 kg (1,690 lb). The final destruction test with this car having been fully conclusive as far as the frame was concerned, the third magnesium frame 917 053 was built to identical specification and eventually became the La Mans winner of 1971.

It may be argued that it was pointless to develop a magnesium frame when the existing cars were already right at the minimum weight limit without even making full use of the titanium and magnesium light weight parts that had been developed but, on the other hand, whatever weight could be saved might have been used to incorporate new developments improving the cars, such as anti-

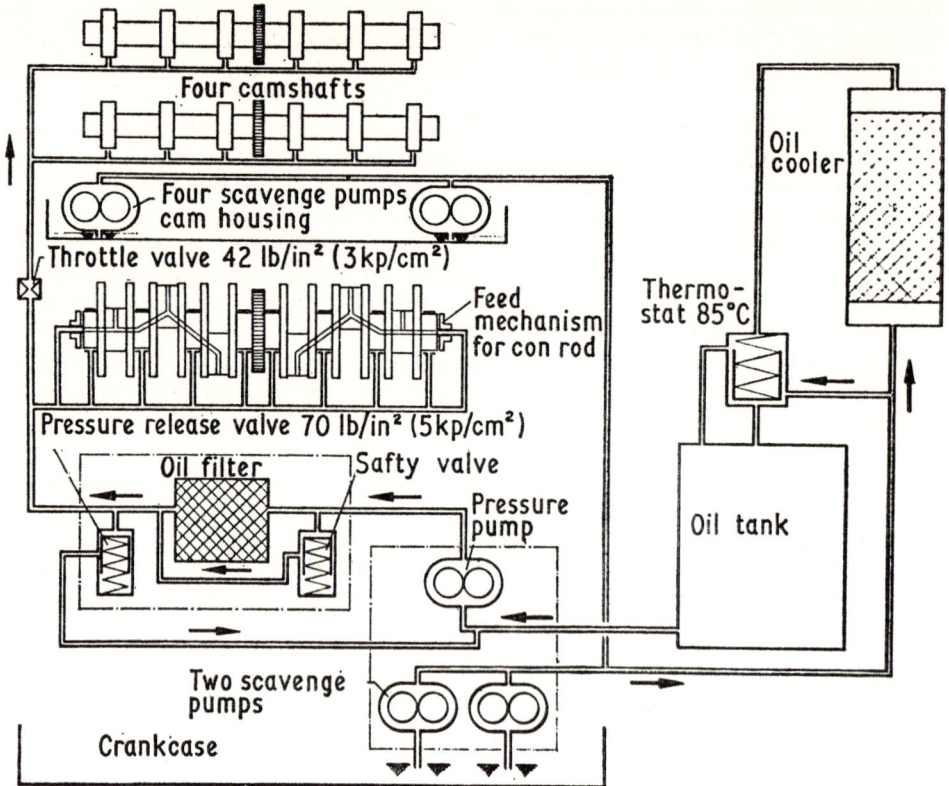

Oil circulation of the Type 912 engine.

lock braking systems, power steering, a cockpit cooling system, etc. Any such plans that may have existed, however, were soon given up when it became known that after 1971, Group 5 cars would no longer be eligible for first rank racing and Porsche turned their attention to the only class of racing for which their experience of light weight construction could be fully exploited—Group 7 racing for which no minimum weight is specified. It was during the winter 1970/1971 that the Porsche management finally decided to transfer the main racing activities from Europe to America and to concentrate the racing department's efforts on developing the 917 to make it competitive in the Can-Am Championship.

Short-tail body developments

Throughout the 1970 season, the short-tail 917, usually called 917K, was run in practically unmodified form as far as the body was concerned. After the Daytona 24-Hour race which was run on 15 in wide rear wheels, the rear part was slightly widened to cover the 17 in wide wheels used in most of the other races except Le Mans, and from this race on, John Wyer, who would not hear of using long-tail cars, added a small adjustable aerofoil at the extreme rear of his team's cars. Much of the experience gained in the development of the 908/03 Spyder and of the 917 PA Spyder which took part in the 1969/1970 Can-Am races was applied in the development of the 917K for 1970: the wedge shape and the louvred air outlets in the front wings to increase the circulation of air in the wheel arches, in the interests of better brake cooling, are evidence of this. At the end of the season, however, some tests were done both on the Hockenheim track and in the wind tunnel to compare the standard tail part with the John Wyer Le Mans tail, a modified Wyer tail and a development of the standard tail sporting vertical fins. The main object of the Hockenheim tests was to get an indication of the influence of the tail part on the maximum speed of the vehicle. The speed was recorded electronically on a 50-metre base, just before the braking point at the end of the straight preceding the East Curve. The straight is too short by far to allow a car to reach its true maximum speed, but the figures obtained give a comparative indication of the drag figures to be expected.

The standard 1970 tail which Porsche usually call 'Daytona 70 tail' and the John Wyer Le Mans tail are identical except for the small aerofoil added by Wyer above the recessed part of the tail. This wing is supposed to make it possible to give the two small rear spoilers a much flatter angle of incidence and consequently produce a smoother air flow at the breakaway point.

On the two modified tails, the waist line prolongation over the rear wheels is flatter, but rises in a gentle curve towards the rear, to produce a smooth spoiler effect. With the John Wyer aerofoil added, it is called the modified John Wyer tail while the Porsche version has two vertical fins.

As registered at Hockenheim, the speeds reached over the base were as follows:

Standard Daytona 70 tail	175.5 mph
John Wyer Le Mans tail	173.0 mph
John Wyer modified tail	175.0 mph
Finned tail	177.0 mph

The test car, 917 032, fitted with a 4.9-litre engine and running on Firestone rain tyres on 9 in wide wheels at the front and 15 in wide wheels at the rear, was driven by Derek Bell. The fact that the results were not entirely consistent with subsequent wind tunnel tests to which the same car was submitted shortly afterwards, may be accounted for by the rainy weather.

For the wind tunnel, the car was fitted with normal dry weather tyres on 10.5-in wide front wheels and 17-in wide rear wheels. Its frontal area was S=1.546 m²

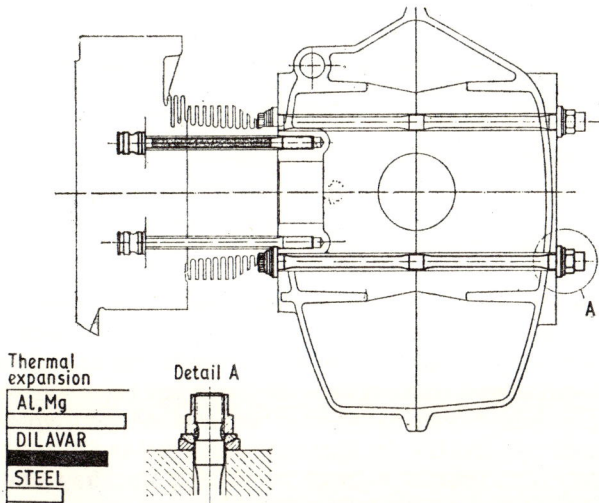

Thermal expansion

AL,Mg
DILAVAR
STEEL

Detail A

Crankcase and cylinder head bolts of the 912 racing engine.

and apart from the experimental tails, the body was to 1971 specification, with the rear part of the front wheel arches rounded and slightly prominent to ease the air flow. As it went into the wind tunnel, the car also had louvres cut into the horizontal part of the front wings, in front of the wheels, in order to let air into the wheel arch and improve brake cooling. A 10 mm (0.4 in) high and 970 mm (38 in) wide front spoiler was set across the front, under the leading edge of the 'nose'. Various combinations and modifications were tried with the following main results:

1. Standard Daytona tail with spoilers at trailing edge of rear wings (wings in the sense of 'mudguards'). Spoiler height 60 mm (2.4 in), width approximately 700 mm (27.5 in); angle of incidence: 40°;
  Drag coefficient Cw=0.447;
  Front lift coefficient Clf= —0.031;
  Rear lift coefficient Clr= —0.287.

2. John Wyer Le Mans 70 tail (similar to Daytona 70, but with adjustable aerofoil between rear 'wings', over central recessed part of tail). Spoiler angle: 15°; aerofoil angle: 6.5°;
  Drag coefficient Cw=0.438;
  Front lift coefficient Clf= —0.018;
  Rear lift coefficient Clr= —0.313.

3. Modified John Wyer tail with lowered rear waistline extension (lower rear wings). Spoiler angle: 11.5°; arofoil angle: 9.5°;
  Drag coefficient Cw=0.384;
  Front lift coefficient Clf= —0.019;
  Rear lift coefficient Clr= —0.192.

4. New Porsche tail with lowered rear waistline extension and vertical fins. Rear spoiler height 70 mm (2.75 in); spoiler width reduced to 630 mm (25 in) each to accommodate fins. Spoiler angle: 36°;
  Drag coefficient Cw=0.417;
  Front lift coefficient Clf= —0.019;
  Rear lift coefficient Clr= —0.287.

5. New Porsche tail with fins and spoiler across the entire width between fins. Spoiler height 10 mm (0.4 in);
  Drag coefficient Cw=0.386;
  Front lift coefficient Clf= —0.037;
  Rear lift coefficient Clr= —0.228.

Summing up the comparison between the old Daytona 70 tail and the new finned tail with full width spoiler—
  Daytona 70 tail: Cw=0.447; Clf= —0.031; Clr= —0.287
  New finned tail: Cw=0.386; Clf= —0.037; Clr= —0.228—
indicates that the new finned tail gives an advantage of approximately 15 per cent in drag with a 20 per cent benefit in front downthrust and a 20 per cent loss in rear downthrust. This could no doubt be adjusted by an appropriate rear spoiler setting to produce practically the same downthrust figures as the old Daytona tail while maintaining the full benefit of a 15 per cent drag reduction. Other interesting data obtained in the course of these wind tunnel tests were that the louvred under-shields in front of the front wheels had a detrimental effect in reducing the front downthrust but they were used with a reduced number of louvres in 1971 to improve brake cooling, the tests having indicated that the lifting effect was reduced when some of the louvres were blanked off. The 0.4-in high spoiler set across the front edge of the body was definitely instrumental in both decreasing the drag and increasing the front downthrust as shown by the following figures:

6. Car as under (4) (new finned tail with separate rear spoilers), each second louvre removed from the front wing undershield, with front spoiler;
Drag coefficient Cw=0.414;
Front lift coefficient Clf= —0.030;
Rear lift coefficient Clr= —0.290.
7. As above, but without front spoiler;
Drag coefficient Cw=0.421;
Front lift coefficient Clf= —0.021;
Rear lift coefficient Clr= —0.318.
On the occasion of these test, some experiments were also initiated to indicate the benefits that might be gained from air boxes producing a ram effect over the intake pipes. These tests were soon followed by others with car 917 030 and gave the following indications:

a) Ram boxes have a worthwhile effect only if they are high enough to project well out of the boundary layer. Forward facing air scoops at body panel level, either above the cockpit or on the sides, have very little effect.

b) Baffles must be fitted inside the air box to equalise the ram effect over the intake pipes.

c) The two ram boxes required to obtain a worthwhile ram effect on the 917 increase the drag by about 5 per cent. Consequently there is little benefit to be expected from their use.

With an eye to future development, another test was carried out on this occasion: two longitudinal 'fences' were added to the crest of the front wings in order to direct as much of the air flow as possible over the sloping front of the vehicle and increase the front downthrust. The effect was quite startling, as the downthrust on the front wheels was more than doubled, with no increase in total drag and only 10 per cent loss of rear downthrust (caused by the fulcrum effect of the front axle). Unless a very high front downthrust is required, however, a continuous spoiler across the front has more advantages as it not only increases the downthrust to an extent that can be very easily controlled and adjusted, but also reduces the drag.

The 'fences' which had been added as a make-shift measure on the 917PA driven by Jo Siffert in the 1969/1970 Can-Am series were not used on other 917s, either in Group 5 or later in Group 7 versions.

Le Mans cars 1970/71

The emphasis which the very fast Le Mans circuit and its very long straight lays on speed, calls for a compromise rather different from that which was set as a target for the short-tail 917s. 1969 had shown that a long-tail 917 could be as much as 20 mph faster than a 1970 short-tail 917 (usually called the 917K). In 1970 it was expected that Ferrari would make a great effort to win at Le Mans and Porsche dared not ignore the speed potential of the long-tail cars. As will be remembered, their task was not made any easier by the fact that mobile flaps were now definitely banned. So it became extremely important to develop a shape for which variations of the angle of incidence caused by humps and dips in the road surface had as little influence as possible on the front and rear lift coefficients. The issue was not made easier by the fact that, whereas in 1970 the short-tail 917's used mostly 10.5- or 12-in wide front rims and 17-in wide rear rims, 15-in wide rear rims were definitely to be used on the long-tail cars in order to reduce the frontal area and the ensuing total drag. The major problem of reducing the

lift variations induced by changing angles of incidence was eventually solved—
at the cost of some increase in drag from Cw=0.33 to Cw=0.36—by giving the
front and rear upper decks a slightly concave shape, a solution which was arrived
at in co-operation with the French design office SERA, directed by Charles Deutsch
of DB and CD racing car fame. But a reasonably satisfactory solution was only
reached after extensive wind tunnel and track tests, in the course of which two cars
were destroyed by accidents, fortunately without too serious injuries to the drivers.
In addition to the concave front deck, the actual Le Mans cars differed from the
ones tried out on the occasion of the pre-practice session in having their tail fins
connected by an adjustable aerofoil. This was adopted from the previous year
when the addition of an aerofoil between the fins had shown that it improved the
drag coefficient, presumably because the slot formed between the aerofoil and the
upper deck of the tail prevented an early breakaway of the air flow. The adjustable
aerofoil also provided an easy means of adjusting the rear downthrust. There had
been no time, however, to try either the concave front or the aerofoil in the wind
tunnel before the race.

Only two long-tail cars were entered for the event, as John Wyer would not
hear of them and preferred to run his own modified version of the short-tail model.
The two long-tail cars were 917 042 entered by Porsche-Salzburg and fitted with
the comparatively new 4.9-litre engine to be driven by Elford and Ahrens, and
917 043 using a well-proven 4.5-litre engine and lent for the race to the Martini
racing team.

The other cars officially representing the factory at Le Mans were two 4.5-litre
917Ks, 917 023 for Hans Herrmann and Dickie Attwood, and 917 021 for van
Lennep and David Piper, and the three John Wyer cars which had a small aerofoil
added to their short-tail body. These were 917 016 for Rodriguez/Kinnunen and
917 017 for Siffert/Redman, both with a 4.9-litre engine, and 917 026 with a 4.5-
litre engine for Hobbs/Hailwood.

In view of their wider speed range, the long-tail cars had a five-speed gearbox
with the following ratios:

4.5-litre: 15:29, 21:29, 23:24, 26:21, 30:21 with crown wheel and pinion
8:37.

4.9-litre: 15:29, 21:29, 23:24, 26:21, 31:21 with crown wheel and pinion
8:37.

In the case of the short-tail cars with a four-speed gearbox, the gearing used
was the following:

4.5-litre: 15:29, 21:29, 24:23, 27:20 with crown wheel and pinion 8:37.
4.9-litre: 15:29, 21:29, 24:23, 32:23 with crown wheel and pinion 8:37.

As all cars were geared to peak at 8,400 rpm, it is easy to calculate that the long-
tail cars were approximately 14 mph faster than the short-tail cars. Despite the
twin batteries and the additional equipment required for Le Mans, the Porsche-
Salzburg short-tail cars weighed only 827 kg (1,830 lb) and the long-tail cars
were approximately 65 lb heavier. The weight distribution was:

917L—34.5/65.5
917K—36.5/63.5

Again the long-tail Porsches were the fastest cars on the track, Vic Elford lapping
in 3 m 19.8 s in practice on the 4.9-litre, but this was only 0.3 s quicker than the
512S Ferrari driven by Vaccarella. The Ferraris too had an elongated tail which,
according to the factory people, increased their maximum speed by 9-10 mph
but it is worth pointing out that the weight of the works cars varied between 924
and 956 kg, which is about 100 kg or 220 lb more than the weight of the Porsches.

The fact that Siffert was only 1.3 s slower in a short-tail 4.9-litre 917 than Elford in the long-tail car, indicates, however, that the higher speed of the 917L was partly offset by inferior handling. The more streamlined body still had a noticeable advantage, however: thanks to a notably lower fuel consumption, the long-tail cars could run longer between pit stops. The fuel consumption of the 917K placed first and of the 917L placed second in the race, both using the 4.5 litre engine, was 6.2 and 7.6 mpg respectively.

The 1970 version of the 917L was a vast improvement on the earlier version, but everyone concerned at Porsche felt that it could still be improved. Data for its further development were obtained during a test organised at the Hockenheimring in November 1970 with Siffert as driver. The object was to make the long-tail car handle as well as the short-tail model, and one step taken to achieve this was to use 17-in wide rear wheels while retaining the 10.5-in rims at the front. The car used for the test was 917 042, now fitted with a new body made of the same very rigid but ultra-light sandwich material successfully used on the 908/03. Compared with the 1970 long-tail cars, the new car was modified as follows:

New flat wrap-round nose;
Larger front brake cooling air intakes;
80 cm (31.5 in) wide oil cooler;
Lowered front and rear wing line;
Enlarged front wing louvres;
Rounded front wheel arch trailing edge;
Widened and lowered rear wings with spats incorporating air inlets;
Naca air inlets for rear brake and gearbox oil radiator cooling;
Rear fins parallel (instead of convergent towards rear);
Cockpit air intake in front of windscreen.

The car which was fitted with a full 5-litre engine still in the experimental stage, was also equipped with special instruments working in conjunction with a timing installation on the track. After the car had been set up properly, an average lap time of 1 m 51.82 s was obtained for the full circuit (without the new chicanes). The highest lateral acceleration (in the slightly banked East Curve) averaged 1.516 g and the best braking deceleration (at the end of the straight leading into the 'Motodrom') averaged 1.408 g. The absolute best figures were:

Lap time—1 m 51.33 s
Lateral acceleration—1.65 g
Braking deceleration—1.50 g

The figures are not peak recordings registered by accelerometers installed in the car and influenced by suspension movements, but are based on electronic timing.

The main object of the tests, however, was to measure the suspension travels in order to obtain the angle of incidence of the vehicle in various conditions. The travels were measured at the spring units and if the static position is taken as zero, the compression is indicated by a plus sign, and rebound by a minus sign.

With the rear aerofoil adjusted to give the best possible handling, the results were as follows:

At speed (approximately 180 mph) on the straight:
Front: left, +22.5 mm; right, +22.5 mm
Rear: left, +20.0 mm; right, +20.0 mm
Under hard braking into the 'Motodrom' (average deceleration 1.408 g):
Front: left, +22.5 mm; right, +24.5 mm
Rear: left, zero; right, zero.

Just to show how sensitive a high speed car is to the position of the aerofoil, here are the corresponding results obtained at 180 mph with the trailing edge of the aerofoil raised an additional 2 mm (0.08 in) :

Front: left, +20.0 mm; right, +21.0 mm
Rear: left, +22.5 mm; right, +22.5 mm.

The very small modification to the aerofoil setting had little bearing on the car's attitude under heavy braking, but the driver reported a deterioration in the car's handling.

From the suspension travels registered, the front and rear downthrusts were calculated as follows:

Over front axle, C_{lf}= —0.448
Over rear axle, C_{lr}= —0.507

Only after the 1971 Le Mans race did the car go into the wind tunnel, and the results show how inconsistent wind tunnel tests can be with actual track tests, useful though they may be for getting comparative results at the development stage. When the same car was tried in the wind tunnel in the state in which it had been raced at Le Mans, with very satisfactory results as far as stability and handling were concerned, and only minor modifications compared with the state in which it had been tried at Hockenheim, the following results were obtained: C_w=0.360 (with a frontal area of S=1.570 m²) ; C_{lf}= +0.005; C_{lr}= —0.177.

Development engineer Singer, who was responsible for both the Hockenheim and the wind tunnel tests, concludes: 'The lift factors obtained in the wind tunnel certainly do not reflect the true situation. The downthrusts on front and rear axles are certainly much higher than those indicated'. And he goes on recalling the figures calculated from the Hockenheim tests, finally concluding that, bearing in mind the development work done, the front and rear lift coefficient of the Le Mans cars could be estimated as follows: front C_{lf}= —0.3; rear C_{lr}= —0.6 to —0.7.

Whatever the credibility of the absolute figures obtained in the wind tunnel, the comparative figures obtained for the car with the front and rear suspensions compressed or extended is of great interest:

a) As has already been said, for the car in the static position they were: C_w= 0.360; C_{lf}= +0.005; C_{lr}= —0.177 (+indicates lift; — indicates downthrust).

The comparative figures obrained were as follows:

b) Front suspension extended 30 mm (1.2 in) (incidence $+\frac{3}{4}°$):
C_w=0.375; C_{lf}= +0.151; C_{lr}= —0.234;

c) Front and rear suspension extended 30 mm (1.2 in) :
C_w=0.380; C_{lf}= +0.044; C_{lr}= —0.228;

d) Rear suspension extended 30 mm (1.2 in) (incidence $-\frac{3}{4}°$):
C_w=0.362; C_{lf}= —0.079; C_{lr}= —0.162;

e) Front suspension compressed 30 mm (1.2 in) (incidence $-\frac{3}{4}°$):
C_w= 0.327; C_{lf}= —0.071; C_{lr}= —0.108;

f) Front and rear suspension compressed 30 mm (1.2 in) :
C_w=0.322; C_{lf}= +0.010; C_{lr}= —0.117;

g) Rear suspension compressed 30 mm (1.2 in) (incidence $+\frac{3}{4}°$):
C_w=0.348; C_{lf}= +0.076; C_{lr}= —0.194.

These figures indicate that the worst conditions are reached when the front suspension alone is extended, but if we go by the figures estimated by the development engineers and based on the Hockenheim track tests (front lift coefficient= —0.3; rear lift coefficient= —0.6 to —0.7) the lift variations indicated by the wind tunnel are, even in the worst cases, insufficient to create positive lift, whatever the attitude of the car. It will also be noted that the drag coefficient is a function of the ground clearance and decreases quickly as the ground clearance is reduced. Comparison between (e) and (f) also shows that the drag coefficient is mainly dependent on the front ground clearance governing the flow of air underneath the car.

The stability of the long-tail car tried in the Le Mans preliminary practice in April 1971 is perhaps the best proof of the fact that under no circumstances was the aerodynamic downthrust reversed, and even John Wyer was so impressed by the handling and general behaviour of the vehicle that he elected to run two long-tail cars in the actual race, for which a third long-tail model was entered by the Martini racing team. Of the three cars 917 042, 043 and 045, the first two had already run in the previous year's race, but they had been stripped to the bare chassis and their new body was made entirely of sandwich plastic material, as originally used for the 908/03 Spyder. This gave improved body rigidity and thanks to the lighter weight of the new body material, the weight of the long, overhung tail was not felt any more. The drivers were unanimous in saying that the handling of the 917L was now as good as that of the 917K, and this was reflected by the fastest ever Le Mans lap achieved, Jackie Oliver taking 917 043 round the course in 3 m 13.6 s when his car was officially timed at 240 mph on the Mulsanne straight, using a 4.9-litre engine. This compares with 3 m 18.7 s recorded by Siffert on the magnesium frame short-tail car 917 052, and indicates that the full benefit of the low drag body could now be exploited without any deterioration in handling.

For Porsche, the development of the long-tail car was mainly a technical exercise, but it was also essential to make quite sure that the World Championship title, which they had won for the third consecutive year even before the French endurance race was run, would not be spoiled by a defeat as it had been in 1969.

While the long-tail cars were being further developed, however, an attempt was made to obtain an equally low drag from a car even shorter than the current short-tail 917. It was designed in co-operation with the French SERA technical office and was notable for its 87 in wide body with considerable side overhang and rounded angles, which were incorporated to reduce wheel arch interference and ease the air flow out of the wheel boxes. Due to its very wide body, this car, bearing the Type number 917/20, had a frontal area of 1.656 m², compared with 1.570 for the normal long-tail models. The first and only car of this type built, 917/20/001, arrived completely untested for the Le Mans pre-practice session in April 1971, but after considerable sorting out and a change of engine, it won the Three-Hour race concluding the practice session, driven by Willy Kauhsen who for some time had been employed by Porsche as a test driver. This cannot rank as a very significant victory as Kauhsen had very little competition, his main opponent being Georg Loos in a privately entered Ferrari 512S.

Following the Le Mans pre-practice, the car was investigated in the wind tunnel exactly as it had been run at Le Mans, with the following results: Cw=0.381; Clf= —0.137; Clr= —0.145. In this state, the total drag for the car S x Cw is 11.5 per cent higher than for the 917L and also fractionally higher than for the 917K with the new finned tail which benefits from its smaller frontal area of 1.546 m² and also has more rear downthrust. Increasing the size of the rear spoiler to obtain more downthrust was hardly beneficial due to the resulting considerable drag increase.

With these data in mind, the car was sorted out, Kauhsen driving, on the Weissach circuit, more adjustments being made to the running gear than to aerodynamics. The improvement obtained is reflected in the lap times which went down from 55.0 s to 52.2 s, and the car's shape turned out to be more efficient than suggested by the wind tunnel tests, as a top gear intermediate between that of the short-tail and the long-tail cars was finally used for the actual Le Mans race.

Engine developments 1970/71

To accelerate its development, the Type 912 engine fitted to the Porsche 917 had been designed to include as many parts and dimensions from the 908 as possible. This proved to be a successful policy as, even very early in its development phase, the engine produced 580 hp and was extremely reliable, no engine failure being reported in the 917's first racing season, except when a valve broke on the very first lap of its very first race at Spa.

But using the same bore and stroke dimensions as the 908, the Type 912 engine had only 4.5 litres capacity and, even if this was enough to beat the new 512S Ferraris, which were up to the 5-litre limit but were notably heavier, in the Daytona 24-Hour race of 1970, and if again the 917 proved to be faster in the Sebring 12-Hour race (which the 917s lost due to front hub failures), the Ferrari challenge was not to be dismissed. It was in the summer of 1969 that news came through that Ferrari would also build a batch of 25 5-litre cars and work was soon started in Stuttgart to increase the size of the flat 12. A new crankshaft giving a stroke of 70.4 mm was designed and the bore size was increased from 85 to 86 mm, bringing the capacity up to 4907 cc. This engine, which was first used in the Monza 1,000 km race of 1970, was otherwise identical to the 4.5-litre engine which, except for the adoption of a cushioned hub in the cooling blower, had remained practically unaltered since the 1969 Le Mans race. The capacity increase raised the power output by 20-25 hp, the 4.9 engine producing just over 600 hp at 8,400 rpm. At this level, an additional 20-25 hp does not make a lot of difference to the maximum speed reached, which varies only as the cube root of the power output, as indicated by the approximation

$$V_1 = V_0 \sqrt[3]{\frac{N_1}{N_0}}$$

according to which, assuming a maximum speed of 215 mph for the 4.5-litre short-tail 917, the 4.9-litre would be only approximately 3 mph faster. Much more important, the bigger engine produced 10 per cent higher torque, this being raised from 376 lb ft at 6,600 rpm to 415 lb ft at 6,400 rpm. This was a big advantage, especially with the four-speed gearbox used for most of 1970 and in which third gear was normally geared some 25 per cent lower than top gear, so that when the driver changed up from third into top after the engine had reached its limit of 8,500 rpm, the revs dropped to 6,400 rpm, ie exactly where peak torque is produced. This is particularly advantageous at Monza and at Spa where, for most of the time, the cars accelerate out of very fast curves, and this was illustrated by the new absolute lap record set up by Elford with the 4.9-litre car of 1 m 24.08 s, which stood as the official lap record even after the Formula 1 Italian Grand Prix the same year. Unfortunately, the car was put off the road when Elford's co-driver, Kurt Ahrens, had a tyre failure, but the Rodriguez/Kinnunen 4.5-litre car beat the works Ferraris into second, third and fourth places.

At Spa, too, the 4.9-litre showed its true potential when Siffert and Redman's short-tail car beat the Ickx/Surtees Ferrari 512S by more than $2\frac{1}{2}$ m after 1,000 km, and Rodriguez set up a new absolute lap record in 3 m 16.5 s, an average of more than 160 mph.

If the difference in the maximum speed of the 4.5- and 4.9-litre engines was only 3 mph, it is worth noting that the gear ratios were usually selected to give the 4.9-litre cars a 6-7 mph higher theoretical speed at peak revs, so that in practice the longer stroke engine was revving a little more slowly at the car's actual maximum speed. A comparison of the gearing chosen for the 4.5- and 4.9-litre cars (all short-tails) at Monza and Spa is given below (crown wheel and pinion, 8 : 37) :

Monza : 14 : 29, 22 : 29, 23 : 24, 26 : 21 with 4.5-litre engine;
         14 : 29, 22 : 29, 26 : 26, 29 : 22 with 4.9-litre engine;
Spa :   15 : 29, 22 : 29, 24 : 23, 28 : 22 with 4.5-litre engine;
         15 : 29, 22 : 29, 24 : 23, 29 : 22 with 4.9-litre engine.

At the end of the 1970 season, Ferrari produced an improved version of his 512S, called 512M, which had more power, less weight (but still some 180 lb more than the Porsches) and better streamlining. One of them, driven by Jacky Ickx, had shown the Porsches a clean pair of heels in the Zeltweg 1,000 km race before it retired, and it beat the privately entered but works prepared 917 of Siffert/Attwood in the non-Championship Kyalami Nine-Hour race. Porsche's answer to this challenge was the improved body with tail fins referred to earlier and a full 5-litre engine in which the cylinder bore was increased from 86 to 86.8 mm. The latter was first used in the Brands Hatch 1,000 km race in April 1971 and had an exact capacity of 4,998 cc. In itself, this 91 cc capacity increase should not have produced a worthwhile boost in power, but at the same time a change was made from chromal to nikasil cylinders, which means that instead of being chrome-plated the bore of the aluminium cylinders was covered by a nickel-silicon carbide layer similar to that used by NSU for Wankel engine trochoids. Rather surprisingly, this change of material in itself produced a noticeable increase in power, due to better friction characteristics and possibly quicker bedding-in of the piston rings. The average power output of the full 5-litre engine came out at 630 hp at 8,300 rpm with 425 lb ft torque at 6,400 rpm. As a matter of interest, the cooling system having been left unchanged, this made the 17 hp absorbed by the cooling blower come out at only 2.7 per cent of the total output.

After the Brands Hatch race the 5-litre engine was used throughout the season in Porsche works cars, except at Le Mans where, for reliability reasons, the well-proven 4.9-litre was preferred to the rather new 5-litre.

Capacity increases and the change from chromal to nikasil cylinders were obviously not the only developments from which the Type 912 engine benefited in the two year period 1970/71, but most of the other work done was not fundamental. As already mentioned, a lot of development was devoted to making the engine lighter by using aluminium alloys or titanium for such parts as shafts, spindles and gears, in addition to more obvious parts like connecting rods and various linkages. Despite the bad bearing properties of titanium and its comparatively poor high temperature resistance, it was even developed for the manufacture of intake valves in which the bearing properties of the shaft were improved by a treatment called tiduran. Such valves have a hollow sodium-filled shaft and run in standard bronze guides. They were never used in long-distance races, for which sodium-filled alloy steel valves were always preferred, but they were found in all 1972 Type 912 engines which ran in shorter events. Titanium is unsuitable for the much hotter-running exhaust valves, but these being smaller than the intake valves, inertia loads are less of a problem.

Transmission developments 1970/71

As already known, a completely new transmission was designed to take the torque of the flat 12 engine. From the engine, the drive went through a three-plate

Fichtel & Sachs diaphragm clutch to a two-shaft gearbox with five forward ratios and reverse, all the forward gears using Porsche-type split ring synchromesh providing a servo action on the same principle as used in two leading shoe drum brakes. Both shafts were supported by two roller bearings, with an additional ball thrust bearing at the front end, the 5th gear pinions being overhung at the rear in order to reduce shaft length between bearings.

Two weaknesses soon showed up in this transmission: the clutch was rather unreliable and was responsible for the retirement of both the 917s which had started in the 1969 Le Mans race. As the linings began to wear, the pressure of the diaphragm spring became insufficient and the clutch started to slip, overheating the bonded organic linings which eventually worked loose. On one of the two cars, the transmission casing was also found to have split at the bell housing. This latter weakness was confirmed by the performance of the 917PA Spyder which ran in the Can-Am series and on which the transmission housing had to be changed several times in the course of the Can-Am season.

The first steps taken in the development of the 917 transmission were to replace the three-plate Fichtel & Sachs clutch with a similar diaphragm spring unit by Borg & Beck which had sintered metal linings and gave no further trouble, and to reinforce the transmission casing, mainly by increasing the depth of the external ribs. The new casing had cast-in oil lines, a result of the bitter experience at Le Mans in 1969 in Siffert's 908, when the external plastic pipes melted due to insufficient cooling.

For most of 1970 only four gears were used in view of the excellent flexibility of the engine, especially when its capacity was increased to 4.9 litres at the beginning of the 1970 European season. With this engine, however, the gearbox input shaft broke on the Rodriguez/Kinnunen car at Spa and the failure was traced to a crack due to stress concentration around a radial oil passage. Both shafts were redesigned and, to avoid radially drilling the most heavily stressed central part of the shafts, the splines were used to convey the lubricant as required. A few months later at Le Mans, the second place car driven by Larrousse/Kauhsen finished with a broken third gear pinion of which the failure was found to have been caused by stress concentration due to flexing of the shaft. This led to an increase in shaft diameter for 1971, and only a limited number of five-gear sets were cut to fit them and they were kept for the Le Mans race in which all the 917s, both short- and long-tail, were fitted with a five-speed box. Before that race only four-speed boxes were used, but the Le Mans five-speed boxes, fitted with different gear sets, were also used for the last two races of the season—at Watkins Glen and Zeltweg—as there was no longer any reason to save them up.

To make quite sure of the reliability of the power train before the Le Mans race of 1971, 917 022 was fitted with a 4.9-litre engine and the latest big shaft 5-speed gearbox was tested for 32 hours on a roller test rig at the Stuttgart University. For this test, the gearbox had ratios suitable for Le Mans and the rear of the car was weighted with 325 kg (720 lb) to simulate weight transfer under full acceleration. The very severe test cycle involved accelerating through all the gears up to 8,200 rpm, then braking and changing down through all the gears to first with double declutching and holding the engine at no less than 6,000 rpm. This was then immediately repeated, each cycle taking approximately 60-64 s.

Although the gearbox was fitted with several experimental parts, some as important as the oil pump and with an oil cooler, used for the first time on long-tail cars only to avoid the need for drag producing air scoops, it went through the test with flying colours though the clutch which was fitted with an experimental, positive return device for the discs was changed for a normal one after seven hours, when it was judged unsatisfactory. After 18 hours the synchronising system of the first, second and fourth gears became weak and after 28 hours the gear lever broke. The test was stopped after 31 h 55 m of running, when the box started to make some disturbing noises. These were found to be caused by a damaged reverse gear pinion. The damage was caused by a worn selector grid which allowed reverse gear to be touched when changing down from fifth to fourth gear.

Brake developments 1970/71

Until 1970, all Porsche racing cars had used brakes of ATE manufacture developed in co-operation with the factory. The 917 was no exception and was originally fitted with aluminium ATE brake cylinder units having four pistons of 34 mm diameter each. The ventilated discs had 12 in diameter and the pads with a 60 sq cm (9.3 sq in) area were lined with Textar V 1431 G linings, 18 mm (0.7 in) thick.

From 1970 onwards, when part of the works cars were prepared and entered by JW Automotive Engineering, the possibility arose of using Girling four-piston calipers which could not be fitted to German-entered cars due to patent rights. As the Girling brakes were found to have a higher efficiency than the ATE units, they were used on all John Wyer-entered cars and also on the factory-sponsored cars entered by the Martini racing team in 1971. The first sets of Girling brakes had larger pistons on the abutment side of the caliper unit than on the trailing side, in order to combat the wedge-shaped wear pattern of the pads, and this scheme was also adopted for a new type of ATE caliper which used 34- and 38-mm pistons. Like the Girling caliper it also had a separate saddle to which the cylinder units were bolted. The saddle was originally made of titanium, later of aluminium. The higher efficiency of the Girling brakes was established at the end of 1970, by which time both the ATE and the Girling calipers used two pairs of 42-mm pistons. Rig tests indicated that for a braking torque of 218 lb ft, the efficiency of the ATE caliper unit was 9 per cent inferior to that of both Girling and Lockheed calipers and, for a braking torque of 360 lb ft, the efficiency of the ATE caliper was only 73 per cent of the Lockheed or Girling unit which both had the additional advantage of being some 2 kg (4.2 lb) lighter. The Girling brake was finally given preference because it could accommodate 20 per cent more lining material than the Lockheed, and pad changes took less time.

Originally the ventilated discs were bolted to a steel flange carried by the hub, as they had been in all previous Porsche racing cars. The first step in the reduction of unsprung weight was taken when the disc was reduced to a ring closely corresponding to the swept area and bolted to a conical part which was itself bolted to the hub. This cone was first made of titanium, then of aluminium alloy, being drilled for weight saving. The weight of the alloy cone was exactly 1 lb while the weight of the disc was 12 lb. Aiming at a further reduction in the unsprung weight, experiments were made with a completely new form of disc: the aluminium 'cone' was extended to include a spider forming the vanes of a ventilated disc. On either side of this spider a ring of a copper chrome alloy, of a size corresponding to the area swept by the brake pads, was riveted. This saved another 2.65 lb compared with the cast iron disc, bringing the total weight down to 11.7 lb, 40 per cent less than the original cast iron disc and steel flange. Such copper chrome discs were actually used successfully in the Daytona 24-Hour race in 1970, but on the more lightly stressed rear brakes only. Experiments in this direction were continued and test runs were made on the Zeltweg track, but the desirable higher coefficient of friction obtained at normal braking temperatures was found to drop sharply as the temperature increased, causing brake fade. A more reliable and cheaper means of increasing the braking efficiency and saving weight was found by drilling the cast iron disc right through the cooling ducts and vanes. Such discs were first used on the Targa-Florio-winning 908/03 in 1970 and the best results were obtained with discs having curved ventilating vanes as these largely eliminate the tendency to crack formation. As indicated by rig tests, the perforated disc has the following advantages compared with a plain ventilated disc:

    1. It is 3.8 lb lighter, which is even lighter than the copper chrome disc.

    2. The coefficient of friction is 15-20 per cent higher and remains very nearly constant over the entire operating range. It is believed that this results from the fact that the linings remain cleaner as all the material rubbed off is taken up by the holes.

    3. The average temperature is approximately 150°C lower, resulting in less heat transfer to the wheel bearings. This was observed in a test cycle run at a simulated speed of 104 mph in which a braking torque of 290 lb ft was applied for 2.5 s at 15 s intervals.

    4. The angle of the wedge-shaped wear pattern of the lining is reduced from 5° to less than 1°.

This last point allowed a return to caliper units with four equal size (42 mm) pistons. It was also found that these perforated discs were totally unaffected by water splashes, any water on their surface being pushed into the holes and centri-fuged out of the disc as soon as the pads are applied. This would make them very suitable for use on normal production vehicles. One would imagine that these perforated discs, called 'Gruyère' discs in the factory jargon, could be the cause of quicker wear, but the tests indicated no difference at all, while in actual racing conditions the wear increase was found to be no more than 5 per cent, the rubbing effect probably being compensated for by the lower disc temperature.

At the time of the rig tests, the perforated discs had already been used successfully in three races on the 917 and they were subsequently used throughout the 1971 season, except at Le Mans where wear is critical and where they were used on one short-tail car only—the one which won.

Other experimental parts were tried in this test series, among them magnesium caliper pistons, titanium pad back plates and a composite brazed brake disc, none of which was found to be mature. In view of the excellent results obtained with perforated discs, an experiment was also made with a perforated pad having 34 3 mm holes spread on its surface, but this brought no improvement in the co-efficient of friction, and pad wear was increased by as much as 60 per cent. A small but worthwhile unsprung weight reduction was obtained by replacing the steel caliper bolts by titanium bolts, in 1971.

The 1971 Le Mans race

A good picture of the stage of development reached by the Group 5 917 coupé is given by the cars entered for the Le Mans 24-Hour race which was the final target for these cars, Porsche having already made sure of the Manufacturers' Championship by the time the race was run. The six cars entered represented three variants on the 917 theme: three were 917L long-tail models, two were 917K short-tail models with tail fins, and the sixth car was the experimental 917/20 with the SERA-designed short and wide aerodynamic body known in the works jargon as the 'Big Bertha'. The accompanying table recapitulates the main features of the two cars most typical of the stage of development reached: the long-tail

Turbo-charged engine installation in 917/10. There is still room for the diagonal tube across the engine bay.

Front pyramid of the 1972 Type 917/10.

Below left: This view of the turbo-charged 912 engine shows the butterfly valve throttle arrangement and the eight atmospheric automatic inlet valves above the intake manifolds.

Below right: The turbo-charged type 912 engine. The two turbo-chargers and the main blow-off valve can clearly be seen.

Porsche-designed front brake of 917/10 turbo-charged Can-Am *car.*

The turbo-charged 917/10 did as well in the European Interseries as in the Can-Am, Leo Kinnunen (seen here leading a McLaren) winning the 1972 series outright with a 4.5-litre car, ahead of Willy Kauhsen's similar outfit.

917 042 entered by the Martini Racing Team for Vic Elford and Gerard Larrousse, a car entirely prepared at the factory and 917 053, the short-tail car entered by the Martini Racing Team for Helmut Marko and Gijs van Lennep which is the magnesium frame short-tail car in which, apart from the frame, many other experimental features were incorporated, to such good effect that the car eventually won the race. Except for the 4.9-litre engine which Porsche preferred to use for its proven reliability, the winning car 917 053 represents the last stage of development of the 917 for Group 5 racing.

It will be noted that in addition to its magnesium frame and to its being the only car using perforated brake discs front and rear, 917 053 was fitted with many experimental parts including a 55-litre (12 gal) oil tank. The only reason for the latter was that, despite its special Le Mans equipment comprising two generators, two batteries and headlights totalling 310 watts, the car was still underweight and the difference up to the regulation 800 kg (1,770 lb) had to be supplied by filling up with oil. It will be recalled that the car on which the magnesium frame was developed, 917 052, weighed only 766 kg.

The 917/20 has not been included in this table as it was purely an experiment. Generally speaking its mechanical specification was similar to that of the long-tail cars, except that it had perforated rear brake discs and a 28:19 fifth gear ratio. Its weight was 813 kg (1,800 lb).

The best lap times obtained by the various types of cars were 3 m 13.9 s by Pedro Rodriguez in long-tail car 917 043 which was officially timed at 240 mph on the Mulsanne straight; 3 m 18.7 s by Helmut Marko in the short-tail 917 053, and 3 m 21.0 s by Kauhsen in the 917/20. The two fastest Ferraris had done 3 m 18.5 s and 3 m 18.7 s driven by Mark Donohue and Nino Vaccarella respectively. The latter, co-driving a works-prepared car with the Spaniard Juncadella, gave the Porsches a good run until his car retired at half distance with a broken transmission, just after it had gone into the lead when the Porsches met various troubles. The Elford/Larrousse long-tail car broke the retaining bolt of the cooling blower which literally flew off, and the engine seized; an oil pipe broke on the Rodriguez/Oliver car with similar results to the engine, and a cracked crankcase eliminated the last of the long-tails, the Siffert/Bell car, when it was in the lead after 16 hours. On both the John Wyer long-tail cars a rear wheel bearing had to be changed, presumably as a result of the excessive load imposed by the rear wing. On the second place 917K of Attwood/Müller the fifth gear dog clutch had to be replaced at half distance, apparently as a consequence of a machining fault. This kept the car standing for 38 minutes and it eventually finished without being able to use 4th gear. Apart from two lost alternator belts, only the winning car was practically trouble-free and it set up a new absolute Le Mans record by covering 5,335.3 km in 24 hours at an average of 222.304 kph (over 138 mph), beating the record set up by a 7-litre Ford in 1967, before the chicane (which increases the lap times by some 6 s) was installed on the pit straight. Jo Siffert also set up a new official lap record with the 917L in 3 m 18.8 s, an average speed of 243.905 kph (152 mph).

It is worth noting that, in the cars of three different types which were managed by Porsche (ie 917 042, 917 053 and 917/20/001), the fuel consumption was practically unaffected by the body shape, which probably reflects that the full performance of the long-tail cars could now be used. In fact, the average lap times of 917 042 were around 3 m 20.0 s, 5 s faster than for the other two cars, while the highest speed reached on the straight and the lower drag (creating a lesser braking effect) of the long-tail car is borne out by the fact that its front brake

Le Mans 1971 – Specifications

	Chassis No 917 042 (long tail)	Chassis No 917 053 (short tail)
Frame	Aluminium tubes	Magnesium tubes
Running gear		
Front		
Camber	0°	0°
Toe-in	30′ per wheel	30′ per wheel
Toe-in variation for 30 mm compression travel	35′ (toe out)	25′ (toe out)
Castor	4°	3°
Rear		
Camber	+45′	+40′
Toe-in	30′ per wheel	42.5′ per wheel
Brakes	Girling Aluminium saddle	Girling Aluminium saddle
Cylinder units	Aluminium pistons, steel bolts	Aluminium pistons, titanium bolts, aluminium centring bushes
Disc	Curved vanes, not perforated	Curved vanes, perforated
Lining	Textar V 1431 G	Textar V 1431 G
Cooling	Air hose, front and rear	Air hose, front only
Dampers	Bilstein	Bilstein
Gearbox	Type 917	Type 917
Ratios	13:26, 18:26, 24:25, 27:21*, 29:19	13:26, 18:26, 24:25, 25:20, 27:19
Final drive	8:37	8:37
Clutch	Borg & Beck diaphragm, 3 discs, sintered metal linings	Borg & Beck diaphragm, 3 discs, sintered metal linings
Tyres		
Front	Firestone 9.0/24.0 – 15 YB 19 Pressure 22 lb/sq in	Firestone 9.0/24.0 – 15 YB 19 Pressure 22 lb/sq in
Rear	Firestone 14.5/26.0 – 15 IB 19 Pressure 28 lb/sq in	Firestone 14.5/26.0 – 15 IB 19 Pressure 26 lb/sq in
Engine	Type 912, 4.9-litre	Type 912, 4.9-litre
Weight		
Front	281 kg ⎫ 823 kg	288 kg ⎫ 800 kg
Rear	542 kg ⎭	512 kg ⎭
Miscellaneous	2 alternators, 2 batteries (special Le Mans equipment) Type 920 steering gear Transmission oil radiator	2 alternators, 2 batteries (special Le Mans equipment) Type 920 steering gear 55-litre (12-gall) oil tank Gearbox support in magnesium

*The other 917/L used 25:20

pads had a maximum life of six hours while they lasted for 13 hours on the short-tail cars and for nine hours on the 'Big Bertha'. The fuel consumptions were 5.8 mpg, 5.95 mpg and 5.85 mpg respectively.

Despite all the efforts put into it by the factory, the 917L never succeeded in winning at Le Mans though its failure had nothing to do with the streamlined body itself. In every one of the three Le Mans races for which the model was entered, the long-tail 917 showed itself to be the fastest vehicle on the track and set the pace of the event, even in the first year when its handling was far from being satisfactory. But even if the long-tail 917s never won, they were extremely interesting technical exercises from which not only the engineers concerned, but the entire automobile industry should benefit.

14

The development of the 917/10 Spyder

THE FIRST OPEN 917 made was the 917 PA taken to America by Jo Siffert in August 1969 to take part in the last six races of the Can-Am series. This was a rather hastily built car of purely experimental character, mainly intended as a development exercise for the 917 Group 5 cars. Its shape was strongly inspired by the 908/03, but there had been very little time to test it at all, and several modifications were made on the spot, mainly of an aerodynamic nature. But the car was sufficiently successful to draw the attention of the Porsche racing engineers to the suitability of a modified version of the 917 for Can-Am and Group 7 racing generally and to prolong its career after 1971, when cars of more than 3-litre capacity would be excluded from the Manufacturers' World Championship. They were faced with a difficult choice, as a developed version of the 908/03, which mainly needed a more powerful engine, could have been very competitive in European 3-litre sports car racing. The reasons why they decided against 3-litre sports car racing were mainly two:

1. The 3-litre capacity limit for sports car racing was linked to a minimum weight clause requiring the cars to weigh no less than 650 kg (1,438 lb) which is 100kg more than Porsche had proved they could reliably get down to with a 3-litre car (though the additional power required to keep the 908 competitive would, no doubt, also have entailed an increase in weight). Light weight construction had for many years been almost a religion with Porsche and to build a comparatively heavy car would have meant giving away a major asset.

2. Clearly a completely new engine of ultra high specific output would have to be designed which had no relation whatever to existing or possible future production engines.

On the other hand, the arguments in favour of Group 7 racing were threefold:

1. As there was no minimum weight requirement, the full experience of light weight construction could be applied.

2. There being no ban on supercharging, the existing flat 12 engine could be turbo-charged, providing an enormous increase in power at a very slight weight and bulk penalty. The flat 12 was still using comparatively simple components of production car size and the experience gained with turbo-charging may be useful for future production designs.

3. Porsche sales in the USA needed a boost, following a reduction in the number of models offered as a result of the Federal anti-pollution laws.

The decision to use the existing flat 12 engine with a turbo-charger installation was not taken simply because there was no other choice. Another comparatively quick approach would have been to make a 16-cylinder power plant using the existing cylinder units from the Type 912 engine. The lesser bulk, lower weight and lesser complication of the supercharged 12-cylinder were the main reasons for its choice, however, as soon as it became obvious that the required power could be obtained with sufficient reliability with the aid of a turbo-charging plant.

In order to gain more experience of Can-Am racing, it was decided that an open bodied car using a 'standard' 5-litre unsupercharged engine would be prepared for Jo Siffert to drive in the Can-Am series, starting from the Watkins Glen race on August 25 1971. This car looked rather like the old 917 PA but had a different front with the body sloping forward in front of the wheels at an angle of about 45° right to the leading edge, and the tail sported two vertical fins which were also added to the 908/03 for 1971. As in the 1971 version of the 917K, these fins had been added as a result of wind tunnel tests. Without any other modifications, the test results were as follows (frontal area 1.465 m²):
without tail fins:
    Cw=0.540; Clf= —0.244; Clr= —0.464
with tail fins:
    Cw=0.508; Clf= —0.262; Clr= —0.424.
While front wing 'fences' produced practically the same lift figures as the fins, the drag coefficient was nearly as bad as for the car in its original state.

As it was sent to America the car had a sandwich body, the latest type of rein-forced five-speed gearbox, and incorporated many lightweight parts such as front aluminium hubs, rear titanium hubs, lightweight Girling brake calipers with alumin-ium pistons and titanium bolts, magnesium steering box brackets and gearbox sup-ports, and aluminium gear change shaft plus all the other usual lightweight parts. Two side tanks were fitted, having a total capacity of 66 gallons plus three-quarters of a gallon in a collector tank. In this state, the car 917/10/002 weighed 743 kg (1,620 lb) without fuel. Before he was killed in a European Formula 1 race, Siffert ran the car in four races of the Can-Am series, finishing second twice, third once and fifth once. Just before 917/10/002 took part in its first race, 917/10/001 had already been running with the turbo-charged engine at Hockenheim and on the Weissach test track. It was then tried in the wind tunnel practically in the same state as it had been tried previously with the exception that it was now fitted with a wrap-round horizontal 'running board'-type front spoiler, 40 mm wide, had a full width 30 mm high tail spoiler, and sported two air intake scoops and one central gearbox oil radiator scoop on its rear deck. Compared with the original version, the drag was practically the same but there was more downthrust on the front wheels and less on the rear wheels. Drag and lift were comparatively little affected by variations in the car's angle of incidence. As an experiment, the nose was replaced with the nose from a long-tail 917 with very little change in the results.

An unexpected finding was that removing the large scoop located at the rear end of the engine bay and directing air to the gearbox oil cooler, and removing the two intake air scoops feeding the two turbo-chargers actually increased the drag coefficient and doubled the downthrust over the rear axle, as shown by the following figures obtained with the long-tail nose:
With the 600 mm wide and 140 mm high transmission oil cooler scoop and twin intake air scoops: Cw= 0.546; Clf= —0.309; Clr= —0.230.
    Without any air scoops: Cw= 0.580; Clf= —0.264; Clr= —0.474.
These figures seem to indicate that the scoops effectively deflect part of the air flowing along the body to its destination, thus reducing the aerodynamic forces acting upon the tail of the car.

Another series of tests was done after two vertical fins connected by an aerofoil had been added to the tail. The aerofoil was 200 mm (8 in) above the rear deck (with an angle of incidence of 6°) and consisted of a fixed main aerofoil set at an angle of incidence of 10° 15′ and an adjustable full length auxiliary flap.

This combination of fins and an aerofoil creating an air slot at the rear, confirmed previous experience by reducing the drag, all other factors being equal. Several tests were made by moving the fins and the aerofoil forward and rearward and measuring the air velocity on the rear deck of the body. The following figures are of particular interest because they show how the downthrust was increased by the fins and aerofoil without any deterioration of the (admittedly bad) drag co-efficient, the best results being obtained with the fins and aerofoil moved well back, where both the speed of the air flow and the leverage over the rear axle is highest.

Car with 917L nose, no air scoops, rear spoiler 65 mm (2.6 in) high:
Cw=0.656; Clf= —0.255; Clr= —0.606.

As above, but with fins and aerofoil, flap angle 28° 30′:
Cw=0.656; Clf= —3.15; Clr= —0.721.

Using the formula

$$F = 0.0075 \times C \times S \times V^2$$

(F being expressed in kg and V in mph) to calculate the drag and lift, we obtain for a frontal area of S=1.465 m² and a speed of V=200 mph, a total drag of 290 kg (640 lb) with front and rear downthrusts of 138 kg (305 lb) and 307 kg (680 lb) respectively. The downthrust forces being led through the springs (as the rules state that no aerodynamic aids may be carried by unsprung parts of the vehicle), it is easy to imagine how stiff the suspension must be made to prevent it from being compressed down to its stops, and to think of all attendant problems. It will also be noted that the down force induced is more than twice as high at the rear as at the front, which helps in obtaining the desired characteristic of more understeer in open, high speed curves than in slower bends.

Though 917/10-002, which Siffert took to America, was fitted with tail fins, there was no time to modify the tail to take the aerofoil but later cars took full advantage of these tests.

Engine and transmission developments

The development of the 912 engine for Group 7 racing took two different forms. One was a further increase in its capacity to nearly 5.4 litres. It was obtained by enlarging the cylinder bores from 86.8 to 90 mm, which gave an exact capacity of 5,374 cc, timing and valve size remaining unaltered. Nikasil cylinders were used as on the 5-litre and the output was raised to 660 hp at 8,300 rpm. With this bore the sealing surface between the cylinders and the heads had become very small and it was necessary to reduce the size of the annular section gasket. Because of this small sealing surface, this engine has not until now been used in super-charged form. It was raced in factory-sponsored cars only in Europe, at the beginning of 1972 and was offered to private customers as an alternative to the more com-plicated and much more expensive turbo-charged engine.

The second and more important line of development was the addition of two Eberspächer turbo-chargers, each fed by the exhaust system of one of the two banks of six cylinders. They run up to 100,000 rpm and are governed to produce a maximum boost of 20 psi. When this pressure is reached in the intake system, a by-pass valve, operated from a pipe connecting it to the right-hand intake mani-fold is opened to direct part of the exhaust gases directly into the atmosphere. Each of the two turbo-chargers feeds its own bank of six cylinders.

One of the big problems of turbo-charging is the slow throttle response, both when the throttle is opened and when it is closed, as the inertia of the gas turbine

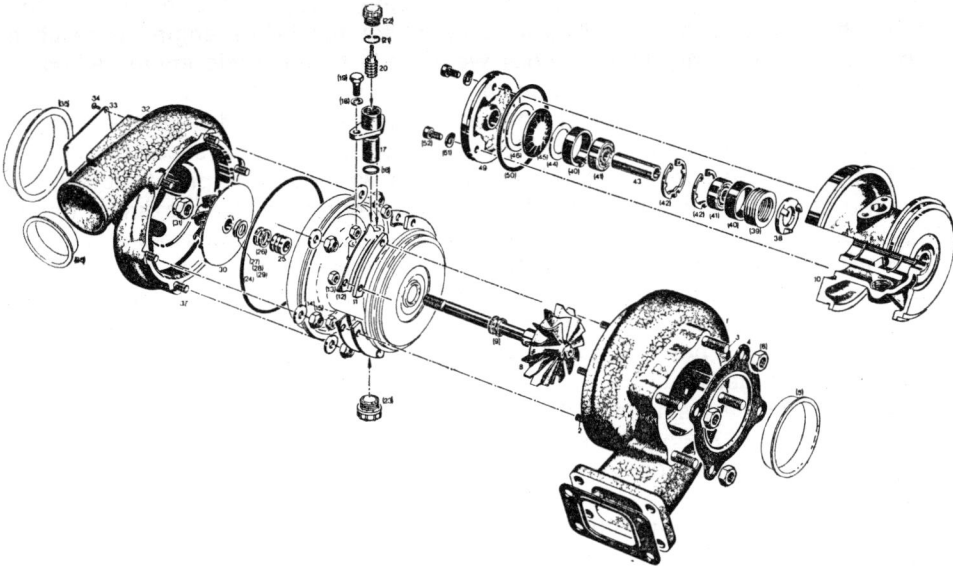

Exploded view of the Eberspächer turbo-charger as used for the Can-Am and Interseries winning 917/10 of 1972.

and compressor wheels cannot be indefinitely reduced. Though, at this stage, Porsche are not prepared to disclose details of the development work undertaken, everyone can see that the throttle slides used on the unsupercharged engines have been replaced by ordinary butterfly valves located as close to the cylinder head as possible, which reduces the amount of compressed air fed into the cylinders after the throttles are closed. As to the delay in throttle opening, a partial cure is effected by four automatic valves incorporated in each of the induction manifolds, which open as soon as the accelerator is depressed and allow normal atmospheric induction to take place if the boost has not reached a pressure at least equal to that obtaining in the inlet manifold. It can also be seen that there is a flap valve on the air pressure line leading from the turbo-charger to the inlet manifold on each side. This valve is operated by the throttle linkage in such a way that the output from the turbo-charger is directed to the atmosphere as soon as the throttle is closed, in order to obviate any back pressure which would cause the turbo-charger rotor to lose speed quickly while it is not activated by exhaust gases. A spring closes this valve as the driver depresses the accelerator. A safety blow-off valve is also incorporated in the system.

Most of the development work was done on the 4.5-litre engine, mainly for the sake of reliability (its crankshaft is slightly stronger thanks to the shorter stroke), but the experience gained was then successfully applied to the 5-litre which in 1972 was used from the start for the works-sponsored cars prepared and entered by the Roger Penske Racing Organisation running in the Can-Am Championship, and has been used only in the United States.

In theory, the limit of the power increase to be obtained by turbo-charging is reached when an increase in boost pressure takes up more power than it produces in the engine. In practice, the limit of the power that can be obtained is set by the thermal and mechanical stresses set up in the engine. But only the pressure and thermal loads are augmented, as the power increase is obtained by raising the induction pressure rather than the rate of revolution. In fact the 950 hp which Porsche set themselves as a target for the 5-litre engine is reached at only 8,000 rpm; very few changes were made to the basic engine to adapt it to turbo-charging and all the main components have remained unaltered. Even the size of the cooling blower wheel could remain unaltered, after the inversion of the 17 and 19 tooth gears in its drive to step up its rotational speed from 0.895 to 1.12 times engine speed. In its 4.5-litre version, as supplied to private customers, the turbo-charged engine produces 850 hp at 8,000 rpm with a maximum torque of 615 lb ft at 6,600 rpm. It is up-dated from earlier units of the same size by the use of nikasil instead of chromal cylinders. Compared with the 528 lb of the original 4.5-litre unsupercharged engine, the weight of either the 4.5- or 5-litre turbo-charged unit, complete with blowers and exhaust system, has gone up to 600 lb. The specific weight has thus come down from 0.92 lb/hp to 0.63 lb/hp for the 5-litre turbo-charged unit.

To take the torque of some 690 lb/ft produced by the 5-litre turbo-charged engine, a completely new, stronger four-speed transmission had to be designed, called the Type 920 transmission. As the former 917 unit, it has a wet sump and additionally a pump circulates the oil through a radiator and also through the hollow gearbox shafts and to jets lubricating the crown wheel and pinion. The splines have been deleted in the titanium half shafts as the Giubo rubber 'doughnuts' have been found quite adequate to accommodate the length variations in the relatively short races in which Group 7 cars are run. The shaft diameter was dictated by destruction tests at Weissach when the original design was proved inadequate.

The clutch is the same as before, except for a stronger diaphragm spring, but the larger final drive unit has moved the drive shafts back 32 mm (1.26 in). However, because the lighter, reinforced 917 gearbox, as used from the middle of 1970 onwards, has proved to be quite adequate for the 5.4-litre unsupercharged engine, it was decided to lengthen the wheelbase of the car only by half the amount to 2.316 m (90⅝ in) so that either of the transmissions could be used with the half shafts at a very small angle in either direction.

Another modification made necessary to accommodate the turbo-chargers was the relocation of some of the tubes in the tail of the frame, which is not a true pyramid design any more. Extensive testing led to some revisions of suspension geometries aiming at reducing camber changes induced by suspension movements while the front anti-dive effect was increased: the reduced steering off-set used since Le Mans 1970 and the modified suspension and steering geometries made this possible, without creating the ill effects experienced earlier when as much as 50 per cent anti-dive was used. With the pivot axis of the upper wishbones converging towards the front of the car and sloping down to the rear, the anti dive effect is progressive while the castor variations are kept to a minimum.

With nearly 1,000 hp available, it becomes extremely important to reduce the dive and squat movements, the overriding factor in the suspension design becoming the need to keep the tyres as perpendicular to the ground as possible when the car is under full acceleration or is being heavily braked, both in order to improve the grip and to prevent local overheating of the tyres. So rather stiff springs and anti-roll bars are used to reduce the body roll which causes the tyres to deviate from the perpendicular position. Lateral accelerations as high as 1.61 g were measured on the 550 ft diameter Weissach steering pad in September 1972 with Willy Kauhsen driving, an extremely high figure if it is remembered that at the speeds of less than 90 mph which were reached, the effect of the aerofoils is only quite moderate, and that the g forces are a calculated average over a complete lap, not a peak recorded by an accelerometer. Nineteen inches wide rear rims were used, fitted with Goodyear 'slicks'.

Having made extensive comparative tests with Girling, ATE and Lockheed brakes Porsche finally decided to design and make their own brake calipers which are now used on all 917 Group 7 cars. They have an aluminium saddle to which the heavily ribbed aluminium cylinder units are secured by titanium bolts. There are four 42 mm diameter aluminium pistons per wheel, as in the former ATE and Girling brakes, and the pistons are 'inverted', as before, to reduce heat transfer. There is no specific clearance adjustment, this purpose being served by the close-fitting rubber seals.

917/10s sold to private owners all have their frame made of aluminium tubes to which the sandwich material body is bonded. Due to the various reinforcements that have had to be incorporated into the chassis to make it resist the stresses fed into it by the immensely powerful turbo-charged engine, the weight of the 1972 vintage 917/10 aluminium frame has risen to approximately 60 kg (133 lb)—still astonishingly light if the forces set up when the car is accelerated fully in the lower gears are kept in mind. But of the two works-sponsored cars run by Roger Penske in the 1972 Can-Am series, one (917/10-011) was built with a magnesium frame which saved 15 kg (33 lb) over the aluminium frame, making it virtually a round 100 lb complete with all the attachment brackets. As some 750 kg (1,650 lb) are quoted by the factory as the weight for the normal turbo-charged car, we may deduce that the magnesium frame version weighs 735 kg though, as was the case with John Wyer, the Roger Penske preparation probably added several pounds to this, a large part being accounted for by the paint sprayed over the body to give it a showroom finish. Weight was also saved on the upper suspension wishbones which are now made of aluminium alloy tubes, following the endurance tests made in Weissach in the spring of 1971 on the second magnesium framed car 917 052.

Entered for the first race for the 1972 Can-Am Championship run on the Canadian Mosport circuit, the turbo-charged magnesium frame Porsche driven by Mark Donohue, who had taken a very active part in its development, immediately showed its paces by taking pole position and leading the race from the start, only to drop back to second place when the driver had to make a pit stop to clear a valve that had stuck in the turbo-charging system. Unfortunately, in practice for its second race, the car lost the improperly secured tail part of its body and Donohue crashed it heavily, injuring himself and destroying the car. The aluminium frame 917/10-003 was immediately put into action and was driven by George Follmer to such good effect that it won the second race of the series on the Road Atlanta circuit. The breakage of a small spring returning a flap valve in the turbo-charging system put paid to its chances in the Watkins Glen race, but even without this mishap, the Porsche would most probably have been beaten by the McLaren team of M20s driven by Hulme and Revson on which Follmer could make no impression. Some time after the race, Helmut Flegl, the engineer in charge of the 917 development, told me that after a private practice session on the Watkins Glen circuit, even before he knew what sort of practice times the McLarens would get down to, he felt sure that the car was not running as it should. His suspicion was that the chassis was not set up properly for the circuit, due to the inability of Follmer, who had little experience of the model, to accurately judge its behaviour, and he based his pessimistic view on the fact that the Porsche computer, which had been fed with all the available data on the track and the known performance data of the car, had indicated a possible lap time around 1 m 39 s, and the best Follmer had been able to achieve was 1 m 40.5 s. Such is the accuracy of the computerised investigation technique developed over the years, since it was first applied to racing by the Zuffenhausen engineers on the occasion of the European Hill-climb Championship series of 1967! It has proved a great help, not only for calculating lap times at which to aim, but also for choosing the right gear ratios for any given circuit even before the start of practice and—more important still— to take the right decision in the innumerable design compromises that must be made at the design stage, when it comes to weighing up such factors as downthrust against drag, chassis stiffness against additional weight, and other similar alternatives.

After the Watkins Glen race, the 'Turbo-Porsche', as it was dubbed and which was constantly improved in details (for instance a new type of Goodyear tyre was used, in conjunction with even wider wheel rims—12 in front and 19 in rear—still with a 15-in diameter), had a magnificent run of successes. The Penske-entered cars (Donohue drove the spare car 917/10-005 after he had recovered from his earlier accident) were beaten only once in the last six races of 1972 (when Follmer ran out of fuel on the last lap) and Follmer took the Can-Am Championship by a large margin preceding the private driver of a 917/10, Milt Minter, while in Europe Leo Kinnunen and Willy Kauhsen took the first two places in the 1972 Interseries Championship, driving 4.5-litre turbo-charged cars (respectively 917/10-004 and 917/10-002, Siffert's 1971 Can-Am car).

The kind of performance the turbo-charged 917/10 is able to develop is hard to imagine, even by drivers of high performance sports cars, as shown by the astounding performance figures calculated by the factory computer and which have been released at a press conference held by Dr Fuhrmann, Porsche's Managing and Technical Director:

0 to 60 mph in 2.1 s;
0 to 100 mph in 3.9 s;
0 to 200 mph in 13.4 s.

When, on being shown an impressive lineup of 25 complete (if not necessarily raceworthy) 917 coupés in the factory forecourt at the end of April 1969, the startled CSI officials ruefully had to accept to homologate the model as a Group 5 'sports car', the general feeling was that Porsche had just invented a new, very expensive way of securing supremacy in the World Championship of Makes series. Even though the model was on sale to private customers, few people thought that more than half the batch produced would ever get as far as a race track for lack of drivers or lack of opportunities to be raced. True, not many of the first series of 917s were sold and most of the bodies had to be scrapped following the complete redesign for 1970, which tests had shown to be essential to make the 917 as stable as it was fast. But most of the mechanical components, including all the engines and transmissions, incorporated in those cars which were never raced were certainly used. Following some up-dating, all the chassis were also used so that in the end, not much was wasted on that first batch of cars. And though originally it had seemed extravagant to build 25 units of such a powerful and expensive model, by the end of 1972, the number of 917s built, including those conforming to Group 7 specification, goes well into the sixties.

The 917 has already become a classic, even though its immensely successful career is still far from having reached its end.

15

Driving the 908/03 and the 917

Nürburgring, April 1970

IT ALL CAME ABOUT because I was unable to attend the Porsche press conference at Hockenheim in December 1969 when a few journalists were allowed to drive the World Championship winning 908 model. To make up for the loss I was invited to drive the latest cars at a testing session. So I drove to the Nürburgring where a 917 with the latest wedge-shaped body and two well worn 908/03s—the first experimental prototypes, as yet unraced—were undergoing development tests before the Monza 1,000 km race and the Targa Florio of 1970.

For these tests the southern loop of the Nürburgring had been hired for four days. Not much work had been done before I arrived on the evening of the second day. As most readers are probably aware, the south loop of the Ring is seldom used for important races and, though I reckon to have lapped the longer north loop more than 1,500 times, I was still unfamiliar with the south loop. It is just as good as the rest of the Ring with up and down slopes and a great variety of corners and bends, though it has been left untouched as far as safety measures are concerned.

After two days of rain, D-day was dry and sunny and the Porsche development engineers Flegl (responsible for the 917) and Bantle (who looks after the 908) kindly let me drive both cars at length, in spite of having to make the best of the fine day. The previous bad weather had slowed up their work considerably.

Hans Herrmann had been taking a 908/03 out for a few laps at a time all through the morning, with the Bilstein shock absorber people watching him at some crucial points. Then he tried the 917 which had arrived overnight from the factory and after a few details had been attended to, 'the beast' was handed over to me.

The cockpit was quite surprisingly comfortable and not in the least cramped, with the seat adjustable over quite a wide range. There is a choice of positions for steering column height (adjustment is facilitated by the rubber universal incorporated in the column), and it even has the luxury of immediate telescopic adjustment. Even with my helmet on there was no suggestion of headroom being limited. By racing car standards, the steering wheel is quite large, and as soon as the car starts moving one finds out why.

Interior body finish is sketchy, the plastic panels being quite rough and the instruments reduced to bare essentials: rev counter, oil thermometer (which in an air-cooled engine replaces the water thermometer) and oil pressure gauge. 'Idiot lights' take care of the rest. The right hand steering column is slightly angled towards the centre line of the car and the pedals are offset correspondingly to clear the big wheel arches.

The gearbox of the 917 has been designed to take a set of four or five gears, this year four gears only have been used. The car I was going to drive—chassis number 917 008 belonging to Porsche-Salzburg—had the four-speed box too. To avoid any possible mis-selection there is a clever blanking plate over the first gear position, cleared only if the concentric catch around the lever is raised, so that pushing the lever straight through from the second gear position will automatically select third. In fact, except for starting, the rather low gearing suited to the circuit never called for the use of first gear, even at the junction between the narrow by-pass road and the track, which is taken at no more than 25 mph so tractable is the big flat 12 engine. Although the engine had had time to cool down while the car was being attended to, it sprang into noisy life at the first touch of the starter. I closed the door (it has no safety catch, as all Porsche doors and lids are hinged at their front end to keep them shut even if the catch fails) and slowly I turned into the by-pass road, the big car as tractable as a road car.

Up to then, the cars with the highest power-to-weight ratio I had driven (2½-litre Formula 1) had about 300-320 bhp per ton. This near 600 bhp Porsche had more than twice as much.

The course starts with a winding downhill section including rather slow corners all of which I took in second. Then comes a short straight. As the engine was not really warm, I had a good excuse to take it easy and changed into third without really pushing the accelerator down. And when the longer straight came, I went into top in the same way. After one lap I felt the 4.5-litre engine was warm enough and, accelerating hard out of the last slow bend, I gave it the gun in second.

What happened then has to be felt to be believed. Surely an ordinary motorist cannot imagine it. The engine just went 'whooooom!', the car literally leapt forward, and it immediately became urgent to change up into third (all in the time it took you to read the first three words of this sentence). In third it was about the same again, but I had to shut off even more quickly as the next corner was coming up at an alarming speed.

It is easy to calculate that with the engine on the power band, the acceleration in second is very nearly 1 g and the amazing thing is that with the big, fat Firestone tyres on 17-in wide rear rims, there is no trace of wheelspin. Another thing that can be calculated is that, assuming a mean acceleration of 0.8 g through first and second gear, 100 mph is reached in 5.3 seconds.

After a few laps I started to get the hang of things and to be able to use the full power up to the braking points (plus a reasonable safety margin), some of which Herrmann had shown me on a preliminary lap we had done in his 911S (I find this is a great help on a circuit which is not perfectly familiar). I also soon found out that fourth gear could be used around several of the faster bends. Surprisingly the noise level is quite reasonable inside the cockpit and in spite of its fantastic performance, the car is not the infernal beast you might think it is. True, my lap times were a good 10 s longer than it *can* be done. But I didn't want to risk anything —also bearing in mind that it is more than ten years since I drove anything with even half the performance. Nevertheless the car felt beautifully stable and well balanced; perfectly neutral in fast curves and understeering only slightly in the slower ones, though there is certainly always power on tap to hang the tail out if you want to.

With the 10.5-in wide rims now used at the front, the car reacts very quickly to any movement of the steering which, at 11.4 : 1 is pretty high geared. It has a strong return action calling for some effort, especially on tight bends, and it is quite lively, though it does not kick back viciously. The brakes, too, call for some strong pushing, but they really stop the car. In fact the grip on the road is such that I never reached the locking point which, with those fat modern tyres, must correspond to a deceleration of some 1.3-1.4 g.

Driving the 917 is a staggering experience and there is no question that you must be extremely fit to drive a car like this for several hours at racing speeds. Not only because everything requires a considerable physical force, but also because with that sort of performance you just cannot relax your concentration for a second.

After a short time the 908/03, which had been attended to in the paddock, came up to the track and I was invited to take its wheel. This was the very first prototype of the new model, the second being the one which had been undergoing tests the whole morning with Hans Herrmann. Both cars, which were taken to Sicily in March for a Targa Florio pre-practice, were still very experimental with some of the aluminium chassis tubes cut or stitched in further lightening endeavours. They also had slightly different bodies, both equally ugly and blunt. These were developed in the wind tunnel, not with the accent on low drag, but rather on reasonable downthrust without spoilers, compact dimensions and lightness (1,200 lb), as this open car had been developed mainly for the Targa Florio and other winding circuits requiring exceptional maoeuvrability and agility. To help front wheel adhesion, the five-speed gearbox is located in front of the final drive, pushing the engine to a rather forward position, while the driver sits with his feet only a few inches from the forward edge of the blunt nose.

For the sake of lightness the cast iron ventilated brake discs are extensively drilled on their working surfaces (they call them Gruyère discs at the factory). Firestone tyres, 13 in, are used on 9.5-in wide rims at the front (11-in rims were also being tried) and 14-in rims at the rear. In this car, the driving position is even more nearly central than in the 917. The five speeds and reverse are selected on three planes with strong self-centring action towards the middle one, and a locking mechanism prevents the driver from jumping a plane and inadvertently going from fifth straight into second instead of fourth when in a hurry.

The cockpit finish is spartan and in addition to a dashboard similar to the 917, you can visually check the anti-roll bar, for it runs right along the dash structure, just above the steering column, so far forward is the driving position.

When taking the wheel of this car, I could not help thinking of the progress made in the last ten years, remembering that this Porsche had the same 3-litre capacity as my Le Mans-winning Ferrari 'Testa Rossa' of 1960, but exactly twice its power-to-weight ratio—even if the 350-360 bhp produced by the Porsche engine is well below par for a 3-litre. In fact, the power-to-weight ratio must be very near the figure for the 917, but somehow it does not feel quite as ferocious, perhaps because the 3-litre has not got the colossal medium torque range of the 4.5-litre flat 12.

With this car more gearchanging was called for, all five gears being used in the course of one lap. And due to the strong self-centring springs, it took me a while to master the gearchange and to be sure of going from fourth to fifth rather than third when it came to changing up. But once this was mastered, the car was a sheer—if earshattering—delight. It handled beautifully and could be flung around bends with the utmost abandon, being especially good in S-bends where its immensely quick reaction to directional changes was marvellous. Except for the rather stiff gearchange, this is a car you drive more with feel than force, and the perfect all-round visibility and beautiful responsiveness quickly inspire great confidence. Even the superb brakes don't take so much force and they check the car without drama, even when used to the limit. Too much power in a corner will, of course, bring the tail out but this is very easily checked and in tight corners such methods can readily be used to help the car round

Altogether I found this to be a much more humane car than the 917, somehow much more on equal terms with the driver. Consequently my lap times were better. I felt that I had driven the 908 with more enterprise than the 917, even if only because I was steadily increasing my knowledge of a circuit I had never driven on before with a really fast car. In absolute terms I would think both cars should be pretty closely matched on this rather sinuous circuit, but whereas I am sure I would be completely exhausted after driving the 917 really fast there for an hour, I would not mind driving the 908/03 in the same way for twice the time, or more. On a fast circuit it would be very different, for in all-out speed, even in this short-tail form, the 917 will probably reach a maximum speed of 220 mph— some 35 or 40 mph faster than the 908/03.

Even if I had not enjoyed these two Porsches so much, I would still be very grateful to those responsible for them for having provided me with this opportunity to confirm one of my convictions about an important point of motor sport history: the nonsense of the widespread belief that the famous 1934-37 Auto-Union racing cars (designed by Ferdinand Porsche Sr) were very difficult to drive because of their very forward driving position. My personal opinion has always been that our present knowledge of the factors affecting car behaviour indicates that this car— with a considerable rear weight bias, small-section tyres and rims and swing-axle rear suspension with static positive camber and considerable camber and toe-in variation—had almost everything to promote bad handling, vicious over-steer and poor straight line stability, and that the forward driving position really had nothing to do with it.

Porsche competition cars 1964—1972 (except 911 and 914 derivatives)

Year	Type	Cylinder	Bore and Stroke (mm)	Capacity (cc)	Compr. Ratio	HP/RPM	Fuel system	Gearbox Gears and Position	Rims Front	Rims Rear	Frame	Wheelbase (mm)	Track Front	Track Rear	Length (mm)	Width (mm)	Height (mm)	Weight without fuel (kg)
1964	904 (Coupé)	4	92×74	1966	9.8	155/6900 w. street exhaust 180/7200 w. racing exhaust	Twin double-choke Weber or Solex	5 overhung	5×15 (Radial) 6×15 (Racing)	5×15 (Radial) 6×15 (Racing)	Box section, steel	2300	1316	1312	4090	1540	1065	c. 650
1965	904 (Coupé)	4	92×74	1966	9.8	185/7200	Twin double-choke Weber	5 overhung	see above		Box section, steel	2300	1316	1312	4090	1540	1065	c. 650
1964/65	904	The type 904 was also used by the factory with 6- and 8-cylinder engines (see 906 and 906/8). It ran with an open body in the 1965 Targa Florio and hill-climbs.																
1966	906 Carrera 6	6	80×66	1991	10.3	210/8000	Twin triple-choke Weber	5 overhung	7×15	9×15	Steel tubes	2300	1338	1402	4113	1680	980	c. 650
1966	906 Prototype	6	80×66	1991	10.3	220/8000	Bosch injection	5 overhung	7×15	9×15	Steel tubes	2300	1338	1402	4113	1680	980	c. 650
1966	906 Long-tail	6	80×66	1991	10.3	220/8000	Bosch injection	5 overhung	7×15	9×15	Steel tubes	2300	1338	1402	4650	1680	980	c. 670
1966	906/8	8	76×54.6	1981	10.4	240/8500	Four double-choke Weber	5 overhung	7×15	9×15	Steel tubes	2300	1338	1402	4113	1680	980	c. 670
1967	910/6	6	80×66	1991	10.3	220/8000	Bosch injection	5 overhung	8×13	9.5×13	Steel tubes	2300	1430	1401	4100	1710	980	575
1967	910/8	8	80×54.6	2195	10.2	270/8600	Bosch injection	5 overhung	8×13	9.5×13	Steel tubes	2300	1430	1401	4100	1710	980	600
1967	907 Long-tail	6	80×66	1991	10.3	220/8000	Bosch injection	5 overhung	8×13	9.5×13	Steel tubes	2300	1462	1403	4839	1720	940	590
1967	907	8	80×54.6	2195	10.2	270/8600	Bosch injection	5 overhung	8×13	9.5×13	Steel tubes	2300	1462	1403	4033	1720	940	600
1967	910 Berg	8	76×54.6	1981	10.4	272/9000	Bosch injection	5 overhung	8×13	9.5×13	Steel tubes	2300	1430	1401	3860	1710	765[1]	450
1968	910 Berg	8	76×54.6	1981	10.4	275/9000	Bosch injection	5 overhung	8×13	9.5×13	Aluminium tubes	2300	1430	1401	3860	1710	765[1]	410–430
1968	909 Berg	8	76×54.6	1981	10.4	275/9000	Bosch injection	5 betw. engine & differential	8×13	12×13	Aluminium tubes	2264	1470	1464	3448	1800	710[1]	c. 420
1968	907	8	80×54.6	2195	10.2	270/8600	Bosch injection	5 overhung	8×13	12×13	Steel tubes	2300	1462	1454	4020	1830	938	600
1968	907 Long-tail	8	80×54.6	2195	10.2	270/8600	Bosch injection	5 overhung	8×13	12×13	Steel tubes[2]	2300	1462	1454	4839	1830	938	620
1968	908	8	84×66	2921	10.4	320/8400	Bosch injection	6 clutch & gearbox overhung	8×13	12×13	Steel tubes	2300	1462	1454	4020	1830	938	660

Porsche competition cars 1964—1972 (except 911 and 914 derivatives)

Year	Type	Cylinder	Bore and Stroke (mm)	Capacity (cc)	Compr. Ratio	HP/RPM	Fuel system	Gearbox Gears and Position	Rims Front	Rims Rear	Frame	Wheelbase (mm)	Track Front	Track Rear	Length (mm)	Width (mm)	Height (mm)	Weight without fuel (kg)
1968	908	8	85×66	2997	10.4	350/8400	Bosch injection	6 clutch & gearbox overhung	9×15	12×15	Steel tubes³	2300	1486	1454	4020	1830	938	660
1968	908 Long-tail	8	85×66	2997	10.4	350/8400	Bosch injection	6 clutch & gearbox overhung	9×15	12×15	Steel tubes	2300	1486	1454	4839	1830	938	680
1969	908/02 Spyder	8	85×66	2997	10.4	350/8400	Bosch injection	5 overhung	9×15	12×15	Aluminium tubes	2300	1486	1454	4000	1830	730¹	600
1969	917	12	85×66	4494	10.5	580/8400	Bosch injection	5 overhung	9×15	12×15 or 15×15	Aluminium tubes	2300	1488	1457 or 1533	4290	2033	920	800
1969	917 Long-tail	12	85×66	4494	10.5	580/8400	Bosch injection	5 overhung	9×15	12×15	Aluminium tubes	2300	1488	1457	4780	2033	920	830
1969	917 PA Spyder	12	85×66	4494	10.5	580/8400	Bosch injection	5 overhung	10.5×15	15×15 or 17×15	Aluminium tubes	2300	1526	1533 or 1584	3905	2100	730¹	775
1970	917	12	85×66	4494	10.5	580/8400	Bosch injection	4 overhung	10.5×15 or 12×15	15×15 or 17×15	Aluminium tubes	2300	1582 or 1620	1533 or 1584	4120	1980	940	800
1970	917	12	85×66	4907	10.5	600/8400	Bosch injection	4 overhung	10.5×15 or 12×15	15×15 or 17×15	Aluminium tubes	2300	1582 or 1620	1533 or 1584	4120	1980	940	800
1970	917 Long-tail	12	86×70.4	4907⁴	10.5	600/8400	Bosch injection	5 overhung	10.5×15	15×15	Aluminium tubes	2300	1582	1533	4660	2032	940	840
1970	908/03 Spyder	8	85×66	2997	10.4	350/8400	Bosch injection	5 betw. engine & differential	9.5×13 or 11×13	14×13 or 15×15	Aluminium tubes	2300	1504 or 1542	1510 or 1506	3540	1950	675¹	545
1971	908/03 Spyder	8	85×66	2997	10.4	350/8400	Bosch injection	5 betw. engine & differential	11×13	15×15 or 17×15	Aluminium tubes	2300	1542	1506 or 1564	3540	2000	675¹	565
1971	917K	12	86.8×70.4	4998⁵	10.5	630/8300	Bosch injection	4 or 5 overhung	10.5×15 or 12×15	17×15	Aluminium tubes⁶	2300	1582 or 1620	1584	4120	2080	940	800
1971	917L⁷	12	86×70.4	4907	10.5	600/8400	Bosch injection	5 overhung	10.5×15	17×15	Aluminium tubes	2300	1582	1584	4615	2080	940	825
1971	917/10 Spyder	12	86.8×70.4	4998	10.5	630/8300	Bosch injection	5 overhung	12×15	17×15	Aluminium tubes	2300	1620	1584	3740	2080	730¹	740
1972	917/10 Spyder	12	90×70.4	5374	10.5	660/8300	Bosch injection	4 or 5 overhung	12×15	17×15	Aluminium tubes	2316	1620	1584	3950	2100	730¹	740
1972	917/10 Spyder	12	86×66 or 86.8×70.4	4494 or 4998	—	850/8000 or 950/8000	Twin turbo-chargers & Bosch Inj.	4 overhung	12×15	17×15 or 19×15	Aluminium tubes	2316	1620	1584 or 1642	3950	2100 or 2150	730¹	750 (Mg 735)

1 without roll-bar
2 907 011 with aluminium tube frame. Weight 600 kg
3 908 012 with aluminium tube frame. Weight 640 kg
4 also used with 4494-cc engine
5 also with 4907-cc engine
6 917 052 and 917 053 with magnesium tube frame
7 917/20: length 3960 mm; width 2216 mm; height 926 mm